PROVERBS OF ASHES

Proverbs of Ashes

Violence, Redemptive Suffering, and the Search for What Saves Us

RITA NAKASHIMA BROCK AND
REBECCA ANN PARKER

Beacon Press
BOSTON

Beacon Press
25 Beacon Street
Boston, Massachusetts 02108-2892
www.beacon.org

Beacon Press books
are published under the auspices of
the Unitarian Universalist Association of Congregations.

Printed in the United States of America

08 07 06   8 7 6 5 4

Excerpt from "East Coker" in *Four Quartets,* copyright 1940 by T. S.
Eliot and renewed 1968 by Esme Valerie Eliot, reprinted by
permission of Harcourt, Inc.

This book is printed on acid-free paper that meets the uncoated paper
ANSI/NISO specifications for permanence as revised in 1992.

Composition by Wilsted & Taylor Publishing Services
Text design by Elizabeth Elsas

Library of Congress Cataloging-in-Publication Data
    Brock, Rita Nakashima.
      Proverbs of ashes : Violence, redemptive suffering, and the
search for what saves us / Rita Nakashima Brock and Rebecca Ann
Parker.
          p.   cm.
      Includes bibliographical references.
      ISBN 0-8070-6796-2 (cloth)
      ISBN 0-8070-6797-0 (pbk.)
      1. Atonement.   2. Feminist theology.   3. Violence—
Religious aspects—Christianity.   4. Family violence—
Religious aspects—Christianity.   5. Brock, Rita Nakashima.
6. Parker, Rebecca Ann.   I. Parker, Rebecca Ann.   II. Title.
    BT265.3 .B76   2001
    234'.082—dc21

                                            2001001372

FOR OUR PARENTS AND GRANDPARENTS

"Mostly [my husband] is a good man. But sometimes he becomes very angry and he hits me. He knocks me down. One time he broke my arm and I had to go to the hospital. . . . I went to my priest twenty years ago. I've been trying to follow his advice. The priest said I should rejoice in my sufferings because they bring me closer to Jesus. . . . He said, 'If you love Jesus, accept the beatings and bear them gladly, as Jesus bore the cross.'"

—LUCIA

"For what credit is it, if when you do wrong and are beaten for it you take it patiently? But if when you do right and suffer for it you take it patiently, you have God's approval. For to this you have been called, because Christ also suffered for you, leaving you an example, that you should follow in his steps. . . . Rejoice in so far as you share in Christ's sufferings."

—I PETER 2:20–21, 4:13

ago would have been between drafts two and three, in the middle of this project. I had assumed her writing about an earlier suicide attempt meant she no longer felt the urge to harm herself. "How did you get to that state? What happened?" I asked.

Rebecca told the story that appears in chapter 5. I had admired her stamina and success as a seminary president. A job that stressful would have been enough for anyone, and I knew she also carried the memory of earlier trauma. But I was unaware of how much it still affected her. She explained the impulse behind her self-harm and her ways of resisting it. I felt anguish knowing the legacy of violence that has marked her life. As I listened I realized that our friendship had changed. In working on this book, whose pages were spread out on the table before us, we had wrestled with deeper, more accurate insights about our experiences and theology. As we moved closer to core truths, we disclosed more about our lives and pushed each other to a clearer discernment of what we needed to write.

When we began our friendship in 1978, as students in a graduate theology seminar, neither of us knew the emotional pain the other lived in. I would not have had the courage then to tell how violence has marked my life. I learned long ago to deny my vulnerabilities and rush to action, to pursue achievements that help me forget the injuries to my soul.

It takes an unusual quality of friendship to free us to speak of our lives as a gift to another. But unfolding to one another the hidden anguish of our lives would take two decades. Our relationship gradually deepened from intellectual kinship to an emotional bond strong enough to hold worlds of pain and memory. Some of the stories I tell here I remembered only as Rebecca and I discussed our writing. Our conversations created a crystalline air in which memory could breathe and be held in words.

REBECCA

In January 1982, Rita and I sat in the cool, Northern California sunshine, sipping coffee at a table on the street. We were in Berkeley to hear Elie Wiesel and John Cobb lecture. I was eager to catch up with Rita, whom I hadn't seen since we were in graduate school together. Now I was in my second year as the minister of a small United Methodist church in Seattle, Washington. Rita was working on her doctoral dissertation.

Rita constantly surprised me. When we were students together she didn't just study theology; she seemed to be having fun at the same time. I heard about ski trips, hot tub adventures, dinner parties, and late-night dancing. She had been born in Japan and traveled all over the world, and her exuberant embrace of life startled me with its freedom and boldness. I, in contrast, was terribly serious and introverted. I had two passions, music and ideas. The rest was straw. I'd never been dancing in my life and wasn't about to start. For most of my life I lived in small towns in southwest Washington state. Seattle and Portland, Oregon, were the biggest cities I'd known, and Canada was the only place outside of the United States I'd visited.

Much of Rita's life was beyond the realm of my experience. But we shared an intense investment in ideas. We knew that thinking mattered. And I was moved by her zest for life. Deep down, I wondered if such freedom was possible for me.

This afternoon, at the sidewalk coffee shop, I listened with interest as Rita described her theological project. "I'm trying to construct a theology that speaks differently about Jesus. Conventional doctrines say Jesus saved the world by dying. But the people who killed Jesus hated him. It's wrong to confuse hate with love. This theology raises profound moral questions for me.

"I've seen what abuse and hate do. I've been working summers with youth from Southern California and Arizona, from every social sector: Beverly Hills, Watts, the Valley, South Central. We call the program a human relations workshop, and the kids come mostly because they are idealistic and want to end racism, sexism, and injustice. We work to empower truth-telling, healing, and community. I've heard stories of abuse and rape that break my heart—from ordinary kids. I counsel some of the religious kids, and the more attached they are to traditional ideas about Jesus, the more likely they are to think of their abuse as 'good' for them, as a trial designed for a reason, as pain that makes them like Jesus. They are often in denial about the amount of pain they live with. It amazes me that they survive and appear so 'normal.' They are wounded, but they have an astonishing passion to be whole. They reach out to others despite abuse, neglect, and hate. We try to help them see the forces that destroy relationships. Finding others who have experienced abuse helps them face their pain more directly and begin to find strategies to resist it. They go back home and do amazing work in their families, schools, and communities."

Rita was writing a theology about the human passion to be whole, to love and be loved, to be hungry for justice in the face of terrible harm, of brokenheartedness. Adapting Audre Lorde's term, she called this passion 'erotic power'—the life-giving spirit of God in every person. She said Jesus could not have incarnated God by dying. Christians claim God is love; if this is true Jesus would have had to receive *and* give love through living, not dying. Love is not an individual possession, but the spirit that breathes through relationships of care. Jesus' vision of *basileia,* the community of God, committed him to the struggle for justice and right relationships; living such a commitment saves us.

"The question of what really saves people's lives is all I'm thinking about these days," I said to Rita. "In the parish, I've had to think about violence in ways I never did in seminary. During my first week as a minister, the son of a leading member of the congregation was arrested on charges of rape and assault with a deadly weapon. I thought I knew quite a bit about life, having lived a quarter of a century in this world. But I didn't have the slightest idea what to do. I went to see Marie Fortune, who directs the Center for the Prevention of Sexual and Domestic Violence. I asked her advice. She said, 'You are his pastor, aren't you?' 'Yes.' 'Then your job is to visit him.' I did. I did my best to help him and his family.

"This year I've been counseling three women in the congregation who are struggling with depression. Each of them has revealed to me that she was raped, physically abused as a child, or the victim of incest. I looked through all my seminary textbooks and class notes on pastoral counseling. I couldn't find a single word about physical or sexual abuse. Theology hasn't taken these realities into account. The only thing I'm finding helpful is feminism."

Rita looked surprised. She'd often introduced feminist ideas into our conversations, but I would change the subject. During graduate school it was our mutual interest in religion, arts, and science, especially process theology, that drew us together. Process theology described reality as relational. It used theories of relativity and the philosophy of Alfred North Whitehead, the mathematician, physicist, and philosopher, to create a theology based in change, creativity, and relationship. Feminism hadn't been common ground for us. Suddenly it was.

"Who are you reading?" Rita asked.

"Mary Daly, Susan Griffin, Adrienne Rich, Audre Lorde, Rosemary Ruether, Alice Walker, Robin Morgan. That's all I'm reading. Feminists. Reading them is like walking into a room full of fresh air, like suddenly arriving in the real world."

RITA

Our friendship took an important turn that day. I'd always liked Rebecca's lovely, generous spirit, which was combined with an extraordinary intellect. But I missed a shared passion for the feminist ideas I found crucial for understanding the world. Still, I had learned a great deal from her. When we were graduate students we'd spent hours in her apartment discussing process theology and our love for the arts.

I was intrigued by her homesickness for the Pacific Northwest, her sense of place, so foreign to my peripatetic life. She described the enveloping hues of dusk as sky and water melded into a soft cerulean shawl of fading light. She spoke of the moist, cool air against her skin and the softness of Puget Sound rain. Her descriptions of backpacking with her brothers in the Cascade Mountains inspired me to learn to backpack myself.

She reminded me of the people I had known in Japan—people who were thoughtful and attuned to others, who were gentle, kind, and generous. Being in her presence felt familiar and comforting. I aspired to, but fell short of, being as good a person as I knew her to be. Even in austere graduate-student housing, the cinder-block walls and linoleum floors of Rebecca's place held great warmth within. I associated it with sophisticated, energizing conversations and her caring, intelligent presence.

But that day in the coffee shop in Berkeley, we began to discuss the critical issues of our lives for the first time. We spoke of our encounters with violence and its devastating effects on people. Both of us were struggling to rethink theology from our feminist perspectives. We wanted to speak to those who had been injured by violence, who were struggling to survive profound betrayals and traumas. We wanted theology to offer healing. We were convinced Christianity could not promise healing for victims of intimate violence as long as its central image was a divine parent who required the death of his child. We wanted theology to redefine salvation—not only as forgiveness for sinners but also as healing for those who had been the victims of sin, for the brokenhearted. We talked of writing a book together.

REBECCA

Few models exist for writing theology that blends intense intellectual inquiry with personal experience. The *Confessions* of Augustine, the African theologian, remains the best example, but theologians have rarely followed suit. And none has tried to write such reflections with a friend. We began in June 1997 to draft a book that was a scholarly, reasoned discussion of the doctrines in Christianity that most troubled us, especially the doctrine of the atonement—the idea that humanity is saved by Jesus' death on the cross. To support our arguments, we used stories from our lives and from people we knew. We disguised events in our own lives in the third person. We did not want our lives to be the point.

After writing three drafts, we realized something was wrong. Despite our best efforts, we had trouble wrestling the project to completion. We had been using stories as illustrations for ideas. But our ideas had not really come first. Life had. The weight of our argument was in our lives. Our theological questions emerged in our daily struggles to teach, minister, and work for social change, and from personal grappling with how violence had affected us. The mask of objectivity, with its academic, distanced tone, hid the *lived* character of our theological questions and our theological affirmations. Friends who read early drafts said, "The stories matter. They carry the ideas. Tell the stories."

RITA

But telling the stories meant we could no longer remain anonymous behind academic prose. We would have to reveal our life struggles. We were taken aback by what this would mean. How much of our lives were we prepared to disclose? What would it take to speak truthfully and respectfully of those whose lives have been closely linked with our own? Would the emotional cost of writing in such a way defeat us? I am a private person who does not share her weaknesses, failures, or pain easily. For Rebecca, especially, the return to harrowing memories of abuse might leave her without protection, without refuge. How could I ask my friend to do this? How could we do this without the shield of academic language, the screen of objectivity?

REBECCA

We were clear that the best way to show Christianity's complicity with violence would be to speak plainly. We needed to say how the theological sanctioning of violence has affected us and those we care about. Neither Jesus' death on the cross nor our own acts of self-sacrifice had saved us. But something had. We wanted to tell what we have tasted and seen ourselves of how life is saved.

Thus, we arrived at the book you hold in your hands, a book in two voices, with two stories to tell, interwoven by the love of friendship. Together our stories witness to a theological vision for resisting violence and affirming life.

RITA

The interweaving of our lives does not erase the differences in our life experiences and cultural backgrounds. Such differences are evident in our stories and their telling. A life-and-death struggle dominates the arc of Rebecca's story, an arc that moves from violence toward recovery. For me the route is indirect. My life began in one culture and was transplanted to another. I was shaped by the relationships and history that touched me, beginning with my earliest life in Japan. As is the case with Asian ways of being in the world, my story is of my families and my relationships.

East Asians and Anglo-Americans tend to see reality differently. For example, in describing an aquarium, white Americans ordinarily will focus on the largest fish. East Asians are more likely to describe the colors, quality of the water, and the overall environment. This holistic way of seeing gives priority to relationships among things, rather than the things themselves. What may appear as directness or clarity in a Western view may appear as narrowness or inaccuracy from an Asian perspective. Indirectness is a mode of communication that allows for more information to be held in a whole.

Rebecca and I have distinct cultural modes of self-presentation, as well as different life experiences. That our different journeys have led us to a shared theological vision is a sign for us: Our insights may be of value to others from a variety of experiences and backgrounds.

We wrote this book together. We struggled through the writing by taking care of each other: reading poetry to each other to start the day, fixing healthy, delicious meals together, hiking in the woods when our minds grew too thick with pain to function, giving encouragement and praise for yet one more difficult page completed, sharing music as we wrote, pausing for intense, focused discussion when either of us got stuck, and ending the day with lighthearted entertainment.

Friendship made this book possible—our friendship with each other and the significant friendships of our lives that we recount in this book. It is inconceivable to us that either of us could have written our stories without the support, the encouragement, the companionship, and the hearing into words of the other. The emotional task would have defeated us working alone, if either of us had possessed the courage to begin it. And that makes this project of inestimable value to us—the realization that our friendship has deepened, that in the writing of this book, we have lived the new theology we hope for and have arrived at a theology neither of us could have conceived alone.

A NEW THEOLOGY BEGINS HERE

At the center of western Christianity is the story of the cross, which claims God the Father required the death of his Son to save the world. We believe this theological claim sanctions violence. We seek a different theological vision.

What words tell the truth? What balms heal? What proverbs kindle the fires of passion and joy? What spirituality stirs the hunger for justice? We seek answers to these questions—not only for ourselves but for our communities and our society. What are the ways of being with one another that enable life to flourish, rich with meaning? When violence has fractured communities, isolated people, and broken hearts, how can life be repaired? We ask these questions not to arrive at final answers, but because asking them is fundamental to living.

We have worked with those afflicted by abuse and violence, whose exposure to war has limited their capacities to feel, whose internalization of messages of hate and disrespect has led to self-destruction and injury to others. We have contended with these realities in our own lives.

In the Bible, prophets and teachers repeatedly contend with their religion's failures and false claims. Job railed against the pious teachings of his day as he struggled with devastating loss and illness. The teachings of his friends reinforced his suffering. "Your maxims are proverbs of ashes!" he protested. Jesus challenged the Temple authorities who oppressed his people: "You have made my father's house a den of thieves!" Judaism and Christianity claim that life is good and that there is an author of life who wants our freedom and joy. Our religious heritage gives us the imperative to confront it when it fails to foster life or advocate for justice.

It also asks us to witness to grace. Grace has come to us in unexpected ways, in the midst of life. We have known healing, courage, restored love—salvation. From these experiences of grace we have arrived at a new theology. We see how to live in resistance to violence; we see how to live in love and in truth without denying bitter realities. We have learned how to use power, how to create places of hospitality for human flourishing, how to be present, how to choose life.

We have felt a fire in the heart of things, intimated in moments of surprise, a power which guards, judges, and continually recreates life. Echoing the biblical poets, we call this fire 'spirit,' this power 'presence.' We have seen how those who glimpse this fire reverence life. We have sensed what Wordsworth called "a presence that disturbs me with . . . joy, . . . something far more deeply interfused." This presence, felt as mystery and offered as faithfulness to one another, sustains and heals life. It calls for justice.

We have experienced life-giving communities that foster knowledge of spirit, awareness of presence. We know that, at their best, healthy communities practice the right use of the powers of life and lead people to experience wholeness, right relationship, and beauty. When this happens, such communities teach us to know ourselves and the world as sacred and sustain an ethic of appreciative care for life.

Violence denies presence and suffocates spirit. Violence robs us of knowledge of life and its intrinsic value; it steals our awareness of beauty, of complexity, of our bodies. Violence ignores vulnerability, dependence and interdependence. A person who acts violently disregards self and other as distinct, obliterating the spaces in which spirit breathes.

We can resist and redress violence by acting for justice and by being present: present to one another, present to beauty, present to the fire at the heart of things, the spirit that gives breath to life.

PROVERBS OF ASHES, FLASHES OF FIRE

The three parts of this book correspond to liturgical seasons in the calendar of western Christianity. The season of Lent leads up to Holy Week and Easter. In liturgical practice, Lent begins on Ash Wednesday, when believers' foreheads are marked with ashes. This mark signifies life bereft of the fire of God's presence. During Lent, as the days lengthen, biblical texts that portray the conflict stirred up by Jesus' teachings and actions are read in worship. The threat of violence against Jesus grows. The Christian community is invited to contemplate the meaning of his crucifixion.

In Part I, "Lent," we tell our experiences of loss, violence, and disruption. We describe how people we have known lost networks of love and were taught life-denying theologies of self-sacrifice. We show how theological claims about Jesus' death have become proverbs of ashes. We turn our faces toward a different theology.

The season of Pentecost celebrates the birth of a life-giving community. On the feast day of Pentecost, fifty days after Easter, the reading is Acts 2. The text portrays a miraculous gift of tongues—a grace of listening and speaking. This gift provides glimpses of fire to a people grieving Jesus' death. The language of Pentecost speaks of bodily transformation—of divine breath and holy fire filling the bereft. A new community is born. Spirit rekindles the people.

In Part II, "Pentecost," we tell what we learned in communities where people found healing and created solidarity for change. Through these experiences, we reveal how life-giving communities and life-affirming theology come into being. We celebrate those who took the journey with us and showed us that human presence and truth-telling have the power to hold life through violence to recovery.

The season of Epiphany recognizes flashes of fire. Throughout the weeks of Epiphany, texts tell how glimpses of the fire of God's presence inspire people to act for justice and liberation. Moses stands before the burning bush. He hears the voice say, "Take off your shoes, you are standing on holy ground." The God he encounters there sends him to lead his enslaved people to freedom. The feast of Epiphany, twelve days after Christmas, celebrates the arrival of the Christ child, welcomed by those who have waited long for a sign of God's presence. The Magi cross the desert to kneel before the baby Jesus. The elderly Simeon and Anna, who have waited all their lives for this child, lift him in their arms with joy. Simeon sings, "Now I can depart in peace for my eyes have seen what was promised" (Luke 2:29–31). But this season of joy is haunted by Rachel weeping for her children, grieving the slaughter of the innocents by King Herod, who seeks to destroy any threats to his power.

In Part III, "Epiphany," we tell the unexpected journeys in our lives that have returned us to childhood to discover love that exceeds our imagining. These journeys include Rebecca's painful descent into memory and a sustained grappling with the debilitating effects of sexual abuse, as well as Rita's discovery of an unknown father and family. Both stories reveal long-kept secrets and the unfolding of sustaining presence. These experiences lead us to the fire that burns at the heart of life, a fire that violence finally, we believe, does not extinguish.

The Postlude brings our voices together in a summary of the theological insights we affirm.

At each chapter's beginning, you will encounter a text from the Bible. These texts weave our struggles and discoveries into a heritage that has helped us understand our own lives as places of illumination. The Bible is a multi-voiced witness to the endeavor to know God and reverence life. As a human document, it is flawed in its grasp of ultimate things, but within it—as in our own flawed lives—we glimpse a mystery that holds us, always.

For you who take the journey with us through our stories of violence, healing, and theological discovery, we wish illumination for your own life, moments of epiphany, and a chance to pause and reflect on what it means, in your own time and place, to love life and to choose it against all odds.

PART ONE

Lent
A Season of Ashes

CHAPTER I

Away from the Fire

Rebecca's Story

"Daughters of Jerusalem, do not weep for me, but weep for yourselves and for your children. For the days are surely coming when they will say, 'Blessed are the barren, and the wombs that never bore, and the breasts that never nursed.' . . . For if they do this when the wood is green, what will happen when it is dry?"

Luke 23: 28–31

"He killed her," Pat said, "With a kitchen knife. In front of three of their children. The baby was sleeping."

She turned and looked out the window, her face still as stone. Her hands gripped the mug of tea so tightly I thought the solid stoneware would crack in her hands. I followed my friend's gaze out the steamy kitchen windows. Gulls circled and cried above the salt marsh, across the slough that edged the main road of town. The rickety old docks, the gas station, and the gravel parking lot of the church looked weary in the dripping rain. It was typical weather for South Bend, Washington, a town that had grown up along the shores of Willapa Bay, a wide, shallow backwater of the Pacific Ocean. Oysters and timber had been its original economic base, but now the town was economically depressed, with many unemployed. It smelled, as it had for nearly a hundred years, of pulp mill smoke and rotting leavings from the sea.

The Methodist parsonage, Pat's home, was perched on the hillside next to the church. Behind the house, Douglas fir, cedar, and big leaf maples climbed the hill, crowded underneath with huckleberry, salmonberry, and sword fern. Against the forest, the bay, the tide flats, and the unceasing rain, the small community felt fragile.

I knew this land. It was home. I'd started life on the other side of this bay, where the Grays River flowed into a similar muddy harbor, and the big towns of Hoquiam and Aberdeen stood. I knew the people—hardy, good-natured, plain. I knew that behind the glassed-in storm porches of the gray-and-white clapboard houses there were interior spaces warmed with sawdust-burning stoves, steaming cups of coffee, friendly conversation, and laughter. As a child, I'd visited these homes with my father when he was making pastoral calls. In my heart, home would always be a place that smelled of coffee and wood smoke, a place where the entry way was crowded with tall rubber boots, dripping slickers, and plaid wool shirts.

I loved it when the men of the church would go out clam digging and come back, with sandy shovels and sloshing buckets, to clean the clams in the big back porch sink of our parsonage in Hoquiam. Their loud voices, happily shouting and teasing, made me feel safe. Life came in from out of doors with a rush of salty wind and rain, the clump of boots, and the clatter of clam shells pouring into the sink.

But I knew better than to think all the homes were friendly. There were interior spaces where children were molested and wives beaten, where voices spoke words that silenced, terrified, and controlled. This hadn't changed.

Pat and I had known each other since junior high. Now we were both United Methodist clergywomen. I'd come to visit her, driving three hours from the neighborhood parish I served in Seattle. Our conversations over tea were a ritual of friendship, and also part of our practice of ministry. Ministry is a lonely profession. By talking together, pouring our hearts out to each other, we eased the loneliness and gained insight into the work we'd chosen.

Pat had tried to help Anola Dole Reed, the woman whose murder she had just told me about. "When I got to South Bend, I discovered there weren't any social services for victims of domestic violence. The closest services were two or three hours away by car. That's too far for a woman who needs emergency shelter. A group of us in the community began to work on how we could offer assistance. With the group's support, I let it be known, quietly, that women in need of a safe space could come to my house."

Pat's choice made sense. It's an ancient principle: church property as sanctuary. When they are in trouble—homeless, hungry, injured in spirit or body—human beings look for haven. Despite religion's failures, people come to churches counting on hospitality for the frightened, harbor for the distressed, shelter for the unjustly persecuted and pursued. Anyone who serves as the minister of a church knows this. People show up on your doorstep expecting the church to be the church, the holy site where divine mercy and strength can be obtained and where human kindness can be counted on. Your job is to keep the sanctuary open and tend the sacred ground.

Pat cared about women who were being battered in their homes. She helped create assistance for them. She turned back from the window and looked down into her tea. "It's just hard," she said, "not to be able to stop it. Almost every woman who's come here for refuge has gone back to her violent husband or boyfriend. She thinks it's her religious duty. I counsel her otherwise. I tell her it's her religious duty to protect her own life and take care of herself so she can protect her children. But my words and this shelter"—Pat gestured around the damp and slightly dilapidated parsonage—"are not enough."

"He killed her," she said, again, this time raising her face to mine and holding my gaze. I understood her sad, angry, and imploring eyes. We had to do something about this, somehow. We couldn't just sit here. Her gaze held questions. Were we destined to be nothing more than compassionate witnesses? Was ministry the art of standing by, while the world exposes its violent hands? Was our job simply to conduct the memorial services, comfort the grieving families, and pray for the children whose remaining parent was the murderer of their mother?

Pat had done more. Working with others, she organized a drop-in support group for abused women. She knew that women needed resources to resist the violence in their lives.

Anola came to the group a few times. Pat offered her support and counsel. When Anola's husband assaulted her, the group gave her the courage to call the police. She was reluctant to press charges, but an activist prosecutor brought her husband to trial. Pat accompanied Anola to court and stood by her as she took the courageous step to testify against her husband. "He knocked me to the floor. He got on top of me and twisted my hand and kept telling me that I'd better start listening to him and do what he wants me to do," she said in court. Gordon James Reed was convicted, fined five hundred dollars, and sentenced to ten days in the county jail.

"While he was in jail, Anola got her ears pierced." Pat smiled broadly, remembering. "It was her act of defiance, a way of saying this is *my* body. He would never have let her do that. She was so pleased with herself. Then he got out of jail. She had to decide whether to let him come back and live at home with her and the kids."

"She let him come home, didn't she." I said with sadness. "Why?"

"She thought it would be the right thing, in God's eyes. In the church she went to, the intact family was celebrated as God's will; father, mother, and children were meant to be together in a loving home. Anola believed that because this configuration of family was the will of God, God would somehow make it all right. For her to break up the family would make her a bad person. Doing the will of God was more important than her personal safety. The possibility that faithfulness to God's will might mean pain and violence could even have been in its favor. A good woman would be willing to accept personal pain, and think only of the good of the family. You know, 'Your life is only valuable if it's given away' and 'This is your cross to bear.' She heard, just like you and I have, that Jesus didn't turn away from the cup of suffering when God asked him to drink it. She was trying to be a good Christian, to follow in the footsteps of Jesus."

Pat counseled Anola to embrace the sacredness of her own life and not to submit to abuse. But it was important to Anola to hold fast to the image of virtue that her church taught her. "I have been trying to hold our marriage together for seven years," she said at the assault trial, "with my head split open three or four times by him." Anola believed God expected her to risk being battered, like Jesus. Her husband reinforced the message, defending his actions saying, "I just kept trying to convince her that we had a marriage here and she had children and everything and that she was destroying it."

Anola allowed her husband back into her home, but she continued to struggle with her decision. She went to her home church pastor for counsel. He, like Pat, encouraged Anola to take care of herself and her children. She came home that evening and told Gordon Reed that she wanted him to leave. He went into a rage. He knocked her to the floor with the baby's high chair and began stabbing her.

Later that night her four-year-old daughter would tell police, "Mommy was bad so Daddy killed her." Her five-year-old son would tell what happened. "I got in the way. Daddy said, 'Get out of the way,' when I tried to stop him. Daddy said he was mad. He said Mommy was a bad woman. Daddy had a high chair and was hitting Mommy. She wasn't crying because she was bleeding. Then Daddy got the knife."

The daughter said, "We thought Mommy had spilled something on her. But she didn't. It was blood. Daddy bent the knife in Mommy's tummy then he went to get the sharp knife. Mommy only used it to cut bread. He stuck her with the big sharp knife. Mommy was on the floor in the kitchen."

"We was crying when Daddy was killing Mommy," the son said.

Gordon Reed stabbed Anola eighteen times using ten knives. The big kitchen knife was still lodged in her neck when the police found her body. He was sentenced to twenty years.

"Her mother came for the funeral," Pat said. "She insisted that Anola be buried wearing her prettiest earrings in her pierced ears. I think it was a way to say, 'My daughter isn't just a victim.'"

"Pat," I said, "the only way you could have helped Anola more is if the whole Christian tradition taught something other than self-sacrificing love. If it didn't preach that to be like Jesus we have to give up our lives in faithful obedience to the will of God."

"But," Pat said, "this *is* what the church teaches. And Anola Reed is dead. I know Gordon Reed is the one responsible. He killed her. But I can't escape the feeling that he wouldn't have had the chance if the church hadn't taught Anola that your life is only valuable if you give it away."

Not long after this conversation with Pat, I spoke at a conference on women's spirituality. I described how a woman's religious home can be a place where she is endangered rather than nurtured, put at risk rather than initiated into freedom and fullness of life. I suggested women need to construct alternative religious ideas that allow for women's lives to be resurrected from the scourges of violence and abuse.

Following the speech, a Lutheran clergywoman raised her hand and said, "On Sunday mornings I go to the church early to prepare the communion table. It is customary in my tradition for the pastor to stand at the table and offer silent prayers before the congregation arrives and the service begins. A few Sundays ago, just before I woke up,

I dreamt I was standing at the table saying the preliminary prayers. Suddenly, the rectangular communion table turned into a stone coffin. The lid was open. I looked inside and saw the skeleton of my grandfather. I felt a surge of fear and revulsion and, at the same moment, a great rush of love.

"This is how I feel about the church. I love the church. It's my home and has been my family's home for generations. And I love the liturgy in all its beauty. At the same time, I feel something is dreadfully wrong. When I preside at the Eucharist, am I not reenacting images and ideas that tell people God wants them to sacrifice their lives? Am I right to do this? Does this give them life? Now when I pray in the church before the congregation arrives, I ask God to forgive me for performing the Eucharistic rite."

Pat and I were approaching a similar contradiction. How could we in good conscience continue to serve a church whose fundamental teachings contributed to the very violence we were seeking to prevent? At the same time, how could we walk away from the sanctuary, from the work of tending sacred ground, and providing ordinary places in the world that are doorways into divine presence, transcendent mercy, healing and hope? This was our chosen work, but clearly it demanded much more of us than repeating the old words and rituals, unexamined.

A few months after my visit with Pat, a quiet knock on the church office door interrupted my reading. Marking quickly the prayer I'd chosen for Sunday's service, I closed the *Book of Worship* and opened the door. A short, brown-faced woman stood on the threshold, bundled up against the chilly Seattle weather.

"Hello, pastor. I'm Lucia. I live down the block and walk by the church on my way to the bus." She gestured to indicate the direction. "I saw your name on the church sign. You are a woman priest. Maybe because you are a woman, you can understand my problem and help me."

"Of course, come in," I said. She sat down on the old sofa next to my bookcase with its load of theology texts bending the shelves. She smiled, an expression both warm and sad.

"I haven't talked to anyone about this for a while," she began, the smile fading, and sadness deepening in her eyes. "But I'm worried for my kids now. The problem is my husband. He beats me sometimes. Mostly he is a good man. But sometimes he becomes very angry and he hits me. He knocks me down. One time he broke my arm and I had to go to the hospital. But I didn't tell them how my arm got broken."

I nodded. She took a deep breath and went on. "I went to my priest twenty years ago. I've been trying to follow his advice. The priest said I should rejoice in my sufferings because they bring me closer to Jesus. He said, 'Jesus suffered because he loved us.' He said, 'If you love Jesus, accept the beatings and bear them gladly, as Jesus bore the cross.' I've tried, but I'm not sure anymore. My husband is turning on the kids now. Tell me, is what the priest told me true?"

Lucia's deep black eyes searched my hazel ones. I wanted to look away, but couldn't. I wanted to speak, but my mouth wouldn't work. It felt stuffed with cotton. I couldn't get the words to form.

I was a liberal Christian. I didn't believe God demanded obedience or that Jesus' death on the cross brought about our salvation. I hadn't forgotten Anola Reed, though I thought of my theology as far from hers. But just that past Sunday I had preached a sermon on the willingness of love to suffer. I preached that Jesus' life revealed the nature of love and that love would save us. I'd said that love bears all things. Never breaks relationship. Keeps ties of connection to others even when they hurt you. Places the needs of the other before concern for the self.

In the stillness of that moment, I could see in Lucia's eyes that she knew the answer to her question, just as I did. If I answered Lucia's question truthfully, I would have to rethink my theology. More than that, I would have to face choices I was making in my own life. After a long pause, I found my voice.

"It isn't true," I said to her. "God does not want you to accept being beaten by your husband. God wants you to have your life, not to give it up. God wants you to protect your life and your children's lives."

Lucia's eyes danced. "I knew I was right!" she said. "But it helps to hear you say it. Now I know that I should do what I have been thinking about doing." She planned to take courses at the community college until she had a marketable skill. Then she would get a job and move herself and her children to a new home.

We stayed in touch as she took each step. Eventually, her husband sought help for himself. Lucia agreed to let him spend weekends with their children. "They got their father back," she said, "and I got my life back."

I was glad for Lucia, and watched her progress with a sense of appreciation for her struggle and her strength. She let go of a theology that didn't support her life, that kept her in bondage to violence. Perhaps, in a critical moment, I offered the words she needed to assist her along the way. But my journey to disenthrall myself from a theology of sacrifice would be longer. Suffering love would haunt me.

The spring I met Lucia, I got pregnant. It was my husband who had proposed that we start a family. We both had finished graduate school, he was busy composing music, and I was settled in the parish. It seemed like the right time. We'd been trying for six months.

I knew I was pregnant the day after Easter. The double-blossom cherry was blooming. The spring rain filled the air with damp fragrance. I felt the life beginning inside of me as if it were an enormous gift. My heart was full of joy.

When I told my husband the news, the blood drained from his face. We were sitting across from one another at a favorite restaurant. I had taken his hands in mine to tell him. The formica tabletop expanded between us as he pulled back and let go of my hands. "I'm not ready to be a father," he said. "I can't do this. I'm not sure I want to stay with you. The only way I can imagine our marriage having a chance is for you to have an abortion." I felt his words as if they were a physical blow—swift, precise, unexpected.

"This is my decision to make," I said, claiming the only ground I could find to stand on.

During the next few weeks I considered my choices. The prospect of losing my marriage and becoming a single mother was overwhelming. I didn't think I could be a single mother and meet my responsibilities as the pastor of a church. I would have to give up my vocation and go on welfare. Worst of all, I couldn't face the shame of being abandoned by my husband. I was afraid I would kill myself. I did not believe that anyone around me would be compassionate or supportive. Years later, looking back, I would know that many of these assumptions were wrong. My family would not have hesitated to help me, had I asked. The church, too, would have stood by me. But, at the time, I withdrew.

I had learned to hide pain early in life. When I was three, four, and five the neighbor who lived around the corner from us had groomed me to trust him. Then he had molested me, orally raping me repeatedly. The anxiety, fear, and pain of that experience and the fierce bond I'd formed with the abuser were traumas I could not and did not tell. He terrified me with threats that silenced me. Living with hidden abuse in turn intensified my dependence on my parents' love and care. I needed them, but was too frightened to tell them why. I wanted still to be the sturdy and happy child that my parents adored. I couldn't ask for their help, so I tried to be like them. They were kind and generous people who put others first. I never saw them angry, upset, or frightened. To keep connected to my parents and the church that was the center of our family's life, I internalized my parents' way of being. It kept me close to them and protected me from terror.

I forgot the sexual abuse. I'd learned to excise part of myself to preserve relationship. It was what a good person did.

When I was in distress, I did not turn to my family or my church. In both places, I had learned that personal need had no place. The good person cares for others, but if she herself is hurt, frightened, confused, or in need, these weaknesses are to be nursed in private, covered over, or solved without bothering anyone else.

In late May, when the lilacs were heavy with purple blossoms, I allowed a doctor to remove from my body what would have become my only child. It was 1982. I was twenty-nine. The abortion was performed in safe, legal, medical conditions.

I chose abortion to save myself from shame, loss, and fears of suicide; to save a child from coming into the world without a father; to save a marriage; and to save the father from something he feared, something he said I could protect him from.

It was a willing sacrifice, I thought. An enactment of love for my husband and hope for our future. But the loss of my child cut deep. I kept the pain secret. Only two friends knew about the abortion. I told one and one guessed. I kept my experience hidden from my parents, brothers, and grandparents. I continued my public life as a parish minister, grateful for work. The daily tasks of church life were a mercy. There were hospital and house calls to make, meetings to attend. The midweek women's Bible study, choir practice, writing a column for the church newsletter—these tasks steadied me.

But our future did not unfold as I'd hoped. My husband and I didn't speak of the abortion. We tried to repair the rift in our marriage, but within a few months, he took an apartment across town. Years later I would piece together fragments of information about his childhood. How he had not been able to remember much of anything from the years when he was twelve and thirteen, except that he feared his father's criticalness. How his sisters said he'd go to bed crying. How his mother would say that she sent him off to boarding school when he was fourteen to remove him from his father's influence. How he was lonesome and homesick at boarding school. How a teacher singled him out for attention and then persuaded him to perform sexual acts. How this teacher was sending him letters still, fifteen years later, filled with sexual fantasies about my young husband. How my husband placed these frequent letters in the wastebasket, unopened.

These fragments didn't add up for me. I couldn't see our marriage in the context of longer histories of disrupted faith, distorted bonds, or sexual abuse. I only knew my present, growing anguish: my grief at losing him and my sense that a hole had opened inside me where life used to be. It would be a long time before I understood that I had bonded with a wounded young man because I myself was wounded in similar ways. I would have to remember the abuse that happened to me, face the sorrow and terror of it, and construct a new self, one not formed around the ideals of self-sacrificing goodness. But this task was one I would only be prepared to take on much later, when the accumulation of sorrow forced me to a deeper consideration of my history.

It was a sad time. I felt keenly the loss of the child whose beginning I had welcomed with joy. I was left with grief and shame, and hid these feelings from my family, friends, and religious community. During the day I did my job, but at night, I wrestled with anguish. I wanted to die. I was troubled that the choice to sacrifice came so easily. It was clear to me that in choosing the abortion I was choosing to make a sacrifice. The pregnancy was a blessing. Letting it go was a loss.

The gesture of sacrifice was familiar. I knew the rubrics of the ritual by heart: you cut away some part of yourself, then peace and security are restored, relationship is preserved, and shame is avoided.

I could have drawn you a picture of the steps. First I bow my head.

I cast my eyes down to indicate my subservience to the other whose will or needs I am obeying. I close my mouth. I do not speak. Then I kneel. I offer my head, my hands, or expose my breast or thigh to the executioner's blade and wait, holding still. He swings, cuts. Then I rise, silently wrap the wound, and withdraw.

Clearly this ritual is a horror. Where did the executioner come from who appeared so readily in my imagination? What if my choice for an abortion was the performance of a ritual that I was trained to enact, not the exercise of genuine moral discernment? I began trying to understand why the gesture of sacrifice was so easy, so familiar to my body, so related to my sexuality, and so futile. Why did I know so well how to do it? Why did the women I knew as friends, counseled as parishioners, preached to in my congregation, know so well how to do it?

I recognized that Christianity had taught me that sacrifice is the way of life. I forgot the neighbor who raped me, but I could see that when theology presents Jesus' death as God's sacrifice of his beloved child for the sake of the world, it teaches that the highest love is sacrifice. To make sacrifice or to be sacrificed is virtuous and redemptive.

But what if this is not true? What if nothing, or very little, is saved? What if the consequence of sacrifice is simply pain, the diminishment of life, fragmentation of the soul, abasement, shame? What if the severing of life is merely destructive of life and is not the path of love, courage, trust, and faith? What if the performance of sacrifice is a ritual in which some human beings bear loss and others are protected from accountability or moral expectations?

My decision for an abortion was the best I could do in the circumstances. The moral position that would ask my husband to keep faith with the child he had fathered eluded me. I lacked trust that the larger community of family, religious community, and society, would care for a child abandoned by its father. I had little insight into the deeper sources of strain in our marriage, or into my isolation. I wanted the child, but I sacrificed the desires of my heart and let go of a life that I cherished.

I do not regret that I had this choice. I firmly believe there are circumstances in which abortion is the most ethical choice, and I am committed to keeping abortion safe and legal. In my circumstance, what I regret is that I lacked moral imagination and therefore moral freedom because I had so deeply internalized the spirituality of self-sacrifice. I didn't exercise much choice. I obeyed a ritual.

The consequence of the ritual was sorrow. Nothing was redeemed or saved. I felt bereft. I grieved the lost pregnancy and my husband's absence. I also grieved an older, pre-existing loss that I did not fully understand. The abortion made me aware of an interior vacuity—an absence of self-possession, of self-protection, of freedom. I was missing an internal space in my own body that was free from the imperative of self-sacrifice. I had no inner sanctuary.

In the midst of my questions, Lent arrived. In the gospel reading for the first Sunday of Lent, Jesus tells his disciples, "We are going up to Jerusalem, and everything that is written about the Son of Man by the prophets will be accomplished. For he will be handed over to the Gentiles; and he will be mocked and insulted and spat upon. After they have flogged him, they will kill him, and on the third day he will rise again" (Luke 18:31–33). The gospel adds, "But they understood nothing about all these things . . . they did not grasp what was said" (Luke 18: 34).

My understanding of this gospel text had been shaped by Bach's cantatas, which I'd played many times as a cellist. One cantata begins with Jesus singing an aria announcing that he has set his face toward Jerusalem. "Don't go! Don't go!" the disciples respond, pleading with Jesus to avoid the dangerous path. But Jesus rebukes them. Then the cello and harpsichord sound out a lilting walk, almost a dance, and the aria of the exemplary believer is sung—an exquisite, joyful duet. One singer proclaims, "With willing feet, I follow thee." The other singer, representing Jesus, dances in harmonious joy. The final chorale is a prayer sung by the whole congregation, "Give us the strength to go with you to Jerusalem."

I had loved this music. When the disciples protested, imploring Jesus not to go, I felt their longing to see a loved one spared. I recognized their protest as a voice of love and I cheered them on. When Jesus responded that he must go, I felt the determination to face whatever had to be faced and I was moved by his strength. This felt like love too. When the exemplary believer sings her joyful duet with Jesus, pledging herself to follow him to Jerusalem and the cross, I wanted to be like her. If only my reluctance to bear suffering for the sake of love could likewise be overcome!

But now I questioned all of this. I didn't tell Lucia to bear suffering for the sake of love. She'd been told that by her priest and all it did was lead to many years of unabated harm. I grieved with Pat that Anola Reed had tried so hard to be a good Christian, and now she was dead. Hadn't Anola Reed, like Jesus, set her face toward Jerusalem? She had been mocked, scourged, and slain. Her young children were the witnesses at the foot of her cross. Their father, her crucifier. Though he was in jail, he still had custody of them. Killing their mother didn't disqualify him from maintaining his parental rights, just as God the Father wasn't denied his for sending his Son to the cross.

My desire to save my marriage had led me to sacrifice the life in my own body. The grief of this would not let me go.

What was the problem here? Were Anola, Lucia, and I just mixed up? Were the teachings of the church sound and good, but our comprehension and application flawed? I didn't think so. We had applied the theology of the church directly to our lives, theology that we had internalized deeply. The music and theology of Bach had seeped into my bones. For others, gospel hymns and praise songs, or the communion liturgy, had become part of them. To offer a willing sacrifice was the highest love. I'd moved to the beat when the gospel choir sang of being poured out, spilled out, and used up for Jesus. And, I'd sung the hymn, "Lord, I am able to be crucified with thee."

My childhood experience had helped me construct an idealized self who lived for others and disregarded her own needs. When I chose to have the abortion, I was fighting to preserve this self. As I struggled with the aftermath of grief, I wanted to maintain the ideal of goodness. These lessons and ideals isolated me and deepened my anguish.

Then Elizabeth, one of my clergywomen friends, told me that her father had forced sex on her beginning when she was four. He raped her throughout her childhood, and the incest only stopped when she left home for college. Elizabeth shared this with difficulty, but she wanted to break the isolation she lived in. I grieved for her pain, and asked whether her religious faith had helped her.

She said, "I identified my father with God. Not 'God is like my father,' but 'My father is God.' When I said this, I believed that my father was benevolent, loving, suffering. I did what I could to ease his suffering, to satisfy and please him. I was torn between two equally

demanding gods. One was far greater, eternal. But the other was intimate, present, and more immediately important to satisfy.

"I thought I was the sinful one, that I couldn't control my body
sexually and couldn't be trusted to keep silent. As I became more
aware of Jesus crucified, I connected my 'betrayal' of my father with
the disciple's betrayal of Jesus. My father would be crucified if I told
our secret."

My friend's account of her childhood faith helped me see further
the anguishing poverty of interpreting Jesus' death as a redemptive
event. Elizabeth was a vulnerable child being violated by a parent.
Her church taught her a good child honors her father as Jesus honored
his when he consented to die at his father's request. At the same time
it taught her to see herself as a sinner whose internal sense of resistance
to abuse threatened the life of her father. By keeping silent she protected her father from "being crucified." Her silence "saved" him and
trapped her in ongoing violation.

I could not keep silent about this theology. I began to argue with
the members of my theological family. Because the teachings of the
church are public, and because I had a public office as an ordained
minister, I argued publicly.

In the Western liturgical calendar there are six Sundays in Lent,
leading up to the observance of Holy Week and Easter. On the first
Sunday the congregation joins Jesus as he sets his face toward Jerusalem and begins the journey to the cross.

I invited the congregation to walk from Galilee to Jerusalem in
the company of the disciples who do not understand why Jesus' death
on the cross is part of God's plan. I suggested we take the disciples'
part—the part of the questioner—and accompany the disciples in
their uncertainty and doubt. Instead of chastising myself or the congregation for 'not getting it,' I asked that we consider what the church
asked us to believe and to examine its merit. If there was life-giving
truth it would yield itself to the sincere searcher who asks honest
questions.

During Lent I presented the major ways Christian theology has
formulated the doctrine of the atonement, the claim that the death of
Jesus on the cross saves us. I looked for the value and meaning in each
interpretation, but I could not let my questions go. I tested every
interpretation against the question, "Would this theology have

helped Lucia or Anola Reed or Elizabeth resist the violence they faced?" Of course my own burning grief was also part of the question. I was reluctant to expose it to public scrutiny, and I knew it would be professionally irresponsible to ask the congregation to take care of my emotional needs. But my experience informed the questions I raised, and I continued in private to struggle for personal resolution.

THE FIRST SUNDAY IN LENT: JESUS PAYS THE PRICE

"Here is how the theological story is told," I said to the congregation.

"In the beginning, human beings lived in the Garden of Eden, in perfect harmony with God. But Adam and Eve disobeyed the commandment of God. Because of their sinfulness, God had no recourse but to demand repayment for the harm they caused. We inherit their sin. The penalty for sin is death. God loves us and doesn't want to punish us. But his honor has been shamed. God is torn between love for us and the requirements of justice. To resolve this problem, he sends his only son Jesus into the world to pay the price we owe, to bear the punishment that all of humanity deserves.

"Anselm of Canterbury formulated the first statement of this substitutionary atonement theology in the twelfth century. In Why Did God Become Human? *Anselm said, 'No one can give himself more fully to God than when there is self-surrender to death for God's honor.'*

"In the sixteenth century, John Calvin developed this theology further, placing more emphasis on the wrath and punishment of God. In his Institutes *he said, 'Not only was Christ's body given as the price of our redemption, but he paid a greater and more excellent price in suffering in spirit the terrible torments of a condemned and forsaken man . . . He bore the weight of divine severity, since he was "stricken and afflicted" by God's hand and experienced all the signs of a wrathful and avenging God.'*

"Jesus struggles with the assignment to be our substitute. He prays, 'Father, let this cup pass from me.' But Jesus loves his father and honors the request even though it means a terrible death. Adam and Eve were disobedient, but Jesus obeys. 'Let thy will, not mine, be done.' On the cross, Jesus bears the punishment we deserve and we are set free."

Summarizing this theology to the congregation, I looked around from the pulpit at the faces of the people of the church. I knew that for some this was the core Christian message. It told them they were loved, forgiven, and freed. The world had done its best to stamp the last bit of self-respect out of them. Life's insults, injustices, and cruelties had persuaded them that they were, in the words of one of the leaders of the church, "nothing but trash." The substitutionary theory of the atonement lifted them up and renewed their confidence. It told them their lives had worth.

Who was I to disrupt this faith or put it down? But I felt compelled not to let the sermon end there. I made my way forward, taking careful steps. It felt like the pulpit was a plow I was pushing through difficult ground. There were land mines and rose bushes planted at random. I wanted the ground to support life and beauty, not to hold hidden bombs that would endanger lives. I continued the sermon:

"I do not want you to lose the knowledge that you are of infinite worth. There is no guilt so severe that you cannot make amends, and no message from life's injustices and humiliations that should define you as trash. Each one of us is the beloved child of God. When this knowledge is shattered in us, there is a divine mercy that will minister to our broken hearts and heal us. But we must arrive at this affirmation and trust by a different path.

"A generation after Anselm of Canterbury wrote this theology, Abelard in his Exposition on the Epistle to the Romans *questioned it. 'Who will forgive God for the sin of killing his own child?' he asked. 'How cruel and wicked it seems that anyone should demand the blood of an innocent person as the price for anything, or that it should in any way please him that an innocent man should be slain—still less that God should consider the death of his son so agreeable that by it he should be reconciled to the whole world!'*

"Offense at a cruel image of God has been present throughout the centuries. In 1805, in his Treatise on the Atonement, *the American Universalist preacher Hosea Ballou said, 'The belief that the great Jehovah was offended with his creatures to that degree, that nothing but the death of Christ, or the endless misery of mankind, could appease his anger, is an idea that has done more injury to the Christian religion than the writings of all its opposers, for many centuries. The error has been fatal to the life and spirit of the religion of Christ in our world; all those principles which are to be dreaded by men have been believed to exist in God; and professors have been moulded into the image of their Deity, and become more cruel. . . .'*

"Do we really believe that God is appeased by cruelty, and wants nothing more than our obedience? It becomes imperative that we ask this question when we examine how theology sanctions human cruelty.

"If God is imagined as a fatherly torturer, earthly parents are also justified,

perhaps even required, to teach through violence. Children are instructed to understand their submission to pain as a form of love. Behind closed doors, in our own community, spouses and children are battered by abusers who justify their actions as necessary, loving discipline. 'I only hit her because I love her.' 'I'm doing this for your own good.' The child or the spouse who believes that obedience is what God wants may put up with physical or sexual abuse in an effort to be a good Christian.

"*Theology that defines virtue as obedience to God suppresses the virtue of revolt. A woman being battered by her husband will be counseled to be obedient, as Jesus was to God. After all, Eve brought sin into the world by her disobedience. A good woman submits to her husband as he submits to God.*

"*Some will say that absolute obedience to God doesn't carry danger, because God is good and does not ask us to be violent. But this defense requires us to be certain that we are always right in understanding what God asks of us. We are fallible. The Bible, some argue, provides an infallible revelation of the will of God. But the Bible is a complex, multi-voiced document. Its teachings can be harmonized only by imposing onto the Bible a uniformity that is not in the text itself. There is no simple revelation of God's will. We have to accept responsibility for our interpretations. Obedience is not a virtue. It is an evasion of our responsibility. Religion must engage us in the exercise of our responsibilities, not teach us to deny the power that is ours.*

"*A God who punishes disobedience will teach us to obey and endure when it would be holy to protest and righteous to refuse to cooperate.*"

I ended the sermon by appealing for a different image of God. We need a God who delights in revolutionary disobedience and spirited protest. Was not Jesus one such as this—a prophet who confronted injustices and risked opposition rather than conform to an empire that enforced its oppressive will through violence?

To myself, I wondered, if Anola Reed had believed in a God who supported protest, might she have protested and resisted her husband's violence, rather than accepted and endured it? If her husband didn't regard God as the divine enforcer of obedience, would he have enforced obedience from his wife with violence? Would they have had more of a chance at life?

THE SECOND SUNDAY IN LENT: SELF–SACRIFICING LOVE
"*Disobedience,*" I said the second week, "*is not universally regarded as the root human sin.*"

"*The nineteenth-century liberal Protestants were disquieted by the image of God as a wrathful, punishing deity. They rejected the substitutionary theory of the atonement and developed a different understanding of the cross.*

"*In* A Theology for the Social Gospel, *Walter Rauschenbush argued against concepts of sin and salvation that 'have too much the flavor of the monarchical institutions under the spiritual influence of which they were first formed. In an absolute monarchy the first duty is to bow to the royal will. When theological definitions speak of rebellion against God as the common characteristic of all sin, it reminds one of the readiness of despotic governments to treat every offense as treason . . . Our universe is not a despotic monarchy, with God above the starry canopy and ourselves down here; it is a spiritual commonwealth with God in the midst of us.'*

"*Rauschenbush defined sin as betrayal of the bonds of care among human beings. The root of sin is not rebellious refusal to obey God, but a deep-seated selfishness. Sin disregards the needs and well-being of the neighbor in a heedless pursuit of self-centered wants. 'We rebel against God and repudiate his will when we set our profit and ambition above the welfare of our fellows and above the Kingdom of God which binds them together.' Selfishness is more than a personal failing. It is a transpersonal evil, institutionalized in social systems that benefit some individuals while exploiting and oppressing many others.*

"*If selfishness is the core human failing, the cure is loving concern for others, the transcendence of selfishness. 'Salvation is the voluntary socializing of the soul.' Individuals are saved by entering into a new life of self-sacrifice, with no thought for self, only love for others. Society is saved by the institutionalization of generosity, the creation of social systems that distribute wealth justly and sustain the ties of community. The kingdom will come on earth, as in heaven, if we will put aside selfishness and build the commonwealth of God together.*

"*The importance of Jesus for liberal Christians is not that he paid the price for sin. Jesus is important because he embodied loving concern for others and called people to love their neighbors. Jesus confronted the oppressive ruler of his day and was not afraid to risk his life doing so. No greater love has any human being than the love that sacrifices self to help and defend others.*

"*Jesus' death on the cross overcame the sin of selfishness. He did not concern himself with saving his own life. Rather, as the gospel says, 'Whoever would save his life will lose it, but whoever loses his life for my sake and the Gospel's will save it' (Mark 8:35).*

"Disciples of Jesus are called to follow in his footsteps. With him, we are to willingly take up our cross and bear the burdens that come with caring unselfishly for others. With his help and inspiration, no amount of pain need sway us from our devotion to serve others. In this way, we will embody God's love for all humanity."

I was preaching the theology I had heard all my life in the Methodist church. During much of my childhood, my own father and grandfather preached this and exemplified it in their lives. So did my mother and grandmother. They practiced unselfish devotion with a stunning and moving consistency. Social gospel Christianity promised healing and progress for society, and gave joy and meaning to the lives of those who followed this path. This was the theology that gave me the image of goodness I idealized and strove to follow. It also had taught me to think for myself and to connect my life to a legacy of social activism.

I wanted to hold on to the joy, courage, and activism I saw in the members of my family. My mother's father, Grandpa Ernst, had a zest for life we all adored. He'd play ball in the house. He'd laugh and tussle with the kids on the floor. On Sunday morning when he preached, the energy would rise in his bright tenor voice, the humor of things would shimmer in the congregation's laughter, and the importance of his vision would move them to tears. He rallied people to fight the good fight, to build the kingdom of God on earth. It would be a kingdom where the Ku Klux Klan didn't have a chance. No longer would the rich sit in palaces while the hungry cried for bread. With high spirits and firm conviction, grandfather cared for the least and he took on the mighty. He manifested a spirit of open-minded inquiry, robust intellectual quest, and passionate social engagement.

My grandmother Ernst was full of life as well. I remember being in church as a small child, standing next to her for the reciting of the Apostles' Creed. My grandmother would begin, "I believe in God the Father, maker of heaven and earth, and in Jesus Christ," then she'd close her mouth until she joined in again on the last phrase, "I believe in the communion of saints." As a child I was impressed that though she was the minister's wife, she didn't do what we were supposed to. "Grandma," I asked one Sunday, "why don't you say 'conceived of the Virgin Mary, descended into hell, rose again from the dead'?"

"Well!" she said, with a bustle of impatience, "Because it doesn't make any sense." My grandmother approached religion like hemming a skirt. She taught me to make the stitches strong enough to be visible on the outside. The lesson was clear. "Don't believe anything unless you can see that it is stitched together well."

My father taught me something similar. When I was twelve, we had confirmation class, and my father was our teacher. Just before Palm Sunday, each child was invited to decide whether or not to join the church. I'd thought about it carefully and announced to my father that I was not going to join. My mother had already sewn me a spring-yellow Easter dress to wear for the confirmation service, but I ignored this fact. Nor did I consider that my father might be embarrassed if his own daughter decided to remain a heathen.

My father, however, did not show the slightest sign of unhappiness with me. He respectfully said, "You have a perfect right not to join the church. But I would be interested to hear your reasons."

I explained myself. "First of all, I don't believe that God sends people to hell." Nothing in my liberal Methodist upbringing had asserted that God condemned people to hell, but I'd gotten the idea somewhere, and I objected to it. "If there is a God," I continued, "God must be at least as good as you and Mother. Neither of you would ever condemn anyone to eternal damnation." My father nodded, appreciatively.

"Furthermore," I went on, "I don't believe that Jesus was the only son of God. I believe everyone is a child of God."

My father said, "Do you know what a person who believes as you believe is called?" "No," I said, surprised to hear that there was a name for my heresy.

"A Unitarian," my father said. Then he added, "I'm a Unitarian in my theology. I agree with your ideas. You can be a Unitarian and join the United Methodist Church. There is freedom to believe as you see fit. John Wesley, the founder of Methodism, frequently preached on the maxim, 'We need not all think alike to love alike.'"

"Oh!" I said, happy to discover this. "Then I'll join the church."

It was the early '60s. My father encouraged the congregation to participate in the civil rights movement. Red-lining was legal in our town, and we mounted a successful campaign to end the practice that created white-only neighborhoods. As the Vietnam War escalated, my father used the pulpit to speak out against it. We lived near a large military base. My father's position stirred up controversy among the many military families in the church, but he had learned from military wives that their husbands were bombing Cambodia even though the State Department denied any U.S. involvement there. He conducted funerals for husbands and fathers who died in an illegal war. The grief of families was multiplied by the government's duplicity. My father would not keep silent.

I was moved by the social witness my father made, and I was persuaded by his instruction to his children: you all have gifts; you will find the joy of life by using your gifts in self-giving service to others. As a teenager, I grappled with the question of my life's calling. Music was my great love, and my time was devoted to cello practice. But I was troubled that a life in the arts might not be justified given the magnitude of suffering in the world. I began to study aesthetics, searching philosophically to answer a burning question: Did beauty matter or was it an extravagance? This search led me to Alfred North Whitehead, whose metaphysics, *Process and Reality,* placed aesthetics at the center of life. It also awakened a passion for intellectual inquiry in me, and I went to graduate school to study with the process theologian, John Cobb. This led me, eventually, to the ministry.

I was deeply committed to the values that had shaped me: social witness, service to others, and an intellectually responsible faith. The courageous activism of my family's religious tradition called me to speak out against wrongs. I needed this heritage of courage now. I had to confront the limits of my theological tradition. For all it had given me, it was not enough as I struggled with the grief that would not let me go.

At night, I was pacing the hall of the parsonage, hysterical with sorrow. My maternal arms were empty. The child I had welcomed with joy was never born. I let him or her go because love cares for the other, and no amount of personal sacrifice for the sake of love is too much. My marriage looked like it wasn't going to survive, despite the sacrifice.

Some nights, not able to sleep, I'd pray. "Dear God, forget about one day at a time. Please help me through one night at a time." And, on the worst nights, "Please, one hour at a time, help me." I wanted to preserve the idealized self I'd modeled after my parents and grandparents. A loving person would bear any pain. I struggled to regain my husband's affection and attention. I prayed for the strength to keep loving him, regardless of the humiliation, rejection, and betrayal I felt.

"Dear God, please give me the strength to never give up on love. Please give me the grace to follow the way Jesus taught, to love no matter what, to endure no matter what. Help me to forgive, help me to forbear, help me to keep my vow of love."

One night, praying this prayer, I received an answer. It came in the midst of my silent pleading, as if it were the voice of God. The answer was one, simple, clear word: No.

This "no" startled me, but I understood its meaning. It meant that some authority, within or beyond me, rejected self-sacrificing love. I pondered this in my heart, wondering if there was another direction that the source of life to whom I appealed in prayer might lead me.

I looked out at the congregation that Sunday morning, and I pushed the plow of my sermon a little further along the rocky ground, with its random land mines and rose bushes.

"As valuable as social gospel theology is, it does not hold all that religion needs to be able to hold. It fails to take into account that in women's lives the central sin may not be selfishness. It may be just the opposite: a lack of a sense of self.

"Women are culturally conditioned to care for others, but not ourselves. We believe that having needs, feelings, ambitions, or thoughts of our own is not good. In this self-abnegation, we enact a culturally prescribed role that perpetuates sexist social structures. The needs and thoughts of men matter, but not ours. Christian theology presents Jesus as the model of self-sacrificing love and persuades us to believe that sexism is divinely sanctioned. We are tied to the virtue of self-sacrifice, often by hidden social threats of punishment. We keep silent about rape, we deny when we are being abused, and we allow our lives to be consumed by the trivial and by our preoccupation with others. We never claim our lives as our own. We live as though we were not present in our bodies."

I paused and took a deep breath. Every eye in the congregation was fixed on me. My words described familiar experiences for the men and women in the congregation, but they weren't used to hearing this from the pulpit. I didn't have the courage to expose how relevant the words were to my own life, but I went on.

"When we aren't present in our own bodies, our closest relationships can

become empty. In sexual intimacy, our husband or lover may feel he is embracing an absence. We ourselves may feel we don't really exist. Intimacy ceases being a joy and becomes an unarticulated loss.

"The Bible suggests that sexism marks the fall of humanity. Exiled from the Garden of Eden, Adam and Eve are cursed with the loss of mutuality. Women will experience their sexuality as a source of pain, and men will lord it over them (Genesis 3:16). Primordial estrangement from God is manifest in social systems of dominance and submission.

"We don't need to be saved from the wrath of God or the sin of selfishness. We need to be saved from the gender socialization that teaches women to abnegate selfhood and teaches men to depend on the service of subordinates. The dynamic of dominance and submission in human relations is the heart of sin. What will save us from this?

"Does Jesus' self-sacrifice on the cross end dominance and submission? No. Jesus' crucifixion was a consequence of domination, not its cure. An oppressive system killed him to silence him and to threaten others who might follow him. Domination still operates in our world and has left many lives bereft of intimacy and joy."

My sermon hit close to home for many. My own pain, albeit cloaked, had entered the public sphere.

Midweek the women's Bible class met at noon, as usual. The women had started the class when their children were young. Now they were in their seventies and eighties, and the group had become small. Every Wednesday, as they'd done for forty years, they packed a brown-bag lunch and came to church to read and discuss the Bible together. The pastor always met with them.

This week, as we were unwrapping our sandwiches, there was an uncomfortable silence. Then one of them turned to me and spoke. "We've talked about this and decided we need to say something to you about your sermons. You have to stop talking about women being oppressed and saying those things happen to women, like battering and rape."

"Why?" I asked, somewhat taken aback.

All at once, all the women burst into tears. One by one they spoke. Marion said, "When I was a child I was raised by my grandparents. My grandfather used to beat my grandmother terribly. He'd go after her, and I thought he would kill her. I'd try to put myself between him and her to get him to stop. Then he would beat me too." When

Marion spoke the rage and grief in her face and voice was as intense as if this violence had happened that morning.

Then Violet said, "Every day of my marriage I have been raped." I was startled to hear this. "What do you mean?" I asked. She said, "In our marriage, I am not allowed to make any decisions. My opinion, my wishes, my thoughts are never honored. He acts against my will. I have no will of my own. That's what I mean by rape."

June Ellen spoke. "My husband doesn't talk to me when he is angry at me. Sometimes I have no idea why. Right now he's angry at me. I cook him breakfast, lunch, and dinner every day, and sleep with him at night, but he won't speak to me. He hasn't spoken to me for three months."

After listening to the women I asked, "How have you lived with these things? Have you talked to one another, helped one another?" They looked around at one another and shook their heads. "We've never said these things. This is the first time we have told each other."

The women had known one another all their adult lives, but they had hidden their memories of abuse and their daily experiences of humiliation. They'd taught Sunday school, run the women's society, raised money for agricultural mission projects in Africa, India, and China, organized food drives and clothing collections for the poor in our own city, managed the church's finances, put out the weekly bulletin, sung together in the choir—but they had never told one another about the daily pain in their own lives. My sermons were disrupting their ability to suffer in silence.

"You are asking me to help you continue to keep your experience silent," I said to them. "Do you really want to do that?" They talked about what it had been like to remain silent. By the end of the conversation, the women were laughing through their tears. The warmth of their affection and their compassion for each other filled the room. They turned to me again, "We think you should keep preaching about what happens in women's lives."

THIRD SUNDAY IN LENT:
THE CRUCIFIED PEOPLE OF GOD

On Sunday the congregation gathered again for worship. In observance of Lent the sanctuary was bare of any decoration. A purple cloth draped the plain altar. A few moments before church, I slipped on my vestments: first the white linen preaching alb, then the purple, raw silk scapular—an elegant apron—that had been made for me by a church member. On its center she had embroidered a crown of thorns interlaced with nails. It rested over my heart as I preached.

"Last week I told you that liberal theology views Jesus' death as an act of self-sacrificing love, an example we should follow. But self-sacrifice has been damaging to women. We cannot offer love to others and never claim the right to comfort, understanding, or self-development for ourselves. This is not good for women's lives or men's lives. It dehumanizes all of us.

"Liberation theology takes an approach similar to liberal theology. But where liberal theology emphasizes self-sacrificing love, liberation theology emphasizes fighting to end oppression and injustice. This means courageously confronting oppressive systems that dehumanize life—even at the risk of violent opposition.

"Jesus is not simply a self-giving person; he is a revolutionary activist. Revolutionary zeal, inspired by Jesus, is not new. In the fifteenth century Thomas Müntzer, peasant and theologian, led an armed revolt in Westphalia (now Germany). The feudal system benefitted a few and left many impoverished. Müntzer said that people could submit to the peasant's lot and die serving an oppressive lord, or they could die fighting to overthrow the feudal lords. Those submitting were the 'devil's martyrs.' Those fighting were 'Christ's martyrs.'

"Not all liberation theologians advocate armed revolt. But all liberation theologians recognize that those who resist oppression risk opposition.

"Latin American liberation theologians speak of Christ's martyrs as the hope of the world, the living presence of Christ. Jon Sobrino, in Jesus the Liberator, calls the voluntary suffering of those who struggle against oppressive systems 'nourishment' for the world. He writes, '[The crucified people] make it possible for this world to recognize itself for what it is, sinful, but also to know that it is forgiven . . . The crucified people . . . make Christ present first and foremost through the fact of being massively on the cross. . . . [T]hey make him present because like the Lamb of God, they carry the sin of the world and by carrying it they offer light and salvation to all.'

"We are called to join Jesus in working to liberate people from all that diminishes life. We are asked to be courageous in this work. I agree with liberation theology's call to engagement. But I remain uncomfortable with its idealization of accepting violence and its glorification of the crucified people of God.

"Any distinction between voluntary and involuntary suffering confuses matters. In each case, the perpetrator of violence remains the same. The perpetrator punishes some for being protesters and resisters. The perpetrator exploits and dominates others. The volunteers in the struggle suffer violation and pain, just as the non-volunteers do. And they all suffer for the same reason: those in power who benefit from unjust systems maintain them through violence, coercion, and exploitation.

"Resistance can disrupt an oppressive system and when widespread enough, it can bring a system down. Resistance is a transforming act. But it is not the abuse inflicted on resisters that brings about the transformation. It is their refusal to cooperate with injustice. Direct action saves people; not the violence of oppressors.

"The violence directed against activists and revolutionaries must evoke grief not adulation. Making the pain of backlash and repression positive cloaks perpetrators. Perpetrators should not be hidden by language that praises the death of martyrs as nourishment for the world. Courageous resistance and hope nourish and change the world. This is what redeems and transforms."

FOURTH SUNDAY IN LENT:
THE MORAL INFLUENCE THEORY

The next Sunday I turned back to the thirteenth century to uncover how liberation theology views the power of the cross.

"Liberation theology upholds an older theology of atonement: Abelard's moral influence theory. Abelard argued against the idea that God was a dishonored lord whose honor was restored by the murder of his own son. Instead, he said the problem is that human beings see neither their sin nor the mercy of God. The death of the Son of God brings human beings face to face with cruelty. Contemplating the suffering of Christ, people will feel remorse and repentance—especially seeing that Christ submitted to violence rather than turning it back on his enemies. A love so great that it withholds evil for evil reveals the mercy and kindness of God. Seeing this, Abelard said, human beings would be moved to stop rejecting God and would open their hearts to receive God's mercy.

"During the civil rights struggle in the United States, Dr. Martin Luther King Jr. understood that peaceful demonstrators would meet with violent hostility. Accept in your own body, Dr. King said, the slings and arrows of their hostility, but do not return it. There is power in undeserved suffering. Your enemy will come to see the error of his ways and will repent.

"*As a strategy to call oppressors and unjust systems to account, the practice of nonviolent resistance can be effective. Important changes have resulted from people's willingness to take risks to confront and transform injustice. But the violence endured during the civil rights movement, including Dr. King's assassination, is anguishing. I am troubled that 'moral influence' theology makes acceptance of violence a strategy to move perpetrators of violence to repentance. This theology assumes every violent perpetrator has the empathy and moral conscience necessary to be moved by the suffering of others. And it makes every victim an agent of God's call to repent and accept mercy. This makes the repentance of the perpetrator more important than the suffering of the victim.*"

In the back of my mind appeared the image of a woman imploring a man to see the pain he was causing her and change his ways. Hadn't I hoped my husband would see the pain he caused me? Seeing my pain, wouldn't he relent in his request that I have an abortion? When that didn't happen, hadn't I believed that he would see how much I loved him by my willingness to have the abortion and to bear the sorrow of the loss? Wouldn't this love move him to stay with me, rather than leave me? Wouldn't he see my beauty and goodness and adore me?

The wrongheadedness of this view of love was painfully evident to me. The suffering martyr moves with an undercurrent of hostility and arrogance. She is better, morally superior. She suffers righteously, indignantly. She languishes into misery, waiting for him to embrace her with humbled heart and passionate gratitude. Even if he possessed the empathy to do so, why must misery become the bond between them?

Oh dear, I thought to myself. This is sick. This is manipulative and evasive. This strategy assumes there is no power available to me other than the power to elicit guilt from another and put him in my debt. This binds the other person through pain. This is not a strategy of freedom, but a rearrangement of bondage. It won't do.

To the congregation, I said:

"*Religion needs to foster a truer regard for life when it is disrupted by betrayal and violence. Perpetrators of violence lose their humanity. So do victims. Strategies for social change must address the consequences of oppression for those who are injured by it. It is not enough to glorify and praise victims for their forbearance or to see them as servants of the perpetrators' conversion.*

"*Without outrage and grief on behalf of victims, we easily return to valo-*

rizing self-sacrifice. Liberation theology often slips back into a glorification of suffering and sacrifice. Leonardo Boff, *in* Passion of Christ, Passion of the World, *writes, 'For Jesus Christ, to open oneself to God meant to abandon oneself to God as a child to a parent. Here is authentic, genuine sacrifice. Human life has an ontological structure of sacrifice.* . . . *[H]uman beings* . . . *can live and subsist in a human way only if they surrender to the Other.* . . . *This is the sense in which Christ was the sacrifice par excellence. He was a being-for-others to the last extreme. Not only his death, but his whole life was a sacrifice: it was wholly surrender.* . . . *Christ would have been a sacrifice even had he never been immolated, had never shed his blood. This is not what sacrifice is. Sacrifice is self-donation: the total gift of life and death.'*

"*This theology will leave an abused child or a battered spouse defenseless. Theology needs to teach us how to be for ourselves and be for others simultaneously, to hold both lives sacred. If either life is being exploited or injured by the relationship, there should be action that will restore ethical relationship and redress the harm. Only then will our concern extend equally to victims and to victimizers. Otherwise, the victimizer is always the object of the victim's concern; but the victim is never the object of his or her own concern.*

"*Theology needs to tend to the healing of those whose lives have been fragmented by violence. The survivor needs healing, not just to change the system, but so she herself can become free.*

"*Theologians may say that the suffering of victims helps heal the world, but who will heal the suffering victims? Who will take the crucified down from the cross and grieve? How will their lives be restored or redeemed, their bitter anguish salved?*"

FIFTH SUNDAY IN LENT: THE DARK NIGHT OF THE SOUL
"*There is another way that Christian theology speaks of the meaning of the cross. It says that in dying and rising Jesus shows us the pathway of life. This pathway takes us through suffering and despair into new life.*

"*Paul speaks of this as dying and rising with Christ. Just as Jesus died on the cross, our spiritual journey requires us to die to all that separates us from God. We have to die to our pride, die to the certainty that our way is best, die to our attachments. A spiritual death is needed before we find our souls renewed in spirit.*

I thought of the women in the Bible class.

"*Sometimes we live for a long time with a certain belief, like the belief that it is best to never speak about pain and abuse in our lives. We hold fast to our belief and live by it. But then something challenges this belief. We see it may not be the best way to live. We defend our old belief, fearing that if we let go of it our life will fall apart. But then we find we can't hold on. Life has asked us to let go. So we let go. We relinquish the way we have held our life together, the ideas that have guided us. It feels like falling, or dying. We are angry, frightened, resentful. But we discover that by letting go we have opened ourselves to something better. Grace comes to us, and we discover a life that is richer, freer, more joyful. We've experienced resurrection.*

"In this mysticism of the cross, Christianity teaches that the process of dying and rising spiritually is the pattern of Christian spirituality in small and large ways. In the lives of the mystics and the saints, this spiritual dying is sometimes a long struggle—the dark night of the soul. In that dark night, we encounter the pain of life full on. We lose a sense of God's presence and struggle with despair.

"Life takes some of us to this place whether we want to go there or not. Our father beats us. We are raped walking home from school. We are drafted into the army and watch our best buddy blown to pieces in front of us. We are traumatized. We enter into the dark night—anguished that human violence can be this enormous. From this spiritual death, we struggle to find life. We cry, 'My God, My God, why have you forsaken me!' (Psalm 22:1).

"Others of us intentionally follow Christ into places of great human suffering. As a spiritual commitment, we volunteer to work on the AIDS ward; we go to the war zone to help refugees; we minister among the homeless; we live among the dying outcasts on the streets of Calcutta.

"The spirituality of dying and rising promises that we will journey through anguish to consolation, through absence to presence, and through death to life because Christ rose from the dead. 'Weeping may endure for the night, but joy comes in the morning'" (Psalm 30:5).

I paused. There were questions I wanted to raise, but I didn't want to take away from what was life-giving in this theology.

I plowed ahead.

"There is spiritual and ethical power in this theology. It affirms that God moves with us through the valley of the shadow of death. The deeper process at work can be trusted and will see us through. 'Light shines in the darkness and darkness has not overcome it' (John 1:5). Trusting this, people commit themselves to be present to human suffering, offering a ministering presence in the face of all that anguishes the human heart.

"But this theology can fail to serve life. It takes a historical event of vio-

lence and misapplies it to a spiritual truth. Jesus' death on the cross was not a spiritual illumination. It was a public execution performed by an oppressive empire. The brutality of this violence is mystified, absorbed into a spiritual affirmation.

"What happens when violent realities are transubstantiated into spiritual teachings?

"You've heard it or said it yourself. A mother loses her son to suicide. In an effort to comfort her you say, 'God has a purpose in this. He sends pain to make us strong. You may not feel it now, but you will learn to give thanks for this experience, because through it, God will strengthen your faith.'

"These words take the grieving mother away from the reality of her lost child. Tragedy is renamed a spiritual trial, designed by God for the mother's edification. God becomes the sender of torture, who injures us then comforts us—a perverse love.

"When Jesus' crucifixion serves as a metaphor for spiritual processes of transformation, or a mystical illumination of God's abiding presence, violence is justified as sacred. In this mode, the infliction of pain can be re-inscribed as a holy action. Violence can be justified as a disciplining of the spirit.

"This theology can lead to the intentional cultivation of pain. For example, in the fifteenth century Catherine of Genoa believed that through denying her body food she would be able to die to earthly appetites and learn to live with total trust in God. In a dialogue between her body and her soul, her body argues that food is important, that if she stops eating bread, she will forget the necessities of the body, and this will make her insensitive to the needs of the poor. Her soul retorts that eating bread takes her away from total trust in God. What good does it do if you save the body, but lose your soul? Her soul wins this argument. Catherine dies of starvation.

"The spiritualizing of suffering makes God the author of all pain, who uses pain to edify or purify human beings. Dying and rising with Christ can easily become crucifying parts of ourselves in internal purgation of the unholy; or crucifying other human beings for a holy cause.

"The mysticism of the cross teaches that violence is God's way of transforming people and communities into greater spiritual well-being. It clouds the realities of human violence in a haze of spiritual glory.

"God is not the author of human violence and does not sanction cruelty and torture. To inflict pain on ourselves is not virtuous and to inflict it on others is not edifying or transforming. Sparing the rod does not spoil the child. It is not godly to beat our children or ourselves.

"We have to face pain more squarely. When grief and loss come to us, we

cannot comfort ourselves by saying God is testing us or offering us a blessing that we don't yet understand. We have to face the pain without this divine sanction.

"We have to learn to grieve full out and face forward, without covering over the realities of human cruelty and violence.

"The dark night of the soul is this difficult. It is a night without comfort, without shield, without warmth. T. S. Eliot expressed this in his Four Quartets.

> *I said to my soul, be still, and let the dark come upon you*
> *Which shall be the darkness of God.*
> *. . . wait without hope*
> *For hope would be hope for the wrong thing; wait without love*
> *For love would be love of the wrong thing; there is yet faith*
> *But the faith and love and hope are all in the waiting.*

The church was quiet after the sermon. I had drawn a pall over the place. People shook my hand after the service, as usual, but they were discomfited. One of the strongest members of the church, well-read theologically, a social activist, and person of prayer, said to me, "I'm not sure I can go where you are suggesting we need to go. It is painful that you ask us to strip so much away."

Another beloved church member was sweet as always, but angry. She shook my hand with her usual kindness and warmth, and said, "I understand that you need to speak from your heart. But I don't come to church to hear about all the violence and pain in the world. I come to church for respite from the pain. I won't be coming here any more. There's another church closer to my home. I know I will receive words of comfort and strength there. I'll keep you and this church in my prayers."

One of the newcomers to the church asked to talk with me further. We met that evening after the newcomer's class. He said, "I like this church and I thought I wanted to join, but you are questioning everything. Isn't there anything that you believe in? I need a faith I can count on, not one where the rug is pulled out from under me."

I wrestled with my parishioners responses. Was I imposing my own struggles on them unfairly? Wasn't it my job to strengthen their religious understanding, not take it away from them piece by piece? Was I going too far?

I remembered the counsel that Bishop Melvin Talbert had given to the ministers in our area. "If you love your people," he said, "tell them the truth. Don't hold back for fear of making them angry. If they withhold funds or threaten to leave—hold your ground. I will back you up. Neither funding nor numbers of people at church are more important than your obligation to speak the truth as you understand it.'"

SIXTH SUNDAY IN LENT: THE CRUCIFIED GOD

There was one more Sunday in Lent before the Holy Week observances would begin, and one more theology of the cross I wanted to examine.

"Jesus' crucifixion shows us that God is with us in our pain. This is what the theology of the crucified God says. On the cross, God experienced the full meaning of human existence. To be human includes humiliation, betrayal, physical torment, abandonment, isolation, and the collapse of hope. On the cross God is finally, fully at one with humanity. This is the at-one-ment, the atonement: that God knows the heart of human sorrow because God is in full union with us, 'even unto death, death on the cross' (Philippians 2:8).

"This theological claim provides a divine companion for suffering humanity, especially the victims of violence and abuse. It tells the oppressed that God is with them. God knows the worst. There is nothing that can happen to a human being that God has not experienced.

> If I ascend to heaven,
> you are there;
> If I make my bed in Sheol,
> you are there.
> If I take the wings of the morning
> and settle at the farthest limits of the sea,
> even there your hand shall lead me. (Psalm 139:8–10)

"The theology of the crucified God speaks intimately to us when we are crushed by sorrow, or struggling to find a way to survive human cruelty. It doesn't minimize pain by saying it is a blessing from God to teach us something we need to know. It doesn't say our suffering will help someone else or be redemptive. It faces the reality of violence without denying it. God is not the one who mystifies or glorifies violence but the witness who fully knows our anguish.

"But for all that is comforting in this theology, something about it chills *me. Did Jesus have to die on the cross for human beings to come to know the abiding presence of God? Jürgen Moltmann, in his book* The Crucified God, *argues just that. He says that God's act of mercy and love on the cross was the total self-annihilation of God by the pouring out of the Father into the incarnate Son. On the cross, God dies. This theology describes a merging of selves in pain and annihilation. What hope is there in this? If God dies on Good Friday because love is the total identification of one being with another, what power will free human beings from being locked in death with God? Is love really the total annihilation of boundaries between selves? Is love's ultimate expression the destruction of the self?"*

This theology ended for me as a suffocating death throe of un-differentiated anguish. It felt terribly familiar, but I couldn't name why. That naming would only come years later, after I had lived longer, and faced more of my own life. I only knew that the crucified God was not a liberator or redeemer.

Hadley Basque invited me to lunch. He'd been listening to my ser-mons and wanted to respond. Hadley was one of the nonbelievers in the congregation. An artist who worked with the homeless in a downtown emergency shelter, Hadley was active in the church but didn't buy into any of the theology. I liked Hadley. I always learned things, talking with him.

"I was a prisoner of war during the Korean War," he began. "I was in the camp for two years. The winters were the hard part. In North Korea the winters are very cold. It snows. The ground freezes. We had to sleep in drafty barracks on thin boards with one thin blanket. In winter, the guards would make charcoal fires in these barracks. They stood around the fires, warming themselves, in front of us. If you wanted to, you could take your blanket and go sleep by the fire. The guards didn't mind.

"You could always tell the prisoners who had given up hope. They would go sleep by the fire. It was warmer there. You could make it through the night without shaking from the cold. But being warmed that way lowered your resistance. The ones who slept by the fire would get sick, pneumonia or flu, or God knows what. They'd last for a while, but they wouldn't make it. They would die.

"Those of us who survived—we were the ones who never went to sleep by the fire."

I looked at Hadley across the table. There was quiet. The restaurant noises clattered around us. I knew what it felt like to sleep away from the fire, but I hadn't known, until then, that it might be a way to survive.

I had told the congregation we had to stop sleeping by the fire. My objection to every theology of the cross was that it mystified violence and offered dangerously false comfort. The restless concern, the fire in my bones, was to face violence in the world more squarely. Theology cloaked violence and taught people to endure it. Christianity's denial of violence appalled me.

You couldn't look at Jesus on the cross and see there, as the old liturgy said, "one perfect sacrifice for the sins of the whole world." You couldn't see the face of love. You couldn't see a model for an interior psychological process of dying and rising. You couldn't see pain inflicted by God for the spiritual edification of believers. All these ways of seeing Jesus on the cross ended up sanctifying violence against women and children, valorizing suffering and pain, or denying loss. You couldn't look on the man of sorrows and give thanks to God without ending up a partner in a thousand crimes.

The actual historical event of Jesus' crucifixion was neither sweet nor saving. In Jesus' time, the Romans occupied all of Palestine. The Roman empire overtaxed the peasants, confiscated peasants' forfeited land, and co-opted the Jerusalem Temple to serve the needs and wants of the ruling minority. The Romans and their collaborators in Jerusalem were unpopular with the peasants of Galilee, who resisted in many ways. Jesus, a Galilean Jewish teacher, resisted Roman exploitation and cultural domination by teaching and healing. A community gathered around him.

The Romans suppressed resistance by terrorizing the local population. Crucifixion was their most brutal form of capital punishment. It took place in full public view, to teach a lesson through terror. Those crucified were soldiers or slaves who had run away from service or enemies of the state, especially those fomenting political insurrection and resistance. Jesus was likely guilty as charged. His demonstration against the Jerusalem Temple would have been interpreted by Pilate, who used the Temple treasury to fund his public works projects, as insurrection. Pontius Pilate was notoriously cruel. Philo, Pilate's contemporary, describes Pilate's "outrages, wanton injuries, constantly repeated executions without trial." Jesus died a violent death, preceded by the torture of flogging, which was meant to score the flesh so deeply that the victim bled to death on the cross, sometimes lingering for days. Often the victim was simply tied to the cross. Jesus was nailed, the worst way to be hung. Seneca wrote:

> Can anyone be found who would prefer wasting away in pain dying limb by limb, or by letting out his life drop by drop, rather than expiring once for all? Can any man be willing to be fastened to the accursed tree, long sickly, already deformed, swelling with ugly weals on shoulder and chest, and drawing the breath of life amid long-drawn-out agony? He would have many excuses for dying even before mounting the cross.

Jesus died relatively quickly, which means his wounds were very deep.

His absence was acutely felt. Many of his followers dispersed, anguished and afraid. A few women remained to tend the body and see to his burial. They grieved deeply. Over the years, Rita and I would contemplate the meaning of Jesus' death. To say that Jesus' executioners did what was historically necessary for salvation is to say that state terrorism is a good thing, that torture and murder are the will of God. It is to say that those who loved and missed Jesus, those who did not want him to die, were wrong, that enemies who cared nothing for him were right. We believe there is no ethical way to hold that the Romans did the right thing. We will not say we are grateful or glad that someone was tortured and murdered on our behalf. The dominant traditions of Western Christianity have turned away from the suffering of Jesus and his community, abandoning the man on the cross.

Atonement theology takes an act of state violence and redefines it as intimate violence, a private spiritual transaction between God the Father and God the Son. Atonement theology then says this intimate violence saves life. This redefinition replaces state violence with intimate violence and makes intimate violence holy and salvific. Intimate violence ends sin. Behind the holy mask of intimate violence, state violence disappears.

The days of Lent were drawing us closer to Good Friday. I began preparations for the Good Friday services at the church. The choir was rehearsing to sing Gesualdo's setting of "O Vos Omnes" from the book of Lamentations.

> Is it nothing to you,
> all you who pass by?
> Look and see if there is any sorrow
> like my sorrow. (Lamentations 1:12)

The anthem was a call to witness and to mourn. This is what we needed to do. We needed to face the man of sorrows, without softening the anguish with proverbs of ashes. His suffering was not unique. Is there any sorrow like his sorrow? Yes. Everywhere. Too often.

We designed a simple service for Good Friday, using the old Tenebrae service, the service of darkness. We set a candelabra with seven candles in the sanctuary. It was evening, and the church was lit with candlelight alone.

Passages from the gospels, telling of Jesus' crucifixion were read. The passages told of betrayal, abandonment, humiliation, torture, a cry of utter anguish, and a surrender, finally, to death. Gradually, we extinguished candles. As each scripture passage was read, another light on the candelabra was snuffed. We interspersed readings of the gospel with other texts of terror from more recent crucifixions, public and private: the Holocaust, the death of a child from battering, the rape and murder of women in our community, the killing fields of Cambodia, the death of species from environmental destruction.

We said no prayers of thanks for Jesus' loving sacrifice; offered no praise to God for divine grace and mercy; made no promises to offer ourselves for sacrifice, taking up our cross and following Jesus. The music held sorrow and lamentation. We joined our voices with the anguished prophet Jeremiah:

> O that my head were a spring of water,
> And my eyes a fountain of tears,
> so that I might weep day and night
> for the slain of my poor people! (Jeremiah 9:1)

A darkness without fire or light descended on us. The old tradition keeps one candle burning, hiding it behind the altar, to symbolize hidden hope. Does any spark of kindness, or life, or divine presence, or holy breath, remain in the Golgathas of this world? We extinguished the last candle. We went together into the night. Without words. Away from the fire.

CHAPTER 2

Haunted by Loss

Rita's Story

By the rivers of Babylon—
there we sat down and there we wept
when we remembered Zion.
On the willows there
we hung up our harps.
For there our captors
asked us for songs,
and our tormentors asked
for mirth, saying,
"Sing us one of the songs of Zion!"
How could we sing the Lord's song in a foreign land?

Psalm 137:1–4

I stepped into the aisle of the school bus and felt a stabbing pain in the back of my head between my pigtails. I turned. A tall, fat white girl stood just behind me. Her flushed face was ringed by frizzy red hair, her narrowed blue eyes blazed, and her mouth was tightened into a scowl. In her upraised fist, she held a sharpened pencil pointed at my eyes.

"Don't you ever step in front of me again, you dirty Jap!" she hissed.

I looked away quickly and hurried off the bus, shocked at her fury and violence. I felt ashamed at being the target of such a humiliating act and vaguely embarrassed for her—that she had so little self-control. I washed the blood off my head in the bathroom and quietly found my classroom.

I had been eager for the first day of second grade in 1957. In first grade, I had walked to a different school. This was my first bus ride. I felt more grown up riding the bus.

I spent the entire day mulling over what happened. I wondered what I had done wrong to provoke such fury, since I had stepped into the aisle just like the boy in front of me. No one else seemed to provoke such violence by taking their turn. I was puzzled about how to tell if a person would be hostile. I thought about how far it was to walk to school and whether I would get lost. I did not know the way from our apartment in Fort Riley, Kansas, to the school on the hill.

My eagerness for school faded. I began to worry and be confused. What was wrong with being Japanese? How would I know what to do if following what other children did caused violence against me? Were there separate, hidden rules for being Japanese?

The next morning, when my mother, Ayako, was fixing my hair, she asked me about the cut on my head. I was too embarrassed and ashamed to tell her the truth; I said I hit my head on the playground. I didn't want to worry her. I had no language to describe what happened, or to explain my confusion, anxiety, and sadness. They remained buried inside me.

I got back on the bus—I couldn't walk to school. I was careful to avoid the fat white girl, and I always looked backward before I stepped into the aisle in front of anyone else. Whenever I could, I sat in the front seat just behind the bus driver, a kindly black man named Melvin. I thought he wouldn't let bad things happen to me. Every day, boarding the bus, I said good morning to him. At the end of the day, we each said, "See you tomorrow."

THE PROBLEM WITHOUT A NAME

Children at school occasionally called me names, like Chink or Jap, and made fun of me by pulling the corners of their eyes up tight. Their taunting made recess time a minefield. Eventually, I figured out who the mean kids were and avoided them, but it was difficult. I grew more homesick for Japan, where I had lived for my first five years. No one there had ever treated me with such cruelty. How does a seven-year-old child defend herself against random and incomprehensible hostilities?

It would be many years before I had an answer. I formed a flesh of bronze to shield myself from arrows of hate. Inside that metallic skin,

I could pretend that I did not feel the sting of scorn, the humiliation of contempt, that I was impervious to hate. My pain remained hidden, as undigested lumps frozen in time. I worked to assure I did nothing to provoke ridicule, nothing to embarrass myself. I became disdainful of my own feelings of vulnerability. As long as I faced outward from my shield, I could deny the pain within. If I could scorn my own weaknesses, I could forestall succumbing to my fear, despair, and homesickness.

Even now, when hurt, I sometimes retreat behind that shield; it gives me an air of imperturbability. I am emotionally hidden, unavailable to others. I can be indifferent or cruel. I ignore my own pain, resorting first to fury. Anger allows me to blame others, to deflect the pain off the surface of bronze. My capacity for empathy disappears. I survived a childhood being Japanese in Kansas this way, but sometimes I feel as though the fat white girl won.

I realized long after I was a theologian that my interest in religion and my focus on the violence done to Jesus are grounded in my childhood experiences of racism. I have concluded that the Christian theological tradition has interpreted Jesus' life in ways that reinforced trauma. I was isolated by the traumatic events of my childhood. The tradition has isolated Jesus as a singular savior, alone in his private relationship with God. Jesus is depicted as unique and separate, carrying salvation on his own solitary shoulders. His relationships to others are described paternalistically, as if they needed him but he did not need them. To be saved, I was supposed to have an isolated relationship with him, to need him when he did not need me.

I knew, from my own experience, that there is no grace in such isolation. Isolating Jesus from mutual relationships carried forward the trauma of violence without healing it. My theological obsession became how to show that vulnerability, mutuality, and openness demonstrate love, that these bonds of love and care reveal the presence of God. If Jesus did not participate in such bonds, if he was isolated, he could not offer any grace.

My family cooperated with the fat white girl by avoiding feelings. The scorn of American children baffled me, but then, so did my mother. She was proud of being Japanese, but her pride was tinged with antipathies. Once when I was seven, we walked down the street in Junction City, Kansas, going to the only Asian grocery store in the small town, which thrived on customers who were the soldiers' Asian wives on the nearby Army base. An Asian-looking woman and girl turned the corner and walked toward us. I was excited to see others who looked like us. "Look, Mommy, Japanese!" I said happily. "Korean," she snapped, in the same tone of voice I had been called "dirty Jap." How, I wondered, could she tell the difference, and what was it about Koreans that deserved such hostility?

In the 1950s, a language to resist racism did not exist for me. My family did not understand racism against Asians. We did not discuss it. I could not name it to myself. In high school, I began to learn about racism, but it was taught to me as a black-white problem, related to slavery. Since I had to place myself in the American picture, and since my father, Roy, was white, I related to racism as a white person. I accepted my responsibility to stand against racism. I was against racism on behalf of blacks. I did not understand racism as something also directed against Asian Americans, against me.

I once had an argument with my father. I had a date with a black guy I met in school. I was around seventeen at the time. My father was adamant that I should not see him. He stood between me and the front door and quoted a biblical text to me from Genesis about "each after its own kind."

"What about you?" I said. "You married a woman of a different race." He looked surprised for a moment, then stepped out of my way as he said curtly, "That's different. Your mother isn't black." I went on my date.

I knew my father's response was wrong, both about segregation and about me and my mother. He pretended that my mother and I were not racially different; he wanted us to be honorary white people, to whitewash us. But his pretense belied my experiences in American schools. Despite his disclaimer, I did not have an internal sense of being white, whatever that might mean, when my appearance marked me as different, when the world treated me as not white.

Strangers had the annoying habit of looking into my face and asking one of the dreaded questions: "What are you?" or "Where are you from?" I knew what they meant—my appearance marked me as strange, as foreign, as someone who did not belong. I wanted desperately to belong. Why did they have to remind me that, in their view, I did not?

My mixed ethnic appearance was ambiguous. I looked like nothing in particular, just not "American." How could I blame the strangers, since I looked strange even to myself? I longed to be blonde and tall, which is what being "American" meant to me. Often, when I passed a mirror, I was startled by my own image. All day, every day, most of the faces I saw were white; my own dark face in the mirror appeared startling, even to me. I compensated for my Asian appearance by dressing in the most conventional feminine clothes my mother could sew, straight out of *Seventeen* magazine—nothing exotic or ethnic to mark me as different. I had little sense of style, but everything I wore was my idea of what "American" girls wore.

As I reached my teens, I noticed that white boys referred to "geishas," asked me if I could do massage, and leered in suggestive ways, as if I could give them something exotic that white girls couldn't. Part of me liked the attention, and part of me knew they were not really interested in me. The behavior of these boys made heterosexual adolescent dating strange, confusing, and fraught with hazards. I did not trust their interest in me. In college, I was eventually relieved of these games. As soon as I indicated my major was religion, the white male gaze would glaze over and turn elsewhere. They must have thought I was training to be a nun. I was not, but the protection from white male predatory behavior, accorded to me by my personal religious search for answers to violence, was liberating.

ISOLATION AND NOSTALGIA

In America, I achieved a successful professional life. I found religious community. I loved several remarkable men. But there were always pieces of me missing, ways I was not present. The anguish of feeling unwelcome in America left me with the vulnerable pieces of myself hidden behind that flesh of bronze. I seldom examined the loneliness of my protective shell, though I felt a spiritual hunger, a yearning for something elusive, indefinite, yet concretely missing. I pursued a career in theology, which is where I thought I might find what was missing.

I associated my pain and isolation with losing Japan. Being Japanese made me the target of inexplicable hostility in America, the pain of which I hid behind a shield of invulnerability, which I thought of as my American self, the part of me that acted confident and impermeable.

Under that shield lay my Japanese self, my real self, I thought. But

I think for much of my life, I have misunderstood my own isolation. Because the violence of racism I experienced was based on my being Japanese, I focused on Japan as the reason I was isolated. I attributed being isolated with my foreignness, not with the hateful behavior of others.

If I had remained in a Japanese cultural world, where feelings are not usually spoken of explicitly, perhaps my stoic endurance of pain would have been understood by my family. Perhaps if someone had understood my silences, my determined cheerfulness, I would not have felt so isolated, so misunderstood. But my mother and I no longer spoke the same language with fluency.

Racism was traumatizing, but pain also came from being different. My Japanese upbringing was often incompatible with American culture. Many times in my childhood, when American playmates invited me on outings, I refused their first offer. Their response was to leave without me. In Japan, a polite person does not accept an invitation the first time it is offered—to do so is self-centered and rude. Modesty and thoughtfulness require one to say no to the first, and even the second offer. This refusal process allows both parties to maintain social grace and reciprocity. If the offer is only polite, and means inconvenience or personal sacrifice, the invitation can be withdrawn after the second refusal with regret. I spent my childhood believing no one liked me, that their invitations were not sincere.

Why was there never a second or third offer in America? After awhile, I grew tired of being excluded, so I accepted the first offer. But I was ashamed of doing so, and I never knew with certainty if I was liked or just tolerated. I felt lonely and ill at ease. I thought of myself as rude and selfish. I learned to put on a cheerful, congenial face to hide my insecurities. In my pain and bewilderment, I clung tightly to my secret nostalgia for Japan, my private memory of people who loved and understood me.

THE PATH TO JI-CHAN AND BA-CHAN

The Japan of my childhood was ruptured by violence. At the end of World War II, every Japanese citizen was expected to serve the country, to rebuild it from ruins and humiliation. My mother, who was seventeen at the end of the war, had wanted to be a physical education teacher. Instead, she volunteered for Red Cross training and English lessons to become a nurse in a U.S. military hospital in Fukuoka City, on the inland sea, near the shore of Hakata Bay.

A twenty-minute train ride from Fukuoka, my grandparents' thatched-roof farmhouse faced the mountains across the valley and sat on the outskirts of the village of Onojo. A gravel path led through the entry gate, which was surrounded by a profusion of pink and magenta azaleas in spring. The path curved gracefully up to the granite flagstones laid before the weathered sliding door. I lived there for most of the first two and a half years of my life. Until I was five, my *ji-chan* (grandpa) and *ba-chan* (grandma) cared for me while my parents worked in Fukuoka.

Ba-chan was from Saga, Japan. Though only about fifty, she was stooped over from years of hard work. I spent so much time with her my first five years that I spoke Japanese with her Saga accent, unlike my mother, who spoke Fukuokan Japanese.

Many afternoons, Ba-chan took her four grandchildren to the local playground. She pushed us on the swing and watched us carefully. The three boys and I were a mischievous gang. We constantly concocted schemes to surprise Ba-chan because she seemed to take such great delight in being fooled. Some days, she and I went without my three older cousins, just the two of us. If we went without the boys, I could persuade her to go down the slide. She made her dignified way slowly up the ladder in her getas. On the platform, she gathered her gray kimono to keep it from flying up and struggled to land on her feet at the bottom. Ba-chan always managed a good landing, which brought a delighted smile to her face. I broke out in happy squeals of laughter as I jumped up and down applauding. She was my favorite playmate, and I spent hours following her around the house imitating her stoop and smile.

Ji-chan kept a store in the village and a garden at home. He was a lay preacher at his Jodo-Shinshyu Buddhist temple. He wrote poetry and was a quiet, reflective man in a house of garrulous women. He was my bathing partner every evening because he bathed first, in the cleanest water. I was the youngest and only female grandchild and the only child living in my grandparents' house. After dinner, Ba-chan warmed the *o-furo,* a large, deep metal tub with a wooden bench inside it. The tub sat in a wooden hut against the back outer wall of the main house near the kitchen. Ba-chan filled the tub with water from the backyard pump and started a fire under it. After my mother scrubbed me clean, I was handed to Ji-chan in the steaming water. He held me in his lap so I wouldn't fall in over my head. As we simmered, we talked.

When we finished our long soak, we put on our cotton *yukata* (robes). Ji-chan slipped me inside the top, above the belt, and carried me around his garden, murmuring to me. My body was hot from the *o-furo,* as was the skin on Ji-chan's chest. Against my arms I felt the soft dark blue of his *yukata,* next to my pink and white one. My hair was wet. I could hear Ji-chan's low, hoarse voice above my head as he walked around the garden. The fall evening air was cool and refreshing after the bath. When I looked down, I could see the tops of his beautiful mums. I could smell their pungent odor, as well as the fragrance of the last of the roses.

Seeing the mums made me a little anxious. Once, I went out in the fall garden alone and looked up at the furry mum stems and droopy leaves. They were a scary, hairy jungle from below. But seeing them from the top and hearing Ji-chan's rumbling voice lulled me into drowsiness. I listened, occasionally offering a comment or question until I could hardly stay awake. I do not remember what Ji-chan said in a language I no longer speak, but I remember his deep voice, the solidity of his body against mine, the tops of the flowers, the fragrance of soap and blossoms, and the cool evening air.

I remember the silence as I slipped into slumber every night on my futon next to my mother, with Ji-chan and Ba-chan in the next room, separated by paper walls. The night stillness was full of presence. I felt my warm body against the cool cotton covers, I heard my mother's soft breathing as she lay beside me, and I sensed my grandparents nearby. Swaddled in silence, I felt safe, loved.

The same quality of silence accompanied Ji-chan and me as we played in the main room of the house. Sometimes he sat beside me, focused and watching, as I played with an origami toy he had made for me. Other times he used his hands to throw shadow animals that danced on the wall, to my delight. In those moments, I felt him more present to me than when he spoke. Words were the leaves rustling on the surface of the ground, and silence was the root network of love— deep, solid, and inexplicable—a presence both elusive and tangible.

Ji-chan's garden was widely appreciated. Every spring, neighbors strolled by the gate to view his azaleas, and in summer, they admired the yellow rose that graced the entry. When Ji-chan and Ba-chan married, he wanted to plant a rose, but Ba-chan disliked them because of their thorns. Ji-chan searched until he found a thornless climbing rose, which he planted for Ba-chan. It climbed around the front door up to the roof. Of the many plants Ji-chan tended with care, the rose became Ba-chan's favorite.

The rose was visible at the end of the curving path from the entry gate. Traditional Japanese houses have curving or kinked pathways to prevent the residents from being followed home by hungry or angry ghosts. Unfriendly spirits can bring terrible luck to a family. Precautions must be taken to protect family fortunes. Every morning, Ba-chan carefully placed a small saucer of food at the entry gate to stop wandering stray ghosts from coming any farther. The only spirits she wanted in the house were our dead ancestors who protected and comforted us. Their faded black-and-white photos were enshrined in the lacquered Butsudan altar, a shiny mahogany cabinet with an array of small doors and drawers. The shrine rested on the woven straw floor in the main room of the dark, cool house. Ba-chan kneeled before it every day, summoned the ancestral spirits with a small brass bell, and fed them tidbits—a tangerine, a rice cake, or a sweet bean pastry. For some reason, our ancestors seemed undeterred by the curving path to the door.

Why is it that hungry and angry ghosts cannot turn corners? Are they too stupid to notice the route has veered? Are they visually impaired? Are they too focused on pursuing their prey to watch the contours of the paths? These specters must be needy or angry beyond reason, their compulsions overwhelming their common sense. Buddhists say that the pain we cannot relinquish causes us to suffer, that we must be willing to face directly into pain, to live through anguish to reach peace. They say we cling most ferociously to our own ego-driven needs, and that no such needs can be satisfied because the ego wants to avoid pain. We carry the burden of our uncauterized, unreleased pain, and we suffer. Our angers and hurts trap us in self-made prisons. They prevent us from experiencing the world flowing within us and around us at each passing moment. This captivity must also be true of the ghosts. I think the dead are not so different from those of us still living.

The Christianity I have studied now for over three decades does not understand the power of ghosts. Christianity is haunted by the ghost of Jesus. His death was an unjust act of violence that needed resolution. Such deaths haunt us. Rather than address the horror and anguish of his death, Christianity has tried to make it a triumph. Rather than understand and face directly into the pain of his death so his spirit can be released, we keep claiming he is alive. We try to use him for our personal well-being, to release us from our own burdens. We keep calling to his ghost to take care of us, instead of letting him go. This haunting has erupted into violence in the name of Jesus: the Crusades, the Inquisition, the Holocaust—the need for punishment, for judgment of the unredeemed, as if the infliction of more pain on others could cure our own. We have not found the curved path that frees us, that will let us heal from and relinquish the trauma of violent death.

JIZO'S PATH

My parents' house in Fukuoka City did not have a curving path. The flimsy wooden door slid open directly onto the wide packed-dirt public alley in front of the house. The three years we lived there, many ghosts slipped through the door. We would be haunted by losses and hungers that would follow us across oceans.

Our only protection came from the tiny shrine at the end of the alley, tucked into the corner of an old wooden fence. In the corner sat a ten-inch granite Jizo, the Buddhist saint who protects children and travelers. Jizo resembled a squat gray bowling pin with an overly large, round bald head, like a baby. He sat serenely on top of three thin stone blocks and waited behind the slatted wooden door of his shrine. He wore a bright red bib, as if he were ready to eat the tangerines and rice cakes arranged before him. He was lit by votive candles. I passed by every day with my mother and father. They held my hands as we walked to Ohori Park to play and look at flowers, or went to the market, or visited the *depato* (department store), where they shopped and I played in the rooftop playground. My Japanese mother was five feet two inches tall, and my white American father was a six-foot-tall red-head, though his hair was already thinning on top. Roy had to bend a little to hold my hand.

Jizo's bib hid the spirits of children who died before their parents.

All dead children's spirits have to cross Buddhist purgatory. They are too small and weak to make it without help. In the expected order of things, the spirits of children would be assisted by the souls of their dead parents. To die ahead of one's parents puts one in jeopardy. Tucked inside Jizo's clothing, the spirits of deceased children can escape the demons and reach heaven.

Jizo statues in every imaginable shape and size dotted the Japanese countryside in the wake of World War II, a parade of parental go-betweens. His saintly presence marked the anguish of mothers and fathers—holding their children between the living and the lost, between vulnerability and protection. A temple near Kyoto gathered thousands of the Jizo and placed them side by side in large square plots, like rice paddies. Today, they huddle together in all sizes and hues, a harvest of grief hewn in stones.

Jizo's journeys across dangerous terrain made him popular with travelers—a Japanese St. Christopher. A powerful travelers' saint, he followed my family over the years to every new home: Naha, Okinawa; Fort Riley, Kansas; Amory, Mississippi; Landstuhl, Germany; and Barstow, California.

Jizo's first major challenge happened when I was five. My American father received transfer orders to leave Fukuoka, and we went across the sea to Okinawa. My mother, baby sister, and I became a nuclear family on a U.S. Army base, where I, who spoke only Japanese, was put in an American kindergarten. I lost my mother tongue, forgetting Japanese within a few months. My mother spoke to me only in her heavily accented English.

Okinawan women took care of my sister and me while my parents worked. Every afternoon, I waited anxiously at the front window, looking for my mother walking home in her white nurse's uniform. As soon as I spotted her, I rushed out the front door and ran to her for a hug.

A few months after we moved to Okinawa, my parents called my grandparents in Onojo. When I was brought to the phone to talk to Ji-chan and Ba-chan, I couldn't understand them. Something in my voice worried them. Ji-chan and Ba-chan bought passage on a boat and came to visit us.

My people are not natural travelers. My grandparents were peasants from the country who had journeyed infrequently by train to local areas. They had never left the island of Kyushu before. Their biggest trip had been after they married in Saga and set up their household three hours away in Onojo. What sense of concern prompted them to undertake the expense and hazard of a sea journey to this unfamiliar place, to this place haunted by one of the bloodiest battles of the Pacific Theater of the war?

When they arrived, Ji-chan and Ba-chan were strange old people to me, people I couldn't understand. They seemed only vaguely familiar. I did not know how to behave toward them. The second day of their visit, Ji-chan had a bright red balloon he showed me. When I reached for it, he pulled it away and told me, in Japanese, to ask for it. In English, I said, "Balloon, balloon!" He held it away as I kept shouting, "Balloon!"

Suddenly, I said it in Japanese and began speaking to him in my mother tongue. With the return of our common language, he was my beloved Ji-chan again. For the next five days, it was as if my grandparents and I had never been apart. After they left, I never spoke Japanese again.

Ji-chan died of leukemia when I was twelve, in 1962. After one expensive transfusion to prolong his life, he called together his children and told them that he saw no point in getting another. They were difficult to undergo and expensive. He had lived a long and full life and saw no need to bankrupt his family to prolong his own existence. He announced he would not go back for any more medical care. He died at home. Ba-chan outlasted him by seven more years and then succumbed to stomach cancer during my freshman year in college. The anchors of my memories of Japan died before I ever saw them again.

I was torn from the Japanese culture that gave my life stability, that taught me how to know, what to see, how to speak, whom to love, and what to hope for. My family moved often. At six, I was transported from Okinawa to Fort Riley, Kansas, to dry prairies and American schools. I spent the first year of junior high in a segregated school in Amory, Mississippi, because my father was forced to go ahead of us on a tour of duty in Germany. I was the only non-white student in the school, just as race riots erupted at the University of Mississippi. During the time of the riots, my science teacher served in the Mississippi National Guard on weekend duty at the University. One Monday, he showed us slides he had taken of the riots: burned cars on their sides, dogs attacking black people, the Guard in riot gear. He referred proudly to the photos of "niggers getting their heads bashed in." I was uneasy all year in that school.

After our year in Mississippi, my mother, sister, baby brother, and I joined my father in Landstuhl, Germany, for three years. My last two years of high school were spent in Barstow, California, where my parents settled during my father's last military assignment. There, I came to love the austerity and beauty of the desert. After college and a master's degree, I left Southern California for two years of graduate study in systematic theology in Basel, Switzerland, where I became a passionate skier. On the surface, I did well in each new place, making good grades, finding new friends, negotiating my way into unfamiliar territories and cultures; my isolation went underground.

Such restlessness defines the U.S. experience for me. Like so many Americans, I have had to reconstruct my life, to make myself anew. Dislocation, the aftermath of violence, trauma, and isolation reach back for generations among American families. Americans have lost languages and lands and lives. Genocide and forced relocation, kidnapping and enslavement, immigration, the need to take refuge from poverty, war, and terrorism, illicit border crossings or sea voyages have disrupted our ancestral legacies. We have had to remake our lives, in our own generation or in the past. Many of us continue to move every several years. We are like the ancient Israelites trying to find a home in the wilderness, unable to go back, uncertain of where we wander. We seem, in our diversities and hyphenated identity groups, restless in our longing to belong. We quest for self and search for places to ground us. We seek what makes space for fullness of presence, for fires that illumine our lives. This search has defined my life.

THE PATH OF CHRISTIANITY

My father, Roy, whose family was Southern Baptist, rebelled from that tradition by declaring himself a Methodist when he signed his enlistment papers to join the Army. To Southern Baptists, Methodists are heretics, though I doubt Roy knew what a Methodist was, except *not* a Baptist. The U.S. military provides non-denominational Protestant services, so I grew up on bases served by a variety of Protestant chaplains, Lutheran, Nazarene, Episcopal, American Baptist, Congregational.

I was active in youth groups, sang in the church choir, and took seriously the stories I was taught in Sunday School. I took most seriously the story of Job. He was presented by my teachers as the ideal of faith—someone who, despite the horrors of his suffering, remained faithful to God. In suffering silently and enduring his lot in life, he eventually received his reward and was vindicated for his faithfulness. While I was not sure what his faith in God meant, I knew what it meant to suffer silently and hope for the best. The story of Job reinforced my Japanese culture's fatalistic philosophy of *shi-katta-ga-nai,* of enduring and suffering patiently because such pain cannot be helped. Job, with his ulcerous sores, torn clothes, and silent, bowed head, was my religious companion in childhood.

Jesus was also presented to me as a silent sufferer on the cross, but there was little reward for him. The resurrection wasn't enough—too isolated and individual a reward. The idea of Jesus dying to save me made little sense. I did not believe I was so bad as to need saving. I knew I wasn't perfect, but I did not think I was a bad person. I did not have an aching hole inside that needed filling with Jesus or salvation. I understood my loneliness as a longing for my family in Japan, not Jesus. Job's isolation seemed more real to me than Jesus' resurrection. Job's reward was a return to relationship, to his family.

I had always, from as far back as I can remember, felt a caring presence in my life, a sense I would be all right no matter what happened. Perhaps it was my ancestors, or Ji-chan or Jizo watching over me, but it had been there longer than I had been acquainted with the Christian God or Jesus, and I did not want to invite Jesus in there. Jesus was dead—a strange, fierce white man. I did not want to get to know him better, despite my Sunday school teachers' glowing accounts of his goodness and obedience.

The Jesus in the Bible I read was neither humble nor gentle. He was argumentative, rude, and self-righteous. Compared to the proscriptions of Japanese etiquette and kindness, Jesus' behavior was not nice, not thoughtful toward others; he was not someone I wanted to emulate. Claims that he still lived made no sense to me. He might haunt people from the grave, but I could not imagine him as alive.

As I lay in bed as a child, I formed an image of Jesus, blond and blue-eyed, gazing upward to a light. I tried to experience him as my friend or someone to hear my prayers. I never found the image comforting. Jesus remained a stranger until I began to study the historical

Jesus in college. When I could see him in his historical context and culture, his struggle against the oppressive powers of his day and his search for justice brought him alive to me, a historical companion on the same journey of hope. But this was not the Jesus I was taught about in Sunday school or church.

Job's restoration seemed a more satisfying resolution for enduring pain. I was a Christian the way a Japanese is Buddhist; I participated in the community and its ritual liturgies, enjoyed them and felt a sense of belonging to my adopted home. And like many Japanese Buddhists and like Job, I accepted suffering.

I encountered fundamentalist Christianity in my senior year of high school, when Joy Clark, a good friend, invited me to attend her father's Conservative Baptist church. I liked her father, Denver, a great deal, as well as his wife, Lillian.

The Clarks came into my life at a time when my father was serving eighteen months of duty in Vietnam. Denver became an emotional anchor for me when my own father was absent and when his return was difficult.

Throughout my childhood, my father had been my emotional companion. My mother was distant and reserved, while Roy was warm and present. Vietnam stole him from me. After he returned, our relationship deteriorated. No one knew then about post-traumatic stress, but I knew my father had changed. Instead of supporting my sense of adventure in life, he wanted to control me, to shape me more strongly into someone who would not make him anxious. We lived in nearly constant power struggles as I tried to hold on to my sense of self and my growing independence. To escape the conflicts, I spent more time with the Clarks.

The youth of the church called Denver "R.C.," for Reverend Clark. Even though I had heard many Christian messages about silent suffering and martyrdom, I found no such piety in Denver or his family. They liked to laugh and to enjoy life. He and Lillian had an easy, open, earthy relationship. The banter between Lillian and Denver sometimes bordered on the bawdy, as though sexual attraction in marriage was a good thing. She was an assertive, outspoken woman, his intellectual equal. They spent a few years after Bible college in Venezuela as missionaries, spoke Spanish, and understood the difficulties of living in another culture and place. When Denver told stories of their time there, he spoke of the people he had come to love, their struggles and presence in his life. He described people with vividness, making them come alive, enjoying their contradictions and foibles.

Denver's enjoyment of life also manifested itself in a major weight problem. The Clarks took me to their favorite restaurants in Laguna Beach, San Clemente, and Los Angeles. Denver delighted in playing, in teasing people, and in good jokes. While I had a cheerful mask, I was at heart a serious, lonely person. When I tended to take myself too seriously, he teased me. His jesting and zest for life broke my isolation and drew me from behind my shell. Some of the frozen chunks of pain in my soul began to thaw.

I had never encountered such a joyous, lively way of being Christian. I had thought of Christian life as pious and serious, as a way to endure suffering, a piety that reinforced my pain and isolation. Though the Clarks had a strong religious grounding, there was nothing martyr-like about it. They often made fun of the gray, dour piety of members of the church, particularly the "church lady" types. The Clarks' Christianity was joyous.

I don't think I had much of a sense of humor until I was around the Clarks. I learned to tell jokes because they took such pleasure in hearing them. My memories of them are laced with laughter and uproarious good times. Our favorite comedian was Bill Cosby. Once, as a surprise Christmas present, I took the Clarks to see a live Cosby performance. We loved his routine about Noah. We laughed for years remembering that night—one word or phrase from the performance would set us off.

Even as we laughed together and they teased me, we had serious theological differences. I thought their creationism and literal belief in the Bible unreasonable. We argued about creation and Genesis. To Denver's credit, he never challenged my right to differ, even though he thought I was wrong. Instead, he organized formal church debates on controversial topics.

The church claimed that Jesus was my personal savior. I tried very hard to believe that claim. I learned the right words to say. I made a confession of faith and was baptized because I wanted to belong to Denver's church. Without being baptized, I was always on the margin, outside. The only time I ever made a formal appointment to see

Denver in his church office was to discuss being baptized. When he asked me about my personal faith, I struggled to say something that might make sense. Whatever I said seemed to satisfy him enough that he agreed to baptize me.

My friendship with the Clarks stood me in good stead as a support system when I entered college. My mother and father had not attended college and did not understand my struggle adjusting to campus life. Denver understood how hard the transition to college was for me and never judged me for the experiments and tangents I pursued, socially or academically, though sometimes he teased me about them. He taught me to laugh at myself and my boyfriends. His support and my desire not to disappoint him protected me from some of the more self-destructive aspects of the counterculture. I did not use drugs or drink. I was twenty-one before I had sex, and I was not self-deceptively swept away or coerced into it. I made a clear, deliberate choice to be sexually active when I decided I was disinterested in marriage.

I have wondered why Denver never rejected or judged me for my independent thinking. Perhaps it was because he also stood to the left of his fundamentalist tradition. He was criticized for supporting Alcoholics Anonymous. He let them meet in the church. Some of the church board thought it was a bad idea because AA did not require people to be saved, and salvation was the only hope for alcoholics. Denver argued that AA clearly helped people in ways the church did not, and that anything that helped people stay sober was good. He thought the church might learn from AA about alcoholism. In the best Baptist tradition, Denver believed in free-thinking and never rejected me for being different from him and the church.

Denver's theology, with its focus on saving souls, was the core of his generous, loving spirit. He believed salvation was a gift from God, given freely through Jesus' death on the cross for sin. He had a healthy regard for the dangers of sin, but enjoying life was not sinful to him. A zestful life was a gift of grace. He gave me a way to be Christian that broke through my isolation, that helped me believe that well-being and joy were the elements of a faithful life, that my spiritual search to overcome the lingering effects of violence was a worthy quest. I flourished in his love.

One of the theological controversies I heard the Clarks discuss from time to time was whether, if one was saved, one could ever lose one's faith and salvation. Unlike some of their Baptist colleagues, Denver and Lillian believed, "once saved, always saved." They were certain that once a person had accepted Jesus as savior, no power on earth or in heaven could separate that person from God. And Denver loved in this way, without conditions. He loved even when differences and hurt were part of the relationship.

Denver sustained that love when I pulled away. In 1972, while I was traveling and just before I graduated from college, I wrote to Denver and asked him to remove me from the list of members of his church. By then, my own theology had evolved so far from fundamentalism, I could not pretend to feel comfortable in his church. He sent me a letter:

> Dear Rita,
>
> Please forgive me for not writing you much, much sooner. I suppose there were a couple of very good reasons. I think I was too hurt to write and second, I didn't know exactly how to write. You know, of course, that you mean a great deal to me and to my family. There is nothing you could do or say that could keep us from loving you.
>
> I know that you are an honest person and I appreciate your honesty in these matters.
>
> I am also confident that "He that hath begun a good work in you will perform it until the day of J.C."
>
> At present you are riding an educational U-2 but I have every confidence that you know the truth and the truth will manifest himself.
>
> I complied with your request and had your name taken from the church roll. I cannot say that did not hurt your second father, mother, or sister.
>
> I said it hurt, I did not say it changed our relationship. We are and want to be, as long as you will let us be, your "other parents."
>
> Maybe I am getting old and nostalgic because I am a grandfather. Whatever the reason, I had to let you know just how I felt and I'm sure you will understand a sentimental old father who loves his daughter very much.
>
> Now, when you get home we will go down to the beach and get burned to a crisp while we discuss the future of the world, mankind, and Rita in particular OK?
>
> It is a typical Barstow day. The wind is blowing hard. It is clear except for dust.

You must be having a fantastic time and we are so proud of you and your accomplishments. It hardly seems possible that when you return you will have graduated from college. Of course it hardly seems possible that I'm a grandfather either, but it is true. See you soon.

Love,
R.C.

By the early 1980s, I had become a feminist theologian and was finishing my doctorate. When I saw Denver for the last time, he was dying of cancer. He walked me out slowly when I had to leave, enjoying a moment in the sunshine of San Clemente, where he and Lillian had made their final home. When we were alone at my car, he said to me, "I know that you have gotten an education that has moved you far beyond what I could have taught you, and you know more than I will ever know. But I need to ask you about your faith. I am not going to be around much longer, and I want to be sure that everyone I love will be in heaven with me. Do you still have your faith?"

I looked at him. "We both know I've taken a long journey away from where I was when I was a member of your church," I said. "But back then, you gave me a solid faith foundation, as well as a wonderful second home when I needed it. I want you to know that I feel good about my relationship with God. I trust it. You don't need to worry about me, I will see you in heaven when my turn comes. I will look forward to seeing you again." He smiled and gave me the last of his wonderful bear hugs.

LOVE AND VIOLENCE

Denver's unconditional support carried me through my conflicts with my father. Roy and I argued frequently about my activities against the war in Vietnam, after he returned from service there. I had a series of leftist, activist boyfriends, none of whom he liked. The one with long black hair, a headband, a beard, and bells on his sandals really set him off. My father was sure I was doing drugs and sleeping with all those "weird, irresponsible" guys.

I stopped living at home when I was twenty because he decided to give me one last beating to make me behave. I had not been "spanked" for years, probably not since I was about fourteen. My father used the word spanking; I called them beatings. Since I was a child, I had felt his punishments were cruel, unjust, and unjustifiable, and told him so every time the issue came up. I also kept a secret strategy of resistance: I refused to change whatever he spanked me for, which meant I was in trouble fairly often. I never felt the punishments I received were fair. I was a well-behaved child most of the time because I liked to please.

There were two main reasons my father punished me, both of which involved his ideas of Southern womanhood from his upbringing in Mississippi. First, he thought I should keep my room tidy. It was always a mess, the bed unmade, clothes in piles on every available chair, and papers and books everywhere. Keeping it straightened was, as far as I was concerned, tedious and unnecessary. Most times, when he chided me for the disorder, I did the bare minimum of straightening up, but the room had an entropic tendency, returning to a state of disorder quickly. When I refused to clean it, he would schedule a spanking.

Waiting for the spanking filled my day with dread. My father scheduled spankings, so he would never hit me spontaneously in anger and so I would have time to think about what I had done wrong. I hated the waiting and the moment when we went into my room for the event. I did not use the time of dread to think about what I had done. Instead, I worked on a variety of arguments for why he should not beat me, which I tried out when the time came. When all the arguments failed, as they inevitably did, I pled with him not to hit me. The worst days were when he told me to remind him to spank me. If I did not remind him, I was punished for both my wrongdoing and my cowardice. I endured his violence and my sense of humiliation by retreating behind my cold, hard shell where I was emotionally inaccessible and under which fury smoldered like molten lava.

The second reason for my being beaten was that I refused to use "sir" and "ma'am" when I spoke to adults. None of my peers in school used such formal language; I thought the terms sounded contrived and fake. Plus, if I used these words, I was sure my friends would think I was being pretentious or obsequious. I tried to explain this to my father, but he accepted no excuses. I was to be a proper Southern woman. I, on the other hand, wanted to fit in with my friends. I couldn't get my mouth to make those sounds, so I was punished periodically for my lack of good manners.

When I received my first spanking around the age of seven, I thought through my humiliation carefully. "If I do what he says, he will think this works. This is how you treat animals, not people. If I change, I will be like an animal. I am not going to let it work on me." I pretended I was emotionally invulnerable to the pain and resolved to resist, rather than give my father the impression that brutality worked to make people better.

Yet I loved him. During my late childhood, he was emotionally present when my mother was distant. On occasional summer weekends we camped on the banks of the local river sleeping in a pup tent and fishing. We talked about life and sat in comfortable silence. His favorite speech to me was: "Be sure you grab hold of a big piece of life and really live it. Don't hold back, go after what you want all out. You only get one chance at life, so live it to the fullest." I took his advice and put aside my shy, reserved Japanese self. My father taught me to pursue my passions by supporting me.

When I showed an interest in and talent for art, Roy made sure I learned copper-enameling, leather-working, and linoleum-carving from instructors at the arts and crafts shop he managed on the base in Fort Riley. He paid for a local artist to give me a year of oil painting lessons when I was ten.

When I was thirteen and we had just moved to Germany, Roy took me to the Army base library to get a card. He gave me a list of writers to read: Hemingway, Faulkner, and Shakespeare. After I worked through my father's list, I found my own favorites: Pearl Buck especially, but also a series of poets: Sandburg, Whitman, Wordsworth, Frost, Tennyson. I learned that year to choose books by authors, not titles. Roy also encouraged my interest in musical theater, driving me back and forth to after-school rehearsals. I flourished with his encouragement and support.

But his beatings always kept me on guard, afraid something I did might elicit punishment. I resented being humiliated, and I was convinced that the way he treated me was wrong. I was determined not to let him control me. I do not know how I arrived at that conviction, since many of my friends were also "spanked." My cousins in Mississippi got the switch often. Physical punishment of children was an unquestioned part of the world I lived in.

I questioned it.

My mother, on very rare occasions, gave my younger siblings a light single swat on the butt when they provoked her. I have no memory of her ever using physical violence on me, except for a slap across the face once when I insulted her. She let me know her disapproval by her behavior: a refusal to look at me, the withdrawal of attention, a curt remark. She never praised me or complimented me directly, so I rarely had her approval, but I always knew when she was unhappy with me.

She left the serious discipline to my father. When he came into my bedroom and closed the door, a serious look on his face, I felt a familiar sense of dread, humiliation, and outrage. He said it was time for the spanking. We discussed how many blows would be appropriate for my offense. He sat on the bed and had me lower my pants. I was instructed to lie facedown across his lap. He counted the blows out loud as he struck me. If I did not cry and say I was sorry, he added blows until I did. He never used anything but his hands across my bare buttocks until I was in my teens.

I stopped crying in early adolescence, no matter how hard he hit me or how long, so the beatings escalated. He tried using a paddle or belt because he didn't think I was sorry enough. But the welts bothered him, so he went back to using his hand which left bruises in the shape of fingers instead of welts. When he was finished, he left the door open and insisted I come out where the family was. I composed myself so they would not see how humiliated I felt.

Late in my second year of college, I brought one of my long-haired boyfriends home to meet my family. My father felt I needed disciplining. He took me to my old room as soon as my boyfriend left. He shut the door and said I needed spanking.

I knew immediately I was not going to let him do it. I told him not to touch me, not to come near me. I meant it. He sat on the bed and told me to take down my jeans. I refused. He commanded me again. "No," I said through clenched teeth, "you are not going to touch me." He got up from the bed and grabbed my wrists to pull me across his lap.

I twisted my arms out of his grasp and stepped toward the door. He grabbed me around the waist, pinning my arms to my side, threw me onto the bed, and moved toward me. I spun onto my back and aimed a kick at his groin. He was a little too far away and was able to grab my right foot before it struck him.

I caught a glimpse of his startled face. He looked at me as if he had never seen me before, as if he saw me clearly for the first time, as if he couldn't believe what he saw.

I kicked at him as hard as I could with my left leg while I pulled the right one free. He leaned toward me to try to grab my arms. I slapped like a whirlwind at his head with my hands. I kicked him in the gut. When he stepped back from the wind being knocked out of him, I rolled off the bed onto the floor and tried to scramble for the door. He sat on me, putting his two hundred fifty pounds directly on my back. I couldn't breathe. When I stopped struggling, he said, "Calm down, I am not going to touch you." His voice was shaking from exertion and adrenaline. He did not look at me. He left the room.

I made sure he would never touch me again. I avoided him as much as possible. I decided not to live at home that summer. However, Ba-chan died in the spring, and, in her sorrow, my mother asked me to come home. She rarely asked me directly for anything. I felt obligated to honor her request. I took a graveyard shift waiting tables so I would not be home in the early mornings when Roy rose. I went out in the evenings before he got home. I rarely ate dinner at home with the family. I spent time with Denver and Lillian.

Roy tried to ground me by forbidding me to use his '64 Ford Falcon, except to go to work. I got rides from friends or walked when I wanted to go out. I refused to tell him where I went, with whom, or when I would return. At the end of the summer, I paid my father five hundred dollars for the Falcon, the amount he had paid when he bought it. When I handed him the money, he looked chagrined. He said he was planning to give me the car. I said, "This way, it's my car, not yours." I resolved never to live under his roof again.

I returned to college for the fall semester. I visited for the holidays and an occasional weekend. The first Christmas morning following that tense summer, the whole family sat on the living room floor in our bathrobes amid piles of brightly colored torn wrapping paper and loose ribbons, our various gifts arranged in neat stacks. My father asked us all to sit on the couch. My mother sat at one end; I was next to her, followed by my sister Jo Ann and brother Raymond. I thought Roy was arranging us for a picture, a holiday ritual. Instead, he stood before us, the twinkling tree behind him.

After a pause, he cleared his throat and said, "I know I have been difficult to live with the past few years. I am sorry for the hurt I've caused and will try to be easier to live with. I want us all to start over again with better relationships." We sat a minute in silence. No one spoke. I think we each mumbled something like "it's OK." My mother got up to make breakfast, and I fled to my room to change clothes.

It was not OK. The vague apology was not enough. My anger at him remained for a long time, long after he died in 1976. I had been isolated by the racist violence and hostility I experienced in school. My father's violence went deeper. Even when I loved someone I had my shield up, to keep myself from being too vulnerable, from risking being hurt the way he had hurt me. My search for a theological understanding of love that breaks isolation, that heals the wounded soul, and that opens the self to the warmth of mutuality, respect, and intimacy was a search also for what would deliver me from my own protective shell. My quest was for access to my own soul, to the capacity to love without barriers.

My mother tried to stay in touch, but I was too angry at Roy to be pulled back into the family by her mild and indirect gestures. She had become a Christian fifteen years after being in America, but her conservative way of being Christian was different enough from mine that faith did not connect us. I do not know why she waited so long, except to honor, perhaps, Ji-chan's Buddhism. But he had put no restrictions on her regarding religion.

When my mother left with Roy in 1955, Ji-chan knew she would eventually make her life in the United States. As she boarded the ship to sail to Naha, Okinawa, Ji-chan said to her, "In his country, people are Christians. Your family wants you to know that, if you decide to become a Christian, it will be all right. We will still love you, and you will still be our daughter." This is the quality of love in my Japanese home that my mother remembered. This is the quality of love I received from Denver. This is the quality of love I needed from Roy, but did not receive.

THE PATH OF GHOSTS
Thirty years later, I was to learn why my mother deliberately cut me off from my Japanese tongue and roots, why there was such distance between us. She did not want me to remember the language or world

that would have given me access to her secret. She sought to protect me from its pain, to be sure I did not know that, in 1948, before she knew Roy, she met and fell in love with a Puerto Rican hospital orderly and amateur boxer. They were two island people in love with the sea and each other.

From war's end until 1952, U.S. military personnel were not allowed to marry Japanese nationals; fraternizing, while inevitable, was discouraged. My mother and this Puerto Rican U.S. soldier, Clemente, moved in together when she discovered she was pregnant. I was born on April 29, 1950. This father named me Rita, for the Hispanic actress Rita Hayworth. For thirty-three years, my first name was the only telltale evidence that he had ever been a part of my life. For those many years, I wondered why I had such an un-Japanese first name.

Six months after my birth, Clemente was sent to Korea, to another war. A few months after his departure, my mother and I moved into Ji-chan's farmhouse to wait for him to contact her. She continued working as a nurse; my grandparents and aunts took care of me. My mother waited months for a word from Clemente; nothing came. Silence. His parents in Dorado sent us gifts: trinkets, clothes. My mother sent them pictures of me in the clothes and Japanese china: a tea set, Noritake plates, all marked "made in occupied Japan."

Months bled into a year, then two. Not a single word from my father. The letters to and from Puerto Rico slowed, then stopped. My mother wanted to go to Puerto Rico to wait for him. Ji-chan would not allow her to leave. He was convinced that Clemente was not a responsible person and would not take good care of us. Ji-chan said Clemente did not have a good heart. He had hurt us too much already.

I have trouble imagining what life was like for my mother then. Japan was patriarchal, poor, xenophobic, and recently traumatized. Our family lived just two hours from Nagasaki. At twenty-two, my mother had a daughter out of wedlock. What Japanese man, of those who survived the war, would marry such a disgraced woman? A son might have given her some status, but I was a girl. Worse, I was of mixed race. On the back of one of my baby pictures sent to Puerto Rico, my mother had written, "look her big eyes."

But I have no trouble imagining my mother's fear, heartache, and disappointment—the endless, sad waiting. Without legal status as

Clemente's wife, she would not know if he had died unless his family told her. If he was not dead, why was there no word? Was Ji-chan right, did he have a bad heart? I can imagine every day the search through the mail, every day the racing pulse and lump in the throat, every day the sinking nausea and heartbreak, the anticipation met by nothingness, the knife of disappointment dulled by repetition and fading hope. Such waiting and wanting has no resolution; it does not have sad goodbyes, a final reconciliation, a death to mourn, or a definitive end.

My mother continued her hospital work. My grandparents, aunts, uncles, cousins, and my mother's nurse friends took care of me. My mother lived with heartache; I lived in a loving, secure home. When I was two, my mother met another soldier, Roy, from Amory, Mississippi, five years older, who had left school after eighth grade. Ji-chan met the red-haired American and liked him. This man, in his opinion, had a good heart and would take good care of us. My mother married Roy in October 1952.

In November 1952, a letter and money order came from Clemente. My mother replied:

> Dear Clemente,
> I was surprise hear from you after such long time, two years. Thank you for money order. I buy Rita clothes.
> I hope you happy. I don't want to break happiness by interfering your life. Just want you to know, I met very nice man and he and I married in October. We very happy. He take good care of me and Rita. You don't need worry. We think best for Rita, she not know about you, so we not tell her about you. Please do not get touch with us anymore.
> Ayako

Clemente was deliberately erased, as if he had never existed.

My mother married Roy in 1952, three years after I thought she'd married him, and three years after the altered marriage license I had once seen in their personal papers, which showed a smudged October 2, 1949. I asked about this date once. I was about eight and had just learned the facts about pregnancy and gestation. I put together in my mind that my parents were married seven months before I was born, but I was a full-term baby, over eight pounds.

My father, who was the person I went to when I needed to talk or ask questions, was peeing in the bathroom. Perhaps I chose the moment because it seemed especially intimate. Our family rarely closed doors, and, in the evenings, we often bathed together as my Japanese family had. As he stood in front of the toilet, I asked if he and Mom were really married in October of 1949. He was quiet for a moment, then said yes, but did not look at me. "Then why," I asked, "was I so big if I was born in April, seven months later?" My father's face flushed a deep red. He finished peeing, zipped up his pants, and, as he washed his hands, he said, "I'll tell you when you're older." What I heard in his voice and lack of eye contact was that I was not to ask, that he did not want to explain to me the problem with the dates. To protect him from further embarrassment and to respect his privacy, I never asked again. Throughout my childhood, my questions about my early life and my parents' early marriage were received with similar messages about not asking personal questions. Eventually, sometime in my early teen years, I stopped asking personal questions altogether.

President Truman only lifted the ban on marriage between Japanese nationals and American soldiers in 1952. My parents could not have been married in 1949. Marrying did not grant Roy an automatic right to adopt me, which is why we went to Okinawa.

Roy had received transfer orders to the United States when I was four. The Immigration and Naturalization Service refused to let me accompany my mother because I was not his legally adopted daughter. Roy appealed—repeatedly. After a series of denials by the INS, he requested an alternative assignment in Okinawa, where I could accompany my mother. During the year in Okinawa, Roy continued his appeals to the INS, all denied. Finally, he turned to his senator.

To clear my entry into the United States, Roy had to sign an affidavit in which he pledged to raise me as a loyal American citizen and as a good Christian. I arrived in the United States as a child of parents from separate nationalities, cultures, religions, and races. The senator who cleared my entry was John Stennis of Mississippi, the infamous segregationist.

To honor the affidavit my father had signed, my parents tried to make me as "American" as possible. Roy worked hard to teach me about American life. He took me fishing and encouraged my interest in painting. I was to speak only English. I was to be a Christian.

I wonder what the Christian promise of heaven meant to my mother, who spent so much of her life in American purgatory. Eleven years after we left Japan, our family stood on the seashore near Los Angeles, the first time we had seen the Pacific since we left Okinawa in 1956. My mother breathed in, was still, and said, "Ah, smell of sea. I remember." Her voice was far away; tears clouded her eyes; she did not look at any of us. It was the most emotionally present I ever saw her.

What would have been my mother's fate had she been alone, without the support of family and friends and without her own income? Alone in post-war Japan, my mother might have aborted me or killed us in a double suicide. She might have given me to an orphanage, or sold me to a childless family or geisha house. Many of the poor in occupied Japan barely survived. We were saved by a loving family, friends, a responsible soldier.

I do not know what it cost my mother to keep me, to decide to save me. Surely it cost her a familiar and comfortable life in Japan, the life my relatives now have. It cost her a professional career. I cannot measure her homesickness and alienation in America, where her Red Cross nursing license and seven years of experience were unrecognized, where her beautiful lacquerware cracked in the Kansas heat, where she searched for foods such as *nori,* tofu, *kokuho* rice, *aji-no-moto,* and *shoyu,* where her own daughter no longer spoke in her mother's tongue and became strange to her.

The gulf of silence between us, haunted by the past and larger than lost language, was the secret she and Roy kept through death: that I was not born his daughter, that I had another father. They believed the secret protected me. Perhaps it did. But that protection came with great losses and hungers.

THE PATH WITHOUT A HOME

Jizo left us in 1972. The ghosts began to catch up with us. The family I thought he had protected through all our travels would slowly come apart by illness, death, and hidden truths that revealed a family built on a lie. I did not know at the time that this year would begin the unraveling of my life.

The second half of my senior year at Chapman College in 1972 began in the most exciting way I could imagine. In early February, I toured the United Nations and boarded the ship, World Campus Afloat, with four hundred other students. We would circumnavigate the earth in four months while taking classes. I enrolled at Chapman for this single reason: Their semester-at-sea program was my chance to return to Japan after seventeen years away. My California State Scholarship Commission Award would have paid for me to attend any school in California, but I applied to no other college—I knew the one thing I wanted. I had been trying to get back to Japan since I'd been torn away.

The separation had been wrenching. I was five and forced to sleep alone for the first time in my life. Ugly faces peeked in the doorway of my room. I no longer slept on futons on the floor, but up on a bed, under which lurked monsters waiting to eat me. I awoke to nightmares for months. I cried out in fear. One of my parents had to sit by my bedside. I missed Fukuoka—my playmates, my family, and my mother tongue. I switched from Japanese into English at the American base kindergarten. From 1955 on, the only link my family had to Japan was through my mother. She corresponded with the family and was the sole source of their news to us.

Through the language, gender roles, and religions of Japan, I inherited an identity. It required little thinking; I knew invisible values and rules, rituals of performance, language, and interactions that were passed on by my family. All these are subterranean, difficult to discern, and yet powerful in their force. I felt secure, loved. I did not think about that world until it was lost.

My memories of home grew distant over the years. I could barely remember Ji-chan and Ba-chan. The faces of my relatives—Aunts Shizue and Fumiko, Uncle Katsumi, and Cousins Itsuo and Yoshiyuki—faded from my memory. They became two-dimensional, black-and-white images, confused with photos in my mother's albums. Fukuoka became an imaginary place where I was safe from the painful losses that marked my American life. My mother encouraged this nostalgia by saying little about it. The few stories that circulated in my memory became worn from overuse.

An American life, conducted in a foreign language and culture, sealed my mother in a chamber of silence. Without her willingness to help me remember Japan, my memories became a nostalgic cocoon that protected me without disrupting my cheerful exterior. I carried the memories deep inside as a magic talisman against the losses I knew in America—the loss of my mother tongue and my mother's emotional presence.

When I was thirteen, I had a recurring nightmare. In the dream, I return to our house in Okinawa and find my mother gone. I know she has been kidnapped.

I rush out into the jungle behind our house running after the kidnappers, trying to save my mother. As I run through the trees, they turn into the pine forests near the base in Germany, where we lived at the time. In the woods, I spot a small house. The doors are locked. I creep up to a window and peer inside. There, in the middle of the empty room, my mother is bound and gagged, tied to a chair. No one else is around, so I tap on the window and shout, "Mama, it's me, Rita!" She turns her head toward me, but there is no recognition in her eyes, only a vacant stare. I awaken feeling hopeless, hollow, and empty.

My removal from Japan ungrounded me. I felt lost as blowing ashes. I searched for a language, for meaningful rituals, ideas, and illumination to shape my life. Because this search required me to create an American life, it led me away from my mother, whom I desperately wanted and needed. I do not know when I finally pulled away from her, but I knew, if I wanted an American life, she could not lead me to it.

My search for a life in the face of such losses has been a religious journey—religious, rather than spiritual, because mine is not just an individual quest, but the seeking of a whole world and community. Religions give language, meaning, and shape to cultures, to ways of being that are organized socially and into which people are born. Theology is how those ways of being are articulated, made into language. My quest for reliable friends and community and for theological answers is how I searched for myself.

When I was a religion major in college, I took several courses to try to understand my Japanese Buddhist roots. We studied the major scriptures of Buddhist sects, their ideas about reality and tenets of faith, their major formative founders and thinkers, the various philosophical schools, and their differences from the indigenous Japanese religion of Shinto. During my trip to Japan in 1972, I realized that what I had worked so hard to learn in class was little help in understanding Japanese religious behavior. What was the Butsudan in people's homes and how did Buddhism fit into everyday Japanese life, if it did? I did not know.

Most Japanese don't even know what sect of Buddhism their family is registered with, and they don't care which it is. They go to Shinto shrines for baby blessings and marriages and Buddhist temples for funerals. They do not meditate. They practice more than one religion. During the year, they visit different temples and shrines, depending on the holiday at the time. They do not understand religions as competing for the same turf. Instead, they divide powers and spirits into different spheres of operation. Differences in functions are simply accepted.

At certain times of the year, when I was a small child in Fukuoka, my mother changed me into my kimono, and the whole family dressed up. We walked the winding path from my grandparents' front door down the dirt street to the train station, where we rode to a temple or shrine with others in traditional festive dress. We walked down stone-paved, narrow, lantern-lit streets, lined with souvenir shops selling pickles, tea, ceramics, toys, and sweet bean cakes. As we neared the temple gates, a booth with big tubs of water beckoned. The tubs were full of tiny goldfish; I tried to catch them in paper nets that melted as soon as they entered the water. I never caught a fish, but I took great delight in trying. Then, we washed our hands and mouths at the fountain at the temple entrance and went in to pray, walk around, and talk. These were religious activities, though I did not understand that at the time, though my classes never mentioned them.

For Ba-chan and Ji-chan, respectful and attentive relationships to the ancestors and the natural world brought good fortune. Japanese culture values harmony in relationships and kinship. Being individualistic or self-assertive was seen as pathological in my Japanese home, which valued humility and generosity. Respectful behavior showed one belonged. Whether one actually believed personally in ancestor spirits was less relevant than participating in rituals that demonstrated one's gratitude and respect for those who have passed on.

The Western version of Buddhism emphasized personal meditation practices, rather than adoption of its Asian cultural forms. European American Buddhism tends to ignore kinship networks, formal ritual, and obligation to family members, living and dead. North American Buddhism prefers to focus on individual spirituality and abstract values such as "respect for nature," or "enlightenment," as a means to help practitioners transcend themselves, their families, and their community obligations. Christianity functions in a similar way in Asia as Buddhism functions in the United States. Converts to Christianity use it to transcend the limitations of family and culture. When religious ideas get separated from their cultural forms, they take on different meanings. They move against a society's norms and grant people more individual freedom.

The values of my American life have often been at odds with my Japanese origins. The anti-religious spiritual search so characteristic of Americans is part of my Protestant upbringing. Protestant Christianity places above all else the relationship of the individual self to God, and U.S. society reflects this with its emphasis on individual achievement, self-assertion, authenticity, and personal fulfillment. The search for individual fulfillment is often based on an antagonism toward organized forms of religion—toward forms of religion that are social and community-based. Socially organized religion is seen as hypocritical or oppressive because people often adapt their behavior in groups to conform to group ideals and expectations.

I was imbued with these individualistic values through a Baptist faith that encouraged me both to embrace a personal, subjective sense of salvation and to think for myself. But ultimately, I found this way of being religious too isolating, too much like the loneliness I already knew through my loss of Japan and my nostalgia for Japan, a nostalgia that disconnected me. An imaginary relationship to a long-deceased savior was no improvement. The disconnect was not about faith and doubt—what Christians meant by faith in Jesus was so foreign to my inner self that I had no way to take it in and make it meaningful. I needed a way of being religious that connected me to others, that broke through my isolation, that gave me living presence. Denver's life had done that, but not his theology.

I hoped my pilgrimage to Japan in 1972 would reconnect me to a lost self and gather the scattered ashes of my soul. Chapman's World Campus Afloat, a college semester at sea, was the means to get there. But before I arrived in Kobe, my world began to fall to pieces.

My family had promised to write while I was on the ship that spring. At each new port—Casablanca, Dakar, Luanda, Capetown, Mombasa—I received long, newsy letters from them. In Columbo,

Madras, and Penang, I stood through mail call with all the others eager for news of home. But there were no letters from my parents.
When we arrived in Bangkok, three ports before I was to arrive in Japan, there was still no letter. I decided to call them, despite the expense.

I stared at the dial of the black phone on the table between the hotel beds. My roommate left to shop before we joined a tour of some
temples and floating markets. I called collect because I had no idea
what it would cost to reach Barstow, California. I heard the international operator talking to a U.S. operator. Finally, I heard the ringing.
My sister's voice was barely audible when she accepted the call. She
called my father to the phone.

"Mother had surgery a month ago. She was diagnosed with ade-
noid cystic carcinoma. It's a cancer in her right facial sinus area. We
didn't want to worry you or ruin your trip, so we decided not to tell
you," my father said. "She lost her right eye, and they're giving her radiation. We won't know for a while whether they got all the cancer.
But don't worry; we're taking good care of her." With that staggering
news, he put my mother on the line. She repeated the same information. Her voice seemed strange, breathy and soft, and she had difficulty saying words clearly. "Don't worry. Enjoy trip. You need anything?"

A decade after I made that call from Bangkok, my mother's death
would tear a hole into my life and fill it with unanswerable questions.
Who was I really? To whom did I belong? What was the truth of my
life and its beginnings?

The ship sailed to Japan in early May, just after my birthday and in
the middle of a major festival week. As we docked in Kobe harbor, I
was packing. Someone knocked on my cabin door. I opened it, and
David, a good friend, said "Rita, honey, there's a sad and worried
looking Japanese couple standing on the dock carrying a sign with
your name on it." I ran up to the deck and spotted my uncle Katsumi
and aunt Shizue holding a piece of white paper that said, "Welcome,
Rita Brock." They looked anxious and a little forlorn until they spotted me waving and shouting. They smiled and waved back. I recognized them from family photos.

Photos of Shizue were rare. Shizue had a disfigured face. When
she was a single woman working after the war at an insurance com-

pany, she attended a company baseball game. A hard-hit line drive struck her face. The accident left her with two nostril holes and some scar tissue instead of a nose. In despair she tried to jump out of the third floor window of her hospital room.

My mother's brother Katsumi, who worked at the same insurance company, visited people who were retired or in the hospital. He visited Shizue. She was embarrassed and would not look at him. She kept her hand over her face. He returned every day. Gradually she relaxed and began to engage him in conversation. Katsumi saw she had a good heart and proposed marriage. His gentleness matched her kindness.

My aunt Shizue and uncle Katsumi traveled north to Kobe to meet me in 1972. Through an interpreter, they let me know we would stay in the Kyoto and Nara area, rather than go to Fukuoka. That journey would have involved many hours of crowded train travel, in pre-bullet-train days. I was deeply disappointed, but tried to make the best of my seven days in Japan.

My aunt and uncle had made *ryokan* arrangements in Nara for the three of us. A *ryokan* is a traditional Japanese inn. We shared one large room together where dinner was served to us. We changed clothes by turning our backs. Shizue and I bathed in the common women's *o-furo*. The three of us wore our *yukata* afterward to walk along the pond nearby and slept on futons on the straw floor. This intimacy with the body, this matter-of-fact relationship to its nakedness and its ordinary functions, is the closest I felt to my childhood home on that trip. The comfortableness with flesh was familiar to me; the ordinariness of physical presence was reassuring in its old resonances to my childhood. As I lay in the dark on my futon, I could hear the soft breathing of the others, just as I had as a very small child.

Each morning, we joined a tour. They took the Japanese language version, and I was put on the English tour. My aunt gave me a small parcel each day of snacks, Japanese children's treats. I saw virtually every significant historical sight in Kyoto and Nara that week, alone. Sometimes my path crossed theirs at a shrine or in a garden. We waved a little forlornly at each other, and my uncle stopped to take a photo of us. To this day, I do not like to take guided tours.

Each evening, when we met for dinner in the inn, my aunt would inquire, "Hamburger *hoishiidesu-ka?*" My aunt and uncle were surprised that I preferred to eat Japanese food. We were almost strangers to each other, separated by their unrevised recollections of me in 1955, by the absence of a common language, by seventeen years lived in different cultures, and by my ideas of Japanese people and their ideas of Americans. I said goodbye to them in Kobe with everything still unreclaimed, still unfinished.

As the ship sailed out of Kobe harbor, I held my end of the colorful paper streamers that spooled off a roll until they ran out or broke. Hundreds of the brightly colored paper ribbons stretched from hands on shore to those on the deck, an old farewell ritual.

I remembered the moment when my mother, father, baby sister, and I left Fukuoka by boat for Okinawa in 1955. We stood on the deck watching Ji-chan, Uncle Katsumi, Aunts Shizue and Fumiko, and Ba-chan on the shore waving goodbye. Each of them was holding a colored spool of paper that ended in my parents' hands. My mother urged me to take one of the spools and hold a connection to those on the shore. I was afraid I would hold too tightly, get pulled into the water, and drown, so I refused. My mother and father tried several times to get me to take the spool, promising to hold tight to me, but I stood on the deck and cried. I refused to take the spool; I refused to say goodbye or wave.

PART TWO

Pentecost
A Season of Fire

CHAPTER 3

Tiamat's Tears

Rebecca's Story

O that you would tear open the heavens and come down,
So that the mountains would quake at your presence—
as when fire kindles brushwood
and the fire causes water to boil—

Isaiah 64:1–2

In the dream, I am standing on Kite Hill, a grassy knoll above Lake Union in Seattle. It is night. Across the black sheen of the still water, the lights of the city are visible in the distance, a silver shimmer on the horizon. But it is the stars that are dazzling. The whole sky sparkles with pinpoints of fire. Looking up into the night sky, I am entranced. I see something moving in the heavens. It's a spinning swirl of light. A spiral galaxy? It grows larger, coming nearer. A flying saucer? I watch, fascinated. It circles downward, speeding towards earth. Now I can see that the lights are multicolored—sapphire blue, emerald green, ruby red, molten yellow. It isn't a flying saucer. It is a great dragon, falling! Its jewel-encrusted body is in a spin as it plummets towards the earth. Wisps of smoke trail from its nostrils. Its fire has gone out. This is why it is falling. It cannot remain in the sky without its fire. Diamond tears are spilling from its eyes. It is going to crash right where I am standing on top of Kite Hill! Alarmed, I scurry to avoid being hit. The dragon thuds to earth. I move towards it and bend down with concern, touching the tears.

From out of nowhere my friend Colleen arrives and takes charge. "We will take the dragon to my house," she announces. We carry the dragon to Colleen's antebellum mansion and up the sweep of stairs. We stretch the dragon around the balcony that circles the interior of the house. There is just enough room for it to be comfortable. We are sweating from the exertion of carrying the heavy, lifeless body. "Now," Colleen says, "we must feed it chicken soup."

I wake up with the dream vivid in my mind. I draw a picture of the dragon, working to make the colors as brilliant as they were in the dream. I draw her tears.

Nearly a year has passed since I aborted the pregnancy that had brought me a moment's joy. My husband and I are no longer living together. He has rented a small apartment a few blocks away. Just before Easter, I'd helped him move, carrying furniture through our neighborhood streets late one night to get him settled in his new place. He said the separation would help him find his way. I had believed that having an abortion would enable our marriage to survive. My husband's departure filled me with sorrow. Sacrifice hadn't saved us. I'd voiced my theological questions publicly in the Lenten sermon series I'd preached probing the Christian doctrine of the atonement. People in the church respected the questions and were grappling in their own ways with the meaning of Christian faithfulness. I continued to keep my personal anguish silent, except in conversation with a few trusted friends. Colleen was one of the friends who knew much of my story.

She had been present Good Friday when the congregation ritually extinguished all fire and light in the sanctuary. We had entered the night of grief together.

Following that service, Easter came round, as usual. The congregation gathered on Kite Hill at dawn, in the rain, and re-enacted the story of discovering a resurrected Jesus. We sang alleluias and went back to the church for pancakes. Spring blossoms filled the sanctuary, and trumpets accompanied our singing. The church was packed with people. In the midst of so much questioning, what could I preach? There is a ghostly skeleton, I said, that we must learn to dance with. We must find how we can hold loss in our arms and move in rhythm with it. I said we cannot live until we learn to embrace life's realities of betrayal, violence, suffering, and grief. How to hold all this in our arms without being destroyed by sorrow I did not know. Maybe music would show us. Maybe ritual would carry us there. But somehow, just as Mary had cradled her crucified son in her arms and wailed, we had to hold the bodies of earth's violated people and voice our grief. Our grief might enable us, the survivors, to act in the world with determination and compassion.

At least, I hoped so.

"Come over and hear my dream," I said to Colleen on the phone. She came in the evening, listened, and studied my drawing. We decided we had to find out more about dragons and we pulled the *Dictionary of Folklore* from the bookshelf in my study. In many cultures, it said, the dragon is the mother creator, the source of all life. Her birth gives birth to the cosmos. Her festivals celebrate the renewal of the world at the new year.

"But my dream dragon is in trouble!" I said.

"She's not the first one to be in trouble," Colleen responded, reading on. In Gilgamesh, the Babylonian creation epic, Tiamat is the great mother dragon. From her body are born all the stars in the heavens. Her son Marduk becomes enraged at her fecundity and determines to slay her. He arms himself for battle and advances upon her, wielding a great sword. She opens her mouth to bellow her rage. Marduk seizes the moment and plunges the sword into her mouth. He kills her, slices her body in two, and casts one half of her carcass into the heavens. The other half of her slain body becomes the foundation for this world. The constellation Draco, seen in the Northern Hemisphere as a spiraling cluster of stars circling the North Star, is perhaps named in distant memory of Tiamat's slain body cast into outer space.

"We navigate by her broken and exiled body," I said to Colleen. "The world as we know it is built on the splitting of the body of the mother of us all; it's built on violence. She's lost her fire. She can't bear to circle the heavens in exile any longer. She's fallen to earth in grief. She is seeking wholeness, reconnection. She is no longer able to sustain a cosmos divided by violence."

"Well," Colleen said, "the dragon in your dream could be you. The creative power of your own body has been disrupted. You must feel like your inner fire has been scattered to ashes."

"That's true," I said. "I feel like I've been thrown to the ground by anguish. Maybe the dream portends a transformation that will come for me."

"It might not be just about you," Colleen added. "Maybe it is about our times. About the healing of women's broken hearts, the mending of our bodies, our search for wholeness. Maybe it's about all of us wanting a world built on some foundation other than violence. Maybe it's about the grief everyone suffers because of the legacies of pain we inherit."

"Maybe it's about chicken soup," I added.

"Chicken soup might be a start," Colleen smiled.

Colleen asked if she could borrow the dragon picture. She took it to the children's improvisational theater group she directed at the church on Thursday afternoons. The children looked at the drawing as Colleen told them the dream-story.

"We'll make it into a play!" the kids said. Colleen listened to the kids talk about the dream and wrote down what they said. From their words and ideas she scripted a play.

"How will the dragon know where to land?" the children asked. "How will she find us? We'll have to signal to Tiamat in outer space so she can see the way. We'll make a pathway of lights for her. Then we'll do a wild and crazy dance to attract her attention."

The play was presented later that spring, on a warm evening fragrant with lilac blossoms, as Pentecost neared. The children staged it in the sanctuary of the church. The audience sat in darkness. Down the center aisle the children laid out a pathway of lights. They danced a wild and crazy dance, banging drums, ringing bells, whooping and leaping and twirling. The dragon arrived from behind the high pulpit and came down to rest in the circle of children. She had a great head of papier mâché, painted after the likeness of my dream-drawing. Her long cloth body was multicolored. When she landed, the fabric deflated in a heap on the floor. She looked like a great popped balloon. Chicken soup was offered her. But it wasn't enough. The heap lay there.

"How can we help her?" the children asked one another. "Her heart must be broken!" one of them cried, "Look at her tears." The children touched the dragon's great head, tenderly.

"We must ask her to tell us her story and we must listen." The children nodded to one another. One of them climbed inside the dragon and her head began to move up and down, as if talking. The children mimed listening. They shook their heads in sympathy. They touched their cheeks and hers, in sadness. One by one, the listening children climbed inside. The dragon's body began to rise, billow, fill. Soon they were all inside. Her long body stretched the length of the aisle. Music filled the sanctuary. And she began to dance.

The play was over. We rose to our feet in applause.

I was moved by the children's sensitivity and by their instinct for ritual. The children of the church created a story of healing. In

Thomas Aquinas' *Summa Theologia* there is a discussion of melancholy. Aquinas observes that there are human beings whose lives are burdened by deep sadness. He wonders whether this sadness makes people more inclined to sin—to do those things that cause harm to others and increase their own despair. After a lengthy discussion of this question, Aquinas concludes that melancholy does indeed have this effect. It worries him. He then asks whether the sad should be held to account for their sins, and concludes that, no, there should be special compassion for those who live with bleak despair, that grief is a burden that should be lifted if possible. But how can melancholy be cured or lessened? Aquinas surveys the known treatments of his day and finally concludes that there are two sources of hope for the chronically depressed: the company of friends and hot baths.

The company of children healed Tiamat. Slain by violence, fallen from her celestial exile, she was restored to life by an act of compassionate listening. A tale of anguish was told and witnessed, and life was restored. The listeners themselves became the rekindled fire that animated the broken heart and body of Tiamat. Communion effected a resurrection. Remembrance repaired a dismembered body.

On Sundays at the Wallingford United Methodist Church, after I climbed the steps into the pulpit, I'd hold still for a few moments and look at the congregation. At the beginning I'd seen a collection of kindly, comfortable middle- and working-class white Americans, who came to church out of habit, duty, or convention. But over time what I could see in their faces began to change. I visited people in their homes. They told me about their lives. I listened. Gradually, people revealed themselves. Their lives contained much more than was immediately visible on their ordinary, seemingly bland faces. They didn't wear their troubles on their sleeves. But everywhere, I saw Tiamat's tears.

There was Sara, in her twenties, who had broken off her engagement to be married because she was traumatized by memories of incest during her childhood. There was John, a minister's son, who had found the courage to tell his parents he was gay. His father denounced him from the pulpit the next Sunday and his family disowned him. There was Janet, who was supporting her husband and two children while he battled the cancer that threatened his life. Janet's boss had passed her over for a promotion and a raise, telling her that men with families needed it more. There was Linda, tireless in her care for others, who had found no personal comfort for the suicide of her son twenty years earlier. And there was Daniel. He was trying to be a good husband and father to his children, but when he had flashbacks from his experiences in Vietnam, he would hit his children in a rage. Daniel was deeply troubled by his lack of control. His girls lit the candles on Sunday morning, timid and frightened.

People kept busy at church with countless activities. They met in small groups to read the Bible, collected food for the hungry, ran a day-care center for children of single mothers, kept a Sunday school going. People met weekly for choir practice, raised money for mission work that alleviated human suffering and that supported the self-development of people around the world. The prayer group prayed for people who were sick or in crisis. Life passages—birth, coming of age, marriage, death—were honored by the church's rituals. Day in and day out, the simple tasks that make life whole were performed.

But as I'd learned from the women's Bible class, the people who were doing these worthy activities were isolated in their own struggles and pain. Illness and death were acceptable troubles, but not war-trauma, incest, homophobia, or domestic violence. These were to be borne in silence.

The church sustained this silence. There seemed to be a tacit agreement that the church was, in part, needed for just this purpose: to cover up violence and injustice that was close to home. An elder, looking back on nearly forty years in the ministry, once said to me, "Church people use religion to cover over their pain, to bury it instead of addressing it. At least the liberal white folk I've worked with do this. I wish I'd understood much sooner how much damage that kind of silence does to people's lives and to the community."

I had learned to keep quiet as well. In hiding my sad experience of abortion and my heartbreak at the disintegration of my marriage, I was behaving just like the members of the congregation. "Love bears all things."

The sermon series I'd preached, examining theologies of the cross, had undone some of this silence. I had begun to mention from the pulpit some of the pain people lived with. I didn't draw attention to individuals or deride the silence. I simply broke it. I mentioned that women were victims of incest, rape, battering, and work-place discrimination. I mentioned that lesbians and gays were treated with harsh rejection by their families and by the church. I mentioned that men were traumatized by war, that children were beaten in their own homes.

It wasn't courage or wisdom that moved me to wrestle publicly with theologies that sanctioned the silent acceptance of suffering. Personal crisis motivated me. But it was more than that. It was something about the church itself, something that went beyond its habits of comfortable silence and rote activity. You could call it a quality of listening.

On Sundays when I'd stand up to preach, I'd be face to face with people I'd come to know. I didn't see them alone. I saw their homes, their workplaces, their extended families, their histories: Mrs. Johnson's tidy living room, its fireplace mantle crowded with pictures of her children and grandchildren, her collection of ceramic dogs displayed in a corner cupboard, the coffee table, with its clean, plastic-lace covering; Julia's cubicle in the city planning department, covered with blueprints, cornered by fabric-covered office dividers, papers held down by a coffee mug, pictures of her children and husband thumb-tacked to the burlap wall; Old Al's armchair set by the picture window, overlooking the dry docks on Lake Union, where the workmen crawled over the rusty hulks of barges under repair. "I've been a tug boat captain most of my life," he said, "Now I like to watch 'em down there, working the waterways, while I sit here and remember. They were going to tear out the dry dock and put in condominiums. No sense of what is beautiful." He snorted.

When I looked at them on Sunday morning, I felt them listening, quietly, patiently. They were waiting for the preacher to say something that was true, something that mattered. It appeared they were willing to wait a long time for this.

Week after week, year after year, people had come to this church and sat under the arched canopy of dark wood that formed the high pitch of the interior. The sanctuary was made from huge Douglas firs hauled down on skids from Mount Rainier, during the middle of the Depression. Many of the people were out of work, scraping to get by. War was on the horizon, but they put their efforts into making a shelter for the spirit.

Now its white plaster walls, simple stained-glass windows, and graceful beams sheltered us. For the people who had been part of this church since the 1930s, there was plenty of room for a young woman minister with a seminary degree to tell them whatever she wanted to about God. There was only one thing they seemed to ask for in their quiet and attentive listening: Say something true. Say something that matters.

The handful of younger people were no different. They hadn't been there for forty years, singing the hymns, passing the silver communion tray with its tiny cups of grape juice, and listening to the preacher and the choir. But they were listening for something, in the same way.

The quality of their listening asked a lot: no bullshit, no pablum, no rote ideas, no shallow theology, no pop psychology—give us the word that matters, the truth that sets us free. How could I meet their eyes if I evaded their request? Even if it meant pushing beyond my own attachment to a comfortable surface that hid difficult questions, I wanted to respond to the trust extended to me. Preparing the weekly sermon, I had to search hard to find the words that mattered. I dug deeply into my limited knowledge of life—thinking, studying, feeling my way. Then on Sunday morning, face to face with them, I spoke. I only rarely attained the quality of speech they were listening for, but every week I reached for it, strained to cross the expanse of silence, utter words that leaned in the direction of honesty. They'd revealed their lives to me, now they listened for my response. I did my best. The congregation heard me into speech—that's how Nelle Morton would have named it.

Nelle Morton was the first woman I heard preach. When Rita and I were studying at the School of Theology at Claremont in the late seventies, Nelle was living nearby at Pilgrim Place, a retirement community. Nelle and her friend, Anne Bennett, were the elder, elegant crones around whom gathered a younger circle of feminist women who called themselves Sister Circle. Rita was active in the group, but I watched Sister Circle from a distance. The women in the group would do things that made me nervous. In class, they would challenge our male professor's use of exclusively male language for God. I didn't disagree with their point, but they were risking the displeasure of the distinguished scholars whose approval I wanted. I hadn't yet

learned the extent to which I had given my power away to men—a re-
linquishment that happened early in my life, in events that I would
only begin to piece back together at midlife. But my awakening to
feminism began at Claremont. The women in Sister Circle had an energy, emotional vitality, and boldness that I was drawn to. What they
were doing and saying didn't go unnoticed by me. Intimations of another way reached me through them, and I tucked what I was learning from them away into corners of my consciousness until I was prepared to make use of it.

The day the seminary community celebrated Pentecost, Nelle
Morton preached. The traditional text for that day speaks of the gift
of the Holy Spirit to the friends of Jesus after his death:

> They were all together in one place. And suddenly from heaven there
> came a sound like the rush of a violent wind, and it filled the entire house
> where they were sitting. Divided tongues, as of fire, appeared among
> them, and a tongue rested on each of them. All of them were filled with
> the Holy Spirit and began to speak in other languages, as the Spirit gave
> them ability. . . . At this sound the crowd gathered and was bewildered,
> because each one heard them speaking in the native language of each.
> (Acts 2:1–4, 6)

Ordinary sermons on this text expound on the miracle of divine
grace that inspires human beings to speak the good news of the gospel. But Nelle took a different tack. She spoke about the power of listening. She said there is a quality of listening that is possible among
a circle of human beings, who by their attentiveness to one another
create a space in which each person is able to give voice to the truth
of her life. Nelle was talking about feminist consciousness-raising,
about the profound accomplishment of women who have broken silences in their lives and found words to make their actual experience
accessible to themselves and to others. She said this was the miracle of
speaking in tongues—the miracle of authentic narrative, made possible by listening that holds still long enough to let the truth be told.
She said that where there is this kind of listening and speaking a new
kind of community is born—a community of life. Nelle said, "We
can hear one another into speech."

At the Wallingford church I preached on Sundays, and weekdays
I visited people in their homes. Pastoral calling was harder than

preaching. I was painfully shy. This shyness wasn't helped by the fact that, on more than one occasion, I'd been sexually harassed making pastoral calls. I'd also received phone calls waking me in the middle of the night from a caller who would ask for my help as a pastor and then assault me with obscene words. Sometimes I'd sit a long time in my car at the curb outside a parishioner's home summoning the courage to get out of the car, go to the door and knock. The tradition in our congregation was for the pastor to come calling, unannounced—a sign, perhaps, that God, too, arrives unannounced. People would stop whatever they were doing to sit and talk with me. At each doorway I dreaded that the door would be closed in my face. I feared that I was disturbing people by this ritual of unexpected arrival.

The door never closed. People welcomed me into their homes and told me about their lives. Though my own grief remained unspoken I moved within a great circle of silent attentiveness, symbolized by the space of the sanctuary and enacted in the conversations I began to have with people.

One afternoon, I paid a pastoral call on Maxine and her husband. They had moved to a retirement home and she'd just had surgery. Their new apartment was a corner room that looked out across Elliot Bay, with the Olympic Mountains in the distance. It was good to see them in a place with so much beauty. The years were wearing on them now. His eyesight was almost gone. She wasn't as strong. They couldn't do as much at the church anymore.

Maxine was reading a letter when my knock interrupted her afternoon tea. She laid the letter down by the worn Bible and devotional pamphlets that rested on the end table, in easy reach of her armchair. She filled a flowered china cup for me, offered me lemon cookies, and picked up the letter.

"My brother Lyle is writing from Southern California. He says the farm workers appreciate the food and blankets they have been able to bring this trip, but they wish they could do more." I knew about the volunteer work that Maxine's brother, a farmer from Iowa, did. He and his wife drove to the Mexican border each winter to help out with the basics: food, blankets, repairs. They offered practical assistance and friendship to people struggling with the debilitating effects of poverty and harsh working conditions. Maxine and her sister Dorris enlisted the women of our congregation to send money and supplies to help as well.

"You know," Maxine mused, "we never thought Lyle would be the one to do something like this. We thought we'd lost him." As I listened, Maxine told me about her brother. In 1945, Lyle came home from the war, the only veteran to return alive to the small town in Iowa he'd left to go to the Western Front. The day he arrived home, the whole town came out to meet him. When the train pulled into the station, the band played. Family and friends waved and cheered, and the mayor stood ready to greet him. But the man who climbed off the train was not the cheerful, high-spirited boy who had gone off to war. The man who climbed off the train was a ghost. In response to the music and cheers, he stared back, mutely. His blank face did not register recognition of anyone—not mother, sister, or friend.

They took him home to the farm. He sat in the rocker in the parlor. He wouldn't speak, he wouldn't sleep, and he would barely eat. No one in that town knew what was wrong. They just knew that Lyle's soul was lost somewhere.

Maxine told me she decided to keep her brother company. Whenever she could she'd sit in the parlor with him and talk. She'd tell him the news from the hardware store in town, or about the potluck at church, who was there, which dress each young woman wore. She'd tell him how the clean laundry had blown off the line and into the tomatoes that morning. When she ran out of things to say, she'd just sit with him quietly, snapping beans or mending socks. Lyle was like a stone. No expression on his face. Rocking.

It went on like this for days that flowed into weeks and on into months. Then one night, late, after everyone else had gone to bed, Maxine was sitting with Lyle, quietly knitting, when the eyes in Lyle's still face filled with tears. The tears spilled over and began to run down his face. Maxine noticed. She got up and put her arms around her brother. Held in his sister's embrace, Lyle began to cry full force, great gusts of sobbing, and Maxine held him. Then he began to talk. He talked of the noise, the cold, the smoke, the death of his buddies. And then he spoke of the camps, the mass graves, the smell. He talked all night. Maxine listened.

When the morning light came across the fields, she went to the kitchen and cooked him breakfast. He ate. Then he went out and did the morning chores.

Maxine touched her Bible. "Weeping may endure for the night, but joy comes in the morning."

I thanked Maxine for telling me this story, and I pondered it in my heart. A traumatized human being was able to return to feeling, to speaking, and to the ordinary tasks of life because another person offered him her presence and was able to remain present to the account of terror and grief without turning away. Maxine was a faithful witness. She waited with Lyle in his silence and frozen feeling. She stayed with him. She heard his testimony without being overwhelmed, listening to the end. Lyle responded by allowing the grief to unfreeze and told his experiences. He became present to himself, able to recount his own memories. However disjointed and fragmented his speech, he was able to organize the thread of experience enough to create words, to tell what he remembered. Lyle began to come back to ordinary life.

He stayed in Iowa and took over the family farm while his sisters, Maxine and Dorris, came out to Seattle. The farm occupied most of Lyle's time, but every year he and his wife drove from Iowa to Southern California to lend a hand to the migrant farm workers who crossed the border from Mexico in search of work.

Many years later, Rita and I reflected on this story. We talked about the power of presence to heal some of the effects of violence. Reliable intimate relationships can help people survive profound violence, terror, and despair and enable them to live beyond their own personal pain. As Judith Herman notes in *Trauma and Recovery,* "Traumatic events destroy the sustaining bonds between individual and community. Those who have survived learn that their sense of self, or worth, of humanity, depends upon a feeling of connection to others." Restored, people return to ordinary life and expand their concern to others—not as self-sacrifice but as self-possession. Present to themselves and to the reality of others, they do not live in denial of violence but in remembrance of presence. They have embraced a greater knowledge of the world, of evil. When we come into such presence of ourselves we are able to take responsibility for our actions and lives, in all their ambiguity. And in that process of taking responsibility, we turn the corner toward the practice of loving, the practice of transforming the world.

While I was thinking and learning these things, I continued to struggle with my inner, unspoken anguish. Maxine's story stayed with me, but I wasn't prepared to trust the steady presence of people around me with the pain I held inside. In the year since my choice to have an abortion, life had become jagged. My theological wrestling, public and private, had not been enough to stanch the flow of my own sorrow. Grief pursued me.

As fall came, my husband remained distant. We'd been living apart for a while now. I began to feel that what had happened to us made less and less sense. I'd been wrapped up in my own grief. But what was really going on in my husband's life? One morning I was to meet him at his place so we could go together to a counseling session. I decided to go a little early. The barren trees were gray ghosts in the cold mist as I walked the few blocks from my house to the apartment where he lived. I'd become suspicious that he wasn't really living there. I found his car on the street near the apartment. The hood was warm. The windshield wipers had wiped away the morning dew. He had just gotten home. Where had he been?

When I got to his apartment I confronted him. "Tell me the truth. Are you involved with someone else?" "Yes." "How long has it been going on?" The truth came out. When my husband and I had begun trying to conceive a child, he had also begun to see another woman. When he had urged me to start a family with him, he was spending afternoons with her, talking. When I became pregnant, he was having sex with her.

I spiraled into a level of anguish and internalized anger that was life-threatening. Why had I trusted without question? How could I have been so out of touch with the actual situation of our lives? Why had I not understood how unhappy our marriage was for my husband? Why had I made it so hard for him to tell me the truth? Was there anyone or anything trustworthy anywhere? I wanted to die.

An unexpected friendship helped me during this time. Chuck was the husband of the woman my husband was involved with. He adored his wife and was heartbroken when she had begun the affair. Their marriage ended. Chuck and I were fellow sufferers in loss and disappointment. Neither of us had wanted to lose our spouses. We were each grieving, and we commiserated.

Chuck had a capacity to hold on to the complexity of things. He was sad and hurt, but he felt that something had been missing in their marriage that had led his wife to look elsewhere for passion. He did not blame her, though he was heartbroken and angry. He was also grieved to see my unhappiness. It all seemed to be more than any of us could bear or fully comprehend. Chuck and I got together every month or two for a good long talk. Talk helped.

The following summer Chuck left to teach in a summer program at Harvard. When he came back in the fall, he stopped by the parsonage. I was delighted to see my friend. He looked great. Tanned and beaming. "It was a terrific summer," he grinned. "I have fallen in love, really fallen in love, perhaps for the first time in my life."

I was delighted for him.

"I didn't know I could feel like this," he said, "and this is the part you aren't going to believe."

"What?" I asked.

"He's a guy."

"Oh, Chuck," I said, "How wonderful!" and gave him a hug.

Chuck told me what this discovery about himself meant for his relationship to God. As a lifelong Methodist he had a strong social conscience and a deep sense of the spirit's presence in life. But he said, "I always struggled with an inner feeling that I was not acceptable to God. The assurance of faith that John Wesley talks about eluded me. I was denying who I was. How could I feel God's acceptance when I couldn't accept myself? Now that I know I am gay and that love is possible for me, I know that God loves me."

I was moved by Chuck's experience and heartened by his new-found joy in life. Chuck had grown up in a society and a church that was inhospitable to who he was. He'd complied with messages that all good people are heterosexual, and that homosexuality is something to be ashamed of. He married a woman he liked and enjoyed. They had a child together. But he wasn't able to bring his whole self to the relationship. Now he had come home to himself and moved beyond the messages of shame.

I needed such a breakthrough myself. Somewhere within me was a deep sense of sexual shame. It blocked my ability to give and receive love. I had little insight into its source. On the surface, I was aware of feeling ashamed that my husband had left me. I felt like discarded trash. I thought my pregnancy had made me repulsive to him, like my sexuality was a crime. I was reluctant to hold my husband responsible for his choices, and blamed myself. The extremity of these feelings was startling to me. I did not know what to do with them, but I could do something about the kind of shaming that had constrained the life of my friend Chuck. Alone at night, waves of sorrow washed me in tears, but during the day, activism was my salvation. I turned away from the painful confusion that haunted me and focused on working for social change.

I formed a resolve: Let there be an end to homophobia, let there be a more hospitable world for sexual difference and diversity, let there be wholeness for human beings—not internalized hatred for ourselves.

It was the early 1980s and anti-gay sentiment was heating up in our city. On the national scene our denomination was preparing to pass legislation that denied ordination to those who were lesbian and gay.

Chuck and Pat, a lesbian woman in the congregation, came up with an idea for what our congregation might do in this climate. Both were active in the church, making important contributions to its life and ministry. But they'd kept a low profile about their sexual orientation. They were only out to me and a few of their friends in the church. Chuck worked for a school district where he would be fired if it were publicly known he was gay. There were no legal protections in place for him.

They wanted to see the church take a proactive stand in support of lesbians and gays. I liked their idea and invited them to present it at the next board meeting.

Tuesday night came around. After preliminary business was taken care of, the board chair called on Chuck and Pat. Each of them came out to the board and told what it was like to be a gay person in a society where the presence of gays was not welcome. They explained how much the church meant to them, and how they wanted its fellowship to be more available to people in the gay community. Then they proposed that the church start a support group for lesbians and gays and that we publish a welcome in the local papers, especially the gay press.

The first response was thundering silence. No one said a word. Then Cecil, the lay leader of the congregation, stood up. Cecil had been converted to Christianity by Aimee Semple McPherson, founder of the Four Square Gospel church. He'd known poverty as a child, and the sting of being called poor white trash. He'd had to quit school after eighth grade to go to work. He was a tough survivor, a self-taught man. The tattoos on his arm were from his years in the merchant marine.

No one ever stood up at board meetings. The meetings tended to be informal. But Cecil cleared his throat to make a speech.

"The Bible is perfectly clear on this question," he said, speaking with firmness. I held my breath. I had no idea where Cecil was going with this. "Jesus said, 'Love your neighbor as yourself,' and as far as I know he put no restrictions on who our neighbor is. I move we do as Chuck and Pat have proposed. There will be some in our church family who will not understand such an action. It will not fit with their understanding of what it means to be a Christian or of how they read the Bible, and we will lose our relationship with them. But if we don't do this, we will lose our relationship to God." Then he sat down.

Cecil's words woke something up in me. He said if holding on to a relationship meant you lost God, you had to let the relationship go. I didn't know how to do this. I had never considered the possibility that love might be willing to break a bond.

The board members began to talk. One said, "Chuck, I didn't know you were gay. But I loved you when I didn't know you were gay, so how can I not still love you now?" Another said, "Do you remember back in the 1960s we had a church member who got fired from his job with the city because he was gay. Remember how he protested and it was in the papers. We stood by him in this church. I don't think we understood very much about what his life was like, but we knew him, and we knew this wasn't fair."

But others were worried. "Of course everyone is welcome in our church. Why should we single out some people and make a big announcement about it? Don't people know they are welcome?" Someone responded, "No, they don't. Churches have gone out of their way to announce that homosexuality is a sin, even though it's hardly one of the major topics on Jesus' mind if you read the gospels. People have every reason to believe they are not welcome. We have to make that welcome clear."

Marge, one of the more conservative women in the church was quiet through much of the conversation. Marge always argued against the church getting involved in social issues—issues that Chuck was often the one to bring up. She was the president of the women's society and carried considerable weight in the church's decisions.

After listening to the debate go back and forth for a while, she spoke. "I've been a member of this church for over twenty-five years, but it hasn't always been easy. In the early '60s, I divorced my husband. People in the church shunned me. They accused me of breaking up our home. They said I wasn't a good Christian, that I was denying my little girls access to their father. I divorced their father because I found out he was abusing them. This was my church, and I kept coming, even though people wouldn't talk to me. It was important for me to be here. I needed the church." She paused, and then, with quiet heat, she slowly said, "I do not want to see any more people shut out like I was shut out because the church is too ignorant or too arrogant to care about people's lives."

Someone said, "Let's vote." The vote was unanimous in favor, with one abstention. The board asked me to preach a sermon the following Sunday announcing the decision. It was the first Sunday in Advent. The lectionary text for the day was 1 John 2:9–10: *"Whoever says, 'I am in the light,' while hating a brother or sister, is still in the darkness. Whoever loves a brother or sister, lives in the light."*

While I was preaching, people began to walk out of the church. Someone slammed the back doors of the sanctuary on the way out, for emphasis.

One longtime member, in her eighties, who had been part of the church for most of her adult life said, "You probably think I'm too old to make a change to another church, but I'm not. I care about Chuck and Pat. I know them both, and I love them. But the action the church has taken is not in keeping with what the Bible says." She and her husband moved their membership. By Christmas twenty-five percent of the church membership had resigned.

The church leaders discussed how to handle the dissent and conflict in the church. We decided that the lay deacons, a group in the church that provided pastoral care to the congregation, would assist me in visiting everyone who had withdrawn or was thinking of withdrawing. We visited every member who disagreed with the action of the church board. In the homes of estranged church members, we listened and prayed together. We agreed to disagree.

Looking back at this time a church member observed that the congregation became strong because it had faced its worst fear: that it would lose members if it took a controversial stand. Many members did leave the congregation. But those who stayed discovered we could weather the loss of important relationships. We recognized that there were many places for people to go to church who believed that homosexuality was a sin. There weren't many religious communities that were openly affirming, proactively supportive of lesbian, gay, bisexual and transgendered folk. We made a choice to provide hospitality where the religious world usually dispensed hostility.

The church was teaching me to accept the loss of relationship for the sake of something more important. I had sacrificed a pregnancy hoping to save my marriage and believing no price was too high to maintain connection. Now I was learning that preserving relationship at all costs was not as important as affirming the human right to be free from abusive treatment. The full impact would only come years later. It would help me face the unholy bond that held me in thrall to a sexual abuser.

New people began to join us. One said, "I left church life when I was young because of the church's hypocrisy. I swore I would never be part of a church again. But I'm joining because this church has taken a faithful stand."

We quickly discovered that lesbian and gay people who had been kicked out of churches weren't going to come to our church just because we hung out a welcome sign. There was no basis for trust that we meant what we said. How did people know that we weren't trying to lure them into the church so we could then convict them of their sin? No one just came to church. They called first, to test the waters. But when a call came into our office that began, "Is this the church that says lesbians and gays are welcome?" we did not always know, at first, if the caller was a person who was looking for a church that would genuinely welcome them, or if it was a person who was angered by our stand.

Nina, our church administrator, became highly adept at handling these calls. In response to the opening question, she would carefully explain that our church affirmed lesbian and gay expressions of human sexuality, that we welcomed people as they were, and that we had no intention of trying to change them. She told me that every caller eventually came around to saying, "The real reason I'm calling is . . ."

One day, the caller said, "The real reason I'm calling is that I am a man, but I like to dress up in women's clothes. If I come to church in a dress, will I be welcome?"

Nina pondered for a second and said, "Is it a really ugly dress?"

The caller laughed and came to church the next Sunday elegantly dressed in a red Chanel suit complete with hat and gloves. She came to the early service. Only about twelve of us were there that morning. We sat in a circle of chairs in the front of the sanctuary, for prayers and hymns, and then the sermon. After the sermon came the greeting of peace. It was our custom that each person turn to their neighbor and say, "The peace of Christ be with you." The response would be returned, "And also with you."

The visitor in the Chanel suit had taken the seat next to one of our fourteen-year-old boys. Carl Jr. was at the gangly, awkward, sullen age. Most Sundays he looked like church was a dose of castor oil. I watched out of the corner of my eye as we began the exchange of peace. Carl Jr. stood up, extended his hand, and said, "The peace of Christ be with you," his voice clear and strong. "And also with you," she responded, clasping his hand and smiling warmly. The sun actually came through the window at just that moment and bathed them in colored light streaming through the stained glass.

After the choice to welcome lesbian, gay, bisexual and transgendered people, the congregation was no longer afraid to take a stand. It became a courageous place, willing to struggle with issues that might stir up conflict, willing to risk the loss of relationship, open to hearing silenced truths.

The social concerns committee wanted the church to raise public awareness of the growing stockpile of nuclear weapons in the world. Mary Brown suggested that we place posters on the city's fleet of metro buses. The posters would depict the increase in stockpiles of nuclear weapons since the end of World War II. Not everyone thought this was a good idea, especially the older members of the church.

The topic came up at the women's Bible class that week for the third time. The women grumbled about how the church was spending too much of its energy working on political issues, and besides, why should we be raising questions about military strategy? It wasn't our place. Myrtle called a halt to the conversation. "Just a minute," she said, "how can you say we have no place having an opinion about this?" She looked around at the women in the group. "Every one of us here knows that our men came home from World War II broken," she said quietly. "We've spent our lives holding together the pieces that war broke. We did our best to take care of them as well as our children. And never speaking of it, always saying it was a good war. We know there is no such thing as a good war." There was quiet in the room as one by one the women silently nodded, remembering. After that, the women in the class supported Mary Brown's project.

Violence, I was beginning to understand, is assisted by silences. To stop violence, silences have to be broken. I'd begun by breaking silence around the abuse of women and children. My sermons stirred up resistance, but the resistance yielded when women began to experience greater connection with one another and less isolation around their own struggles. When the church took a stand in support of lesbian and gay people, the transformation began with silences being broken. First Chuck ended an internal silence and overcame the divide in himself created by internalized homophobia. Then church members began to speak more honestly with one another about their memories and experiences. It was just as Nelle Morton had said. Hearing one another into speech gave rise to a new community, a community of life.

The question for me was, could I move beyond my isolated grief and enter more fully into life? Could I break the hold that self-sacrificing love had on my heart? Staying away from the fire, leaving behind the proverbs of ashes, could I answer the question my despair left me with: Is there anything that can save us in the aftermath of violence and betrayal?

Then one of our neighbors got murdered. She lived alone, just around the corner from the church, an elderly widow on a fixed income. Someone had broken in, beaten and raped her, then robbed her of her meager belongings. This was the second murder within just a few months in our neighborhood.

There was a church board meeting the evening of the murder. Karen, a new member, said, "How can we do all this mundane business when a woman was just murdered down the block? Shouldn't her murder be on our agenda?" The people sitting around the table in the Sunday school room where we met nodded in agreement. We took care of the ordinary agenda quickly, and then turned to a discussion of the murder.

"What I'm concerned about," said Karen, "in addition to the

tragedy and horror of what has happened, is the effect this will have on the people in our neighborhood—especially the women who live alone. This could have been one of our own little old ladies—Myrtle, or Ida, or Rose. She was just like so many of the elderly women who come to our church. They live alone. They've been widows for many years, some of them. They don't have much money. They live on their Social Security check. They're in church every Sunday. They come to the women's society luncheons. Maybe they will be afraid to come to church. I just see them becoming so isolated by fear."

"Isn't this something we can do something about?"

We weren't sure what kind of action to take, but the church board voted that night "to do something." The question was, what could we do? Karen took the initiative to gather information and ideas.

We called a neighborhood meeting. The church sanctuary was full that night, as neighbors, distressed and worried, came together to plan some kind of response. We'd invited the chief of police to talk with us. He said, "We can put more patrol cars on the street, but it isn't going to solve the problem. Patrol cars respond to crime, but don't do much to deter it. It's expensive, and doesn't accomplish very much. What really creates security is when people care about their neighbors. You don't need to arm yourselves with handguns because you are afraid. You don't need to put in expensive security systems, though there are plenty of people who will be eager to sell you one. But that's not a good option for folks in this neighborhood who are on fixed incomes. What you need to do is take some simple, inexpensive security measures—like dead bolts on doors. But most importantly, neighbors need to know each other's names, know something about each other's schedules, and make a promise to look out for one another."

The police chief's words made sense. We were concerned that fear and isolation would increase, that people would feel a need to arm themselves, that a climate of closure and withdrawal would descend on the neighborhood, and that our elderly and those who lived alone would be the most affected. We needed to strengthen ties of connection and mutual support.

Violence severs the bonds of connection among human beings. It denies ties. Security, peace, well-being could be restored by neighbors knowing one another and promising to look out for one another.

The church and the community council called a second community meeting to present our plan. This meeting was festive—with music and good food. We announced that we would recruit a captain for every block in our neighborhood. The one hundred block captains would be in charge of bringing their neighbors together for dessert or a potluck meal. They'd share basic information on how to make everyone's home a bit harder to break into. For those who couldn't make the changes themselves, they'd find someone on the block who could. People would be invited to share their daily patterns with one another: when they headed for work, when the kids came home from school, when they went out to the church for an evening meeting.

An atmosphere of caring and generosity blossomed. Block captains came for a workshop in the church basement, and everyone learned how to install a dead bolt or make stoppers for windows. Throughout the neighborhood people began meeting in one another's homes—getting to know one another better and promising to look out for one another.

A year later, the crime rate in our neighborhood had dropped by more than half. We had gone from the second highest crime rate in the city to one of the lowest. We had learned about one another and built ties of connection and care throughout the neighborhood.

What I was learning at the church was in sharp contrast to the theology of self-sacrificing love I wrestled with. It wasn't the willingness to bear pain, or carry the burdens of others that transformed life in the places where life had been harmed by violence. It was strong relationships among human beings who offered their presence to one another.

I began to understand that violence is resisted by those who reverence the sacred presence of human beings and themselves embody such presence in the world. Individuals and communities protect life by taking actions that keep faith with their knowledge of something other than the lessons of oppression, or abuse, or violence. The practice of loving involves more than obeying an ideal, applying a principle, or imitating a model. Loving acts emerge from the grace we have come to know in the presence of one another. It is by being faithful to the power of presence that we learn to love.

Loving resists violence by introducing *in the flesh* the truth that violence denies. We counter violence, not with words or arguments, but with our very lives, enacted in daily, ordinary deeds of love. Knowledge that is disrupted or destroyed by violence is restored through actions that embody love. This is the liberating quality of truth. "You will know the truth and the truth will make you free" (John 8:32).

It was difficult for people to speak and to hear about sexual abuse, incest, battering of children and spouses. And the silences around sexual orientation had caused considerable harm. Breaking them, though stressful, was also healing. But the silences kept around men's experience in war were the deepest silences I encountered in the church.

Only after the congregation had become a site of open conversation around topics once forbidden did I begin to hear from women, and then from men, about war. Myrtle's comment in the Bible class, "we all know our men came home from the war broken," haunted me as much or more as the revelation from them of the physical and emotional abuse they had lived with in silence.

Daniel came to me for counsel about how to be a better father to his two small girls. He told me he had moments when he flipped out. "I'll be doing fine," he said. "We'll be playing in the yard. I'll be teaching them to ride a bike, or playing catch. Then something will happen, and I'll be back in 'Nam. All around me, I see fire. I hear yelling. Then I snap out of it. But Sandy is crying hard, in front of me, screaming, 'Daddy, Daddy, why did you hit me!'" Daniel looked stricken as he told me this. His normal affect was kindly and quiet, though a bit tense. He worked as a dentist. "What should I do?" he asked me.

I didn't know. I was not prepared for this, any more than I had been prepared for incest and battering. This was the early '80s. There hadn't been much publicity yet about post-traumatic shock in Vietnam vets. I didn't have a name for what Daniel was dealing with. Neither did he. I didn't know what resources there were for him, nor did I think I could help him. As I recall, he eventually found a group for Vietnam vets and told me it was helping some. But after a while he dropped out of the church.

I began to listen more carefully to the men in the congregation, to hear where the silences were. The devastating consequences of war for those who serve in active combat were becoming clearer to me.

So, too, were the resources that people found to put life back together in the aftermath of violence, even when it took a long time.

Bill asked me to come see him. He'd been diagnosed with an inoperable brain tumor. "I want you to hear my testimony before I die," he'd said on the phone. Bill was Marge's husband. They lived out of town in a small house, shaded by trees, close to the edge of the lake. There was a quietness there, and I felt the warmth of their home when I settled in by the fire. Marge disappeared into some other part of the house. We all knew that the brain tumor was far advanced, but Bill could still talk cogently.

"I'm not afraid to die," Bill began. "I want you to know that. And I want you to hear why. I was in the Korean War. They made me a sergeant and gave me a group of men to command. They were good guys. I loved them. Every one. Especially Sam, my best buddy. He was sweet and honest. He never said a hurtful word. He was always there when you needed him. We made it through some tough spots in that jungle. But the men were getting tired. Run down with sickness, the heat.

"One day, a message came through from my commanding officer, ordering us to make an ambush the next day. I knew where we were in the jungle. I knew where the enemy was. I knew if we made the ambush there was no chance that we could succeed at the objective or get out alive. It was a suicide mission."

"I argued with the commanding officer. I told him the mission would fail, and that it was a stupid idea to send us in there. I went so far as to tell him that even if he gave the order, I would refuse to lead my men into there. He told me I was betraying my duty as a soldier, that I was letting personal feelings get in the way of my responsibility, that if I wasn't going to carry out the command I wasn't an American, I wasn't a soldier, I wasn't a man. I felt ashamed of myself for questioning. The next day, I gave the order. We went in. It was bad." Bill stopped speaking for a moment, composing himself. "Most of my men were killed."

Bill hunched over and wrapped his arms around himself. "I was holding Sam in my arms when he died." It was quiet for a moment.

"I broke down then. I wasn't good for anything anymore. They sent me home. In my eyes, I had failed in every way: I had questioned my superior officer. I had faltered in doing my duty. And when my men were killed, I couldn't take the pain. I began to drink. I wanted the shame to go away. I wanted to bury the pain. I drank for the next twenty years. My family fell apart. My wife and children were disappointed in me. Angry. Hurt. She took them and left. I drank more. Slowly but surely I was killing myself."

"Then I met Marge." Bill sat up, caught my eye, and smiled. I thought of Marge's words to the church board—her insistence that the church not be ignorant or arrogant about people's lives. "Marge was tough. She told me I was worth something but I was treating myself like shit. She knew—she'd been there. Thanks to Marge's love I got into AA. I stopped drinking. I began to feel all the things I'd buried and think all the things I couldn't bear to think. It was rough, but the other guys in AA listened to all the crap I had to say about myself, about the world. They just listened. Didn't tell me I was right. Didn't tell me I was wrong. Didn't blink. Then I really began to come to my senses, like the Bible says."

"I saw the truth. Back there in Korea, I was *right* to have questioned my commanding officer. I was *right* to feel the order should be disobeyed. And when I broke down because my buddies died, I was *right* to cry."

As Bill spoke he placed both his hands on his own chest. "This is my manhood," he said, tapping a rhythm with his hands upon his body. "That I can feel. That I can care. That I can grieve. That I can love. That I hate war. That I had the courage to question. That I was willing not to obey."

"I'm not afraid to die now, because I know what love is. I know where God is." Hands again, pressing against his own flesh. "This is what I wanted you to hear from me before I die." He took my young hands in his old ones and looked at me. "It is important for you to know this. You are a preacher. Tell my story. People need to know what I'm telling you. *You* need to know what I'm telling you."

Bill had hated himself. But his life had been saved by a listening community, the tough encouragement of his wife, and by something in himself that rebelled against the suppression of his capacity to think, feel, and act.

Perhaps Bill understood the depth at which I needed to hear what he knew. Perhaps he could see in my carefully guarded eyes, in my mask of competence and good cheer, that inside I was in deep trouble. I'd lost my marriage. I'd had an abortion as an act of sacrifice that led to nothing but sorrow. The isolation in which I surrounded myself accumulated. I could not break the spiral of anguish and self-directed anger. I turned and turned on myself. For nearly two years, night after night I had been pacing the parsonage halls, caught in a relentless rage and grief.

One night, I came to the end of my will to live. I just wanted the anguish to stop. It was spring. A cold, clear night. I lived at the top of the hill above Lake Union, and sometime after midnight I left my house and started walking down the hill. The water would be cold enough. I could walk into it, then swim, then let go, sink down into the darkness and go home to God. The thought was comforting. I had no second thoughts. I was set on my course.

At the bottom of the hill, I had only the small grassy rise at the edge of Kite Hill to cross before I came to the water's edge. I crested the familiar rise and began the descent to the welcoming water when I was caught short by a barrier that hadn't been there before. It looked like a long line of oddly shaped sawhorses, laid out to the left and to the right, the width of the grassy field. In the dark I couldn't see a way to get around either end, but it looked like I could climb over the middle. I quickened my pace, impelled by the grief that wouldn't let go of me. As I got closer, the dark forms before my eyes seemed to be moving. I squinted to understand what I was seeing.

The odd bunchy shapes were a line of human beings bundled up in parkas and hats. The stick shapes weren't sawhorses. They were telescopes. It was the Seattle Astronomy Club.

Before I could make my way through the line, one of them looked up from his eyeglass and, presuming me to be an astronomer, said with enthusiasm, "I've got it focused perfectly on Jupiter. Come, take a look." I didn't want to be rude or give away my reason for being there, so I bent down and looked through the telescope. There was Jupiter, banded red and glowing! "Isn't it great?" he said.

It was great. Jupiter was beautiful through the telescope. The amateur astronomer focusing the lens didn't know me. He didn't know why I was there. He assumed I was there because the night sky was a wonder to behold. Across the sheen of dark water, the lights of the city shimmered. Over head, the sky was wild with pinpoints of fire.

I couldn't kill myself in the presence of these people who had gotten up in the middle of a cold spring night, with their home-built Radio Shack telescopes, to look at the planets and the stars.

Sure on this shining night
Of starmade shadows round,
Kindness must watch for me
This side the ground. . . .
Hearts all whole
Sure on this shining night
I weep for wonder . . .

We had sung those words in church choir, and I knew them by heart. The warmth of Samuel Barber's music and the sweetness of James Agee's poetry embraced that moment, held my life in that moment, when I could not hold myself. The poets, the amateur scientists, and the splendid night sky kept me in this world.

It would be wrong to think of this moment as one in which joy triumphed over despair, or love of life defeated desire for death. Such a view assumes that bad feelings need to be excised, or suppressed by stronger, better feelings. Peace or happiness or even survival are imagined to be accomplished by cutting something out, or dominating some aspect of the self. Viewing the soul this way internalizes violence.

I did not defeat negative feelings of anguish and despair because I saw something more lovely and good. Rather, I became able to feel more. My feeling broadened. Pain, sadness, and despair were not eliminated or overcome. I embraced them within a larger heart. All the feelings and memories I had couldn't be held by a decision to die. I could only hold everything with a decision to live.

The habit of self-sacrifice had created in me a fragmented and isolated interior life. An impulse for self-directed violence had displaced ordinary, commonplace matters. But when I experienced the unexpected continuities of ordinary life, my presence of mind was restored. The choir and its music filling the sanctuary, the fellowship and activism of the congregation—these sustained me. The ordinary inclination of human beings to share what pleases them, the delight of being awake to the beauty of the night sky, the cool air, the grass beneath my feet—these returned life to my senses. The commonplace translated itself into a deeper knowing. There is a web of connection we live in that is greater than sense can tell.

Shortly after that night, I had a dream: I am sleeping alone in the upstairs bedroom of the parsonage. I wake to the sounds of someone trying to break into the house. I can hear the intruder pushing hard, then prying open the front door of the house one floor below. Terrified, I get up. Where can I run to? The window of the bedroom is too small to escape through. The sounds of someone in the house draw nearer. I know the intruder is intent on finding me, is searching the house for me, wants to hurt me. I begin to barricade the bedroom door with whatever I can find. I push the dresser up against it. Pile up shoes, boots, books, a chair. The intruder is coming closer, is at the bedroom door. I pray the intruder won't be able to get in. I can feel the intruder's pursuit like an intense heat. The intruder pushes the door open, knocks over the barricade, crashes through all the boots, shoes, books, and strides toward me.

Light comes in from the hall and I can see her clearly. She is a short, sturdy, tough-looking middle-aged woman, with gray hair, cut short and plain. I immediately recognize her. She is my future self. She reaches me and puts her arms around me. She says, "I know the pain you are in now. I'm so sorry." I feel encompassed by a warm, strong love.

Waking from the dream, I know I am going to live. I know that my future self will be a person who can break through the walls of isolation and fear created by pain and lead me to presence. The dream disrupted the state of mind in which I had been unable to imagine a future. It introduced a person to come, as if she were present now.

Neither the dream, nor my night-sky epiphany, nor the blessings of ordinary church life, took away grief or repaired the torn interior space of my life. But they broadened my consciousness to embrace memories of the religious community, immediate experiences of the world's beauty and the kindness of human beings, and a vivid sense of future possibility. Restored breadth of feeling enabled me to make a decision to affirm rather than do violence to life—even when the violence I contemplated was turned onto myself.

I was not saved that night by an act of sacrifice. I was saved by a restoration of presence, a presence that I had lost and that was returned to me, by life.

CHAPTER 4

Life in My Hand
Rita's Story

Look, my eye has seen all this, my ear has heard and understood it. What you know, I also know; I am not inferior to you. But I would speak to the Almighty, and I desire to argue my case with God. As for you, you whitewash with lies; all of you are worthless physicians.

Your maxims are proverbs of ashes, your defenses are defenses of clay. Let me have silence, and I will speak, and let come on me what may. I will take my flesh in my teeth, and put my life in my hand. See, he will kill me; I have no hope, but I will defend my ways to his face. This will be my salvation, that the godless shall not come before him. Listen carefully to my words, and let my declaration be in your ears. I have indeed prepared my case; I know that I shall be vindicated. Who is there that will contend with me? For then I would be silent and die.

Only grant two things to me, then I will not hide myself from your face: withdraw your hand far from me, and do not let dread of you terrify me.

Job 13:1–4, 12–21

"We're going to shoot all the black students in your college if you don't expel them immediately," the phone caller threatened the Chapman College president. He identified himself as representing the Santa Ana Minutemen, a white supremacist group. It was fall 1968, the first semester I attended the school in Orange, California. Word of the call leaked from the president's office.

Student leaders called an emergency meeting to discuss the threat from a group considered to be more dangerous than the Ku Klux Klan. The meeting hall was jammed. By the time my roommate Bonnie and I got there, we had to stand in the entry doors. The first white speaker was adamant the college must protect the black students.

Black student leaders were outraged by the threat and spoke of the students' commitment to their education. They would not leave. But many were afraid for their lives.

As the discussion intensified, it became clear the black students did not trust the white administration to ensure their safety. Someone suggested human shields. Everywhere black students went, they would be surrounded by volunteers forming a wall of human flesh around them. The Minutemen would have to shoot the white students first. This idea gave everyone a chance to help, to do something more than worry or talk. The suggestion developed into a concrete strategy.

Every morning, black students gathered in front of the residence halls and went to and from the main campus inside a huddle of other students. I wanted to participate, but I was tentative. I had a vague sense of uneasiness that I could not make conscious or explicit. Should I be outside or inside the huddle? Was I white or black? Would the Minutemen shoot an Asian?

When no shots were fired, the shield activity slowly ceased. But something else, something unexpected happened. Relationships among the students changed. The extended contact generated new conversations. The black students told others about their experiences of racism—about what it was like for them to try to shop or eat in the town of Orange and about how badly some professors and students treated them. A group of student leaders, black, white, and Asian American, formed an organization to work on interracial relationships and on integrating Orange.

BECOMING ASIAN AMERICAN

I did not enter college an activist, but these events altered the trajectory of my life. I began to think about the larger political world that impacted me. I was introduced to ideas about oppressive social systems, policies, and laws. Previously, I had thought of racism as individual attitudes and behaviors, as personal prejudice. Now, I could see that ethical people had to organize collective actions to change harmful systems. Not to do so was to acquiesce to evil.

For the first time, I saw myself as part of a group, Asian Americans, with our own history in the United States. A Japanese American couple who were juniors, Cliff and Gwen, introduced me to this new identity. Gwen was a resident assistant in my dorm. Cliff was student body vice-president. Asian American leaders were a new phenomenon to me. Cliff told me about the beginnings of an Asian American civil rights movement in California. He taught me about racism against Asian Americans. I remembered pain I had buried for years. Suddenly there were words for the baffling and cruel behavior of white Americans.

I became divided against myself as I developed a political consciousness. Discovering racism against Asians meant I noticed it more. There were times I wished not to know, times when I could detect subtle, indirect racism that was not overtly hostile: the assumption that my Asian-looking face made me a foreigner, the expectation that I speak Japanese and be an expert on Asia, the suggestion that I fit exotic, Orientalized stereotypes of femininity.

My tendency toward quiet resignation and perseverance had compromised my ability to thrive. I accepted without question the standards of European whiteness as "American" and spent my childhood and adolescence doubting that I could be "American" at all. I had a split female identity: I mimicked white femininity and, at the same time, I complied with stereotypes of Asian femininity that white males imposed on me.

I learned that exclusion by race or ethnicity and the internalization of the norms of the dominant culture are American experiences. This knowledge helped me understand the racism I'd experienced and inspired my commitment to work for change. I had to make this commitment if I was to remain present to myself, to be aware of my experiences and their complexity, and to remain alive to hope.

This new awareness of racism cost me my innocence and ended my ability to adapt to stereotypes unquestioningly. I struggled to purge the norms and exclusions I had internalized. I had grown up in an era when Asian Americans were seen as the "yellow peril," not a model minority. I had worked hard in school to be nice and high-achieving, to disprove the negative stereotypes imposed on me. I began to grasp how I had acquiesced to racism by believing I was the one who had a personal problem. I thought that I could solve the problem by being nice and accommodating, and that I could change people's attitudes with my behavior. I learned to recognize the difference between suffering that required stoic endurance and wrongs that I could resist, between the consequences of my own acts and the aftereffects of oppression and other people's violence and hostility.

Cliff was my mentor. He urged me to get involved in school politics. In high school, I had been a student body officer, cheerleader, and salutatorian at graduation, but I did not consider myself a leader. I continued my cheerleading activities in college because they felt familiar, and I enjoyed the exuberant athleticism. The political activity was new. Cliff helped me think of myself as someone who could be a leader in a different arena, if I wanted to be.

Because I had high math aptitude scores and did well in science, I entered college on full scholarship, intending to become a brain surgeon. But nothing in my formal education was as interesting as the drama of activist work, as personally transforming of my soul. I went to class, but my attention was elsewhere. I joined demonstrations against racism and the U.S. war on Vietnam and dated activists. Though I was a straight-A student in high school, my first semester in college I got a B in zoology, a C in chemistry, a D in calculus.

My academic career was saved by one course. Because activism had become my overriding, life-saving passion, I asked the activists I admired to recommend a good course. Their choice was unanimous: Literature of the Old Testament, taught by a seventy-year-old professor. "Why a Bible class?" I wondered.

A MESSAGE FROM THE WHIRLWIND

The first day of the course, a short, wrinkled old man in a blue suit walked in, carrying a massive pile of books. He spread them on the desk in front and sat behind it. His round head, wispy gray hair, faded blue eyes, and wrinkled neck were visible just above the desk and books. He introduced himself as Willis Fisher and described the course. It had an overwhelming load of reading, papers, and exams.

I could hardly understand him. He shook and had trouble controlling his breathing. He spoke in wavering, staccato bursts, broken by jerky breaths. I thought, "How am I ever going to get through this course? I can't understand him!"

Within ten minutes I forgot about his speech problems. Dr. Fisher said the Bible was not a narrow rule book to follow without question or a seamless, consistent document. He said it was a series of books by different human authors, a record of people wrestling with God, each in their own time and place. It contained great literature, which we must seek to understand.

We would learn about the worlds of the writers, their historical times, and the religious questions that preoccupied them. The meanings of the books began in the past. Whatever they meant now required translation into our world. Dr. Fisher suggested we argue with the biblical writers, challenge their ideas, and come to our own conclusions about the books' views of God. Never before had I heard an approach to the Bible that was intellectually both appreciative and critical.

I remembered my arguments with Denver about creationism and evolution. It dawned on me that the writers of Genesis could not have known about evolution, and my attempt to apply the six days of creation to Darwin was naive. "But," I thought, "the writers of Genesis were probably using the best theories of their time. If they had known about evolution, surely they would have created a religious way to use it."

My doubts about creationism had made me skeptical that the Bible was the word of God—I did not think God was so stupid as to ignore science—but I didn't know what else to think of it. Denver's fundamentalism presented the Bible as God's promise of personal salvation and as literally true. Dr. Fisher's picture of the Bible was richer. The Bible was a vast world of ideas for reflection and insight. It presented the stories of many people who made commitments to ideas larger than individual salvation or success. "This course is going to be great," I thought.

It was more than great. It was life-changing. Throughout the course, Dr. Fisher emphasized the tradition of classical Hebrew prophecy—the books of Amos, Hosea, Jeremiah, Ezekiel, and Isaiah—and its demands for justice. His emphasis came from his Methodist roots and perhaps also from being raised by an unmarried suffragist aunt named Sadie. Methodists accept the Christian responsibility to work for justice and build the kingdom of God. Dr. Fisher pointed out that Jesus said nothing new about God. Jesus was a faithful Jew and what he preached about divine justice and forgiveness was found in the prophets. "Hmmm," I thought, "Jesus is an interesting character, an advocate for justice."

Dr. Fisher's Methodist bias resonated with a slow shift taking place in me. My activism against racism and the U.S. war on Vietnam had become a core life commitment. I could no longer see success as individual fulfillment. I had begun to connect my early experiences of racism and violence with larger social systems. I became committed to changing those systems. Dr. Fisher helped me see my activism as an enduring religious commitment, as more than a political activity, as grounded in my soul and in a long legacy of religious seekers.

For the first time, in Willis Fisher's class, what I studied in college touched me at my core and brought important pieces of my life into a whole. I did far more than the formidable course requirements that semester, easily earning an A. I knew I wanted to learn all that Dr. Fisher could teach me, so I signed up for every course he offered, semester by semester. By the time I had taken four courses with him, I was halfway to a major in religion, so that became my major. My grades were never a problem.

When I took Dr. Fisher's upper-level seminar, Poetry and Wisdom Literature of the Old Testament, I chose the book of Job for a research project. I had never read the entire book before, but I was curious about the story of Job's faithfulness that I learned in Sunday school. I had found his silent suffering and unwavering devotion to God comforting.

I read three translations of Job. I read all Saturday afternoon, completely captured by the text, its soaring, beautiful language. My childhood image of *shi-katta-ga-nai,* of Job's broken, faithful suffering, faded after the first few chapters. By the time I reached the final speeches of God from the whirlwind, that image of piety was completely gone. I was stunned.

Job raged against his suffering; he asked to die.

> O that it would please God to crush me, that he would let loose his hand and cut me off! . . . Is my strength the strength of stones, or is my flesh bronze? In truth I have no help in me, and any resource is driven from me. (Job 6:9, 12–13)

Job indicted God as a bully, and he clung to the only thing he knew, which was his integrity and self-knowledge. He chose to trust himself instead of being faithful to God, claiming his life as his own.

> I will take my flesh in my teeth, and put my life in my hand. (Job 13:14)

When his friends defended God at his expense, Job argued against them. The more they pushed their piety, the more Job stood against it. In my imagination, Job changed from a broken, pious man into a defiant, dignified person, wounded and alone, but unbowed.

I read as much as I could about Job: commentaries about its message; exegetical research on the words, language, history, and editing of the text; and even the Archibald MacLeish play *J.B.* I wanted to understand its grappling with evil and suffering.

Most scholars concluded that a long-ago editor had added the three chapters that comprise the prose morality tale of Job. The pious story, with its happy ending, framed the middle thirty-nine poetic chapters. The emotionally wrenching poetry was threatening to the religious sensibilities of the editor. This anonymous editor softened the nihilistic blow of Job's rage against God by having Job repent and be rewarded in the end. But what did the searing poetry mean? I found every explanation for it unsatisfying.

Job's aloneness and defiance felt familiar. At a level that was not conscious to me then, I saw myself in him as I defied Roy and his violence against me. I felt my personal resistance undergirded and any temptation to be passive and acquiescent to authority challenged by Job's example.

I gave my report in class. I said I liked this Job better than the Sunday school version, even though I didn't understand the poetry. Job's fury against the unfairness of his life, against a powerful God who could help him and did not, and against pious friends who defended God made emotional sense to me. There wasn't a satisfying idea of God in the book. I could only find a noble idea of humanity, of integrity and personal dignity in the midst of unjust suffering.

God finally replies to Job's accusations at the end of the poetic section, but it is an odd response. The divine speech from the whirlwind recites the miracle of creation and depicts life in its wildness and power. The answer to Job was a vision of nature. Perhaps it was enough. I knew I thought of my life as enlarged by love for a numinous universe—awesome, beautiful, and powerful. My personal existence was transcended by a power I did not fully understand. This power was not there for me alone, but belonged to the universe itself, and I belonged to that universe.

> Where were you when I laid the foundations of the earth? . . .
> Or who shut in the sea
> With doors when it burst out from the womb?

When I made the clouds its garment,
And thick darkness its swaddling band . . .
Who has cut a channel for the torrents of rain,
And a way for the thunderbolt,
To bring rain on a land where no one lives,
On the desert, which is empty of human life,
To satisfy the waste and desolate land,
And to make the ground put forth grass?
(Job 38:4, 8–9, 25–27)

When I finished, Dr. Fisher took off his glasses and looked at me. "Do you think," he asked, "that getting twice as much back at the end of his ordeal justifies God having put him through it? Was Job faithful to God?"

I thought carefully before I replied. "No reward," I said, "can make up for the pain Job experienced. I don't think what happened to him can be compensated by anything. If I had died, I would want my parents to miss me, even if they had another child. I would not want them to be happy, as if I never existed. It's like God tried to buy Job back in the end, like guilt money. Job took comfort in nature, not in personal gain."

"Job was not faithful to God. A God who would use a human being as a pawn to prove a point is not a God I would worship. Job was faithful to what he knew best, his own life and thoughts. I don't know why he repented at the end or what he was repenting of, but I didn't like that part. I don't think he had anything to repent for, except maybe thinking he could trust such a God. He was a good person who suffered for no reason."

The whirlwind spoke to me. I decided a religious person did not endure suffering stoically and hope for a reward. A religious person struggles to live with integrity in the larger framework of life and trusts her own feelings and experiences, as I had trusted myself as a child against Roy. I began to believe this, but it would take many years for that message to take hold in my behavior. I could resist overt violence, but I had developed a habit of enduring emotional pain and hoping my acquiescence would bring change.

During my second course with Dr. Fisher at the end of my sophomore year, he invited me to his office for a conference. It was late afternoon, and slanting sunlight fell across his desk. He had me sit in a chair next to the desk and wheeled his chair around so we were facing each other. In the golden light, I could see the tiny white hairs on the back of his hands and the stray flakes of dandruff on his glasses. He asked me what I planned to do after graduation. I said I did not know. He suggested I consider graduate school. "But," I said, "I don't like school." He asked me why. "A lot of my classes are not very interesting to me. I have a hard time studying." He noted that I was getting straight A's in religion. "Yes, but that's different. I *like* my religion classes."

"Well," he replied, "in graduate school you won't have to take classes you don't like. You can study religion. A bachelor's degree in religion won't get you much of a job. I think you should go to graduate school because there is more you can do with an advanced degree in religion. Besides, you have a fine mind, you would do well in graduate school, and your cross-cultural background will give you a distinct perspective from which you will make important contributions to the field."

I was speechless. No one had ever told me I had a fine mind before. I had considered myself lucky in school, or maybe just clever and ambitious. And I had worked so hard to fit into white culture. How had he noticed I had a cross-cultural perspective when I tried not to have one?

Dr. Fisher said the religion department had an encouragement for its majors. The Layne Foundation would pay tuition for my last two years in college and a master's degree if I went to a seminary. He wanted to recommend me for the scholarship. I said I neither wanted to be a minister nor go to seminary. He said, "You can do an academic degree, even a doctorate, at a top seminary. They don't just train ministers. At the best seminaries they also train scholars, and you would make a good one."

I told him I would think about it and asked for a list of schools I should investigate. He suggested Harvard, Claremont, Boston University, and Chicago. I thought about his advice for a few weeks and decided, since I had no other plans, that I should take it. I chose the School of Theology at Claremont because Dr. Fisher had taught there most of his career and because I did not want to leave California.

My religion major brought me to the attention of the Chapman chaplain's office. Chaplain Bill Carpenter was an important mentor for student activists fighting racism in the city of Orange and protesting the American war on Vietnam. He was a charismatic figure, admired by campus leaders and the faculty and administration alike. Because he invited me to participate in chapel activities, I became part of a community of student activists. I saw how being in a community tied me to a long legacy, which gave weight and depth to my advocacy for justice.

Eventually, I joined the denomination of Bill and several activist friends: the Christian Church (Disciples of Christ). The Disciples avoided creeds, which made sense to me. A faith journey should be open-ended, not prescribed by dusty doctrines. Members were expected to read the Bible and draw their own conclusions, which I knew how to do. The focus of the denomination was on two rituals, baptism of adult believers and communion. I appreciated the idea that the communion table belonged to God and not to denominations, that it should be open to all. The college chapel services reflected this sense of hospitality, ecumenical inclusiveness, and commitment to justice-making.

As long as I was in college, I did well on my own. Chapman College was small and friendly. I found community and a meaningful life there.

At twenty-two, I graduated from college with several honors. Becoming an activist and religion major in college had joined my inner pain, spiritual search for healing, and intellectual energies with a larger world of people struggling against injustice and war. My life had been made whole by claiming a religious identity of integrity and resistance to violence and by participating in actions against injustice. But I could not discern how to shape a future out of this conjoining. The chaplain had made a career of faith and activism, but I did not see myself in him. I knew no women ministers and could not imagine myself in such a role. I was a searcher, not a proclaimer. I resisted authority; I did not want to be an authority. It mattered to me that the college faculty believed I would succeed, but I was not sure I believed in myself.

I returned from Japan a few days after graduation without the nostalgic haven that had given me a retreat from both Roy's beatings and my schoolmates' racism. Memories of Japan had been my shelter from hate and harm. I had been forced by reality to relinquish that illusion.

My flesh of bronze had become who I was: an American in a home-
land that had been unwelcoming and puzzling. College had helped
me understand that American self as Asian American—but always,
part of me clung to the talisman of virtual Japan, the balm that
soothed my isolation. Now it was gone.

My decision to pursue a master's was more a stalling action than a
goal or direction. I hoped further schooling might give me space to
put a life together, to take my life in my hand. I had trouble admitting
my fears. To have done so would have meant facing how alone I felt,
how lost I was in trying to make a life of my own.

The summer after graduation, I read the *Female Eunuch,* by Ger-
maine Greer, *Sexual Politics,* by Kate Millet, and the first issue of *Ms.*
magazine. Discovering kindred spirits was reassuring. The feminist
concern for justice for women extended the political analysis I knew
as an activist against racism and war. Feminism also offered me an understanding of some of the personal conflicts of my life. I had always
felt torn between being smart and being adequately feminine. I did
not find domestic life interesting. I knew that life would be more exciting and rewarding with meaningful professional work, but wondered how lonely it would be without a mate. I thought of it as an
either/or choice—a husband or a career. The compelling vision was
feminist freedom and integrity, but a vision is not a life.

SEARCHING FOR AN ANCHOR

In June a Disciples church in Pasadena asked me to direct its high-
school youth program for the summer. The job paid enough to support me.

At the Pasadena church I met T.C., a member of the church and a
doctoral student in science, and this meeting forestalled my having to
confront my uncertainties about the future. He was tall and nice-
looking, with warm brown eyes and hair. We shared anti-war sensibilities, and he liked smart women. He was scrupulously ethical. I
knew I could trust him, and his calm quietness and career commitment quelled my anxieties. His emotional blandness, manifest in a
quiet, highly rational, thoughtful self-control, reassured me.

I had trouble reading his signals. He spent hours working with me
in the youth program, attending the events I planned, and talking to
me at length at other times, after church or on retreats. Through it all,

he kept an even, gentlemanly distance, never crossing into behavior that might mean more than a collegial interest in me.

Except once, when, at a retreat, he told me something so deeply personal I was stunned. He said he was having difficulty with a role he was given in a skit that made a joke about suicide. When he was thirteen, his father had killed himself. He paced nervously as he told me this, but his recitation was carefully controlled, with little emotion, the delivery flat. The pinched words squeezed themselves quickly out of his mouth, as if the passage from memory to words burned. As he paced, he clenched and unclenched his hands. He did not look at me as he told me that his father shot himself.

What that experience might have done to T.C. was beyond my comprehension. I felt awful for him. I also felt honored that he confided in me, an odd elation that came with the thought that, perhaps, he cared more about me than I could discern. I felt protective toward him, a sense of protectiveness that, over the course of the years we were together, kept me from making emotional demands of him. I was afraid that such demands might push him away.

Toward the end of the summer, I asked T.C. how he felt about our dating each other after I left the job at the church and started my master's. He explained that he had an awkward situation in his lab with a woman who worked there. He was interested in seeing me, but it would have to be secret so she wouldn't know.

I agreed to the terms, partly because I thought I had no other choice—his scientific work was the central commitment of his life—and partly because I felt noble and generous supporting him in his difficulty. T.C. made me peripheral to his life, and it seemed normal—I'd always felt peripheral in America. Feeling marginal and isolated were so much a part of my life that it did not feel strange to accept compromising terms for a relationship I wanted very much.

I believed T.C. was going to have a stellar career. I could share his life along with his commitment to science. T.C.'s clear goals provided an anchor for my own future, which yawned as an amorphous void before me. My feminism was mostly vision, outrage, and ideas, not a plan for my life. If I stayed with him, I would not have to construct a plan. I could attach myself to his life.

T.C. and I finished our degrees in 1974. He had six choices for a post-doctoral research appointment and asked me where he should go. I suggested he take the one in Switzerland because I could study theology there at the local university. In addition, we both liked to ski. He hadn't actually expressed an interest in having me accompany him, but I proceeded as if he had. I did not ask directly because I was afraid of the answer.

During the two years we had been dating, his emotional mildness kept me uneasy, uncertain if he cared enough about me to continue our relationship after graduation. I kept my anxieties to myself. I remained uncertain about his feelings and uncertain if he wanted me in his life. This uneasiness was familiar from my childhood, the anxiety of wondering what only one invitation meant. I was used to enduring it.

I concluded that his choice of Switzerland meant he wanted me to be with him and made plans based on that assumption. I couldn't imagine what else to do with my life at that point, and he offered no resistance, though he was not overly enthusiastic about my joining him.

He went first to find a place to live. For over two months, I stayed with a friend, waiting for word from him. I began to fear he had abandoned me. Finally, I received a short letter telling me about the apartment he had rented, the only communication I received from him after his departure. Part of me was afraid my deepest fears were true —that he didn't want me there. But I couldn't face having to make alternative plans for my life. I bought a ticket and joined him in mid-November.

We created a life together marked by the adoption of European habits: train travel, visits to great cathedrals and museums, classical music concerts, weekend hikes or ski trips in the Alps, wine with dinner, exquisite coffee, and elegant, civilized dinner parties. I refined my high-school German and enrolled in systematic theology courses at the distinguished university in town.

I never adjusted well to life in Switzerland. I looked like an illegal foreign worker, dark and Mediterranean—a population subjected to racism. Though my German grew increasingly correct and clear and I could understand the muddy Swiss version of German, I was treated as if I were stupid by shopkeepers. Clerks in department stores ignored me. No matter when I entered a store or where I stood in line, I was often served last and treated rudely. I was sometimes told they were out of something I saw another clerk provide to a Swiss customer. I searched until I found the few stores where the proprietors were friendly, even though frequenting them required taking extra time and trams.

THE LAST LETTER

A year into our time in Switzerland, Roy sent me a letter. He wrote occasionally with news of home but this letter was different. The tone was preachy and sanctimonious. It chided me for living with T.C. and not marrying. Roy told me I would be unhappy until I settled into a traditional wifely life. I wrote a heated response. T.C. suggested I not send it. I decided to take his advice. I did not write to my father after that. Communication with him ceased.

Near the end of our two years in Europe, T.C. and I visited northern Italy. When we returned home late at night, we wearily climbed the flight of stairs from the sidewalk to the entry. To the right of the doorway were now-unused mailboxes for the two apartments in our building. For some reason, I glanced at the old mailbox. A piece of paper had caught my eye. It was a telegram to me.

The telegram, sent that morning, was from my sister Jo Ann. My father Roy had died of a heart attack. They were delaying the funeral for a week, in hope that I could attend. T.C. and I were to leave in two months; it made no sense for me to go home and return. I would fly home to my father's funeral, then travel to Texas, where T.C. had a new research position waiting, and find an apartment for us.

On the long flight across the Atlantic, I felt relief. I was grateful that Roy had died before my mother, so my brother Ray, who was thirteen, would not be raised by him alone. I felt the disquiet of other feelings stirring below the surface, but I did not examine them. I preferred the numbness I felt.

I wondered if my decision not to send my angry letter to Roy had been a mistake. A flurry of letters might have kept some connection alive and allowed us to resolve our conflicts about my life. It was typical of T.C. to avoid conflict whenever possible, but my father and I connected through our heated arguments. Roy had died while we were in a stalemate.

My sister picked me up at the Los Angeles airport for the three-hour trip. I had driven that road to Barstow so many times since I was sixteen that I marked my life by its contours—from the smoggy valleys of the Southland, up Cajon Pass, straddling the San Andreas fault, across the Joshua tree studded vistas of the Mojave Desert. I traveled it first in high school with Baptist church friends, to the beach at San Clemente. At the turn down the mountains, over Cajon Pass, we saw the Inland Valley through the early morning haze and talked about the waves we would ride. At night, as we rounded the top of the pass, asleep, sunburned and exhausted, the shimmering lights of Victorville awakened us. The stars abruptly multiplied their number and wattage, like fireworks in the dark high desert sky.

During my first two years of college, I drove to Barstow on weekends to do my laundry, see friends, or bring a new boyfriend to meet my parents or the Clarks. In reverse, the Joshua trees whipped by until the gradual climb to Victorville turned down Cajon Pass and the brown smoggy air swallowed me. I used the drive to think and reflect. The highway was my route home for the holidays during ten years of college and graduate school. Back and forth on the road between Barstow and Los Angeles, I tried to come to terms with the conflicts between my father and me.

Now I rode to his funeral. Jo Ann told me about the details of his heart attack and the funeral plans. At the top of the pass, the Upper Mojave Desert spread out before us. The suffocating, hazy smog of the brown valleys yielded suddenly to the crystal sharpness of that astonishing sun-blinding desert sky.

Virginia Ann, a cousin from Mississippi, greeted us when we arrived. Bleary-eyed from tears and travel, we hugged each other. Other relatives from Mississippi also came, but she was the one I most hoped would be there. She was my father's first cousin, but she was more like his sister, closer than all his siblings to him. I'd known her since I was in first grade.

During the six years my family lived in Fort Riley, Kansas, we made the long drive to Mississippi each August. Most of the month, we helped my Grandpa Brock, Aunt Pearl and her husband Opal bring their cotton crop in, but we especially looked forward to the days we spent with Virginia Ann and her side of the Brock family.

They were a high-spirited, good-natured, vivacious family. Meals always involved laughter and teasing. Each of Virginia Ann's three younger brothers was a practical joker. Her father, O.C., my grandfather's brother, had a dairy farm. O.C.'s wife, Laura, was a small, smart, lively, funny woman and a fabulous cook. She was famous for her pickled okra and cucumbers. She dyed them bright green. Quarts of rich, fresh milk from the cows disappeared at every meal with Laura's biscuits or cornbread.

They were our favorite relatives. Virginia Ann and my mother had grown close over the years. I was a flower girl at Virginia Ann's wedding and had a crush on her younger brother Robert. He took me for rides on the farm's horse and told me about his college classes. He was excited about reading existentialist philosophy, especially Nietzsche, which cured his desire to be a minister. He became a teacher instead.

Virginia Ann learned early in life how to manage three rambunctious younger brothers because her mother had epilepsy. I heard stories of how one of the family members would come in from chores and find Laura in seizures on the kitchen floor. They seemed to take her disability in stride, caring for her as they'd been trained to and coping as best they could.

During those six years of visits, I decided I wanted to grow up and be like Virginia Ann. She was so different from my self-effacing, long-suffering mother. Virginia Ann finished two years of college before she left school to marry, which made her the best educated among the women on my father's side of the family—the usual pattern was to marry young and leave high school. I loved Virginia Ann's easy laugh, high spirits, and mischievous streak. In her later years, after being widowed, Virginia Ann became the first female deputy sheriff in her county, then a successful store detective.

It was good to see Virginia Ann again and to have her support for my mother during the week that was ahead.

Denver preached my father's memorial. He spoke of my father's sense of responsibility—how his children and wife could always rely on him for help. When my mother was stricken with cancer, Roy built a wooden shell over the back of his Toyota pickup so that my mother could lie down for the four-hour drive back from the big Navy hospital in San Diego. Roy slept in the truck in the hospital parking lot while she received her radiation and chemotherapy treatments. They couldn't afford a motel, but he wanted to be there for her. He took care of her as she recovered from the treatments. When the first round was done and she felt better, he took her to Las Vegas for the weekend where they danced like teenagers until dawn.

At the cemetery, my father received a veteran's funeral with a twenty-one-gun salute. I remember the lonely crack of rifle fire in the clear still air. My mother put the widow's flag in a box with my father's letters to her from Vietnam.

I was sorry that I had never answered his last letter.

MY FLESH IN MY TEETH

I stayed in Barstow two weeks and then took the train to Texas. T.C. arrived two months later. The next fall, in 1977, I drove to California to start a Ph.D. program in Claremont, California, while he stayed in Texas.

Through the first two years of my doctoral work, T.C. paid the tuition, and I earned my own living expenses. This tangle of financial obligation complicated how I felt about him. T.C. had supported us in Switzerland because I had a student visa and couldn't work. In exchange for his support, I took care of most of our household needs and chores—a role uncomfortably close to being a conventional wife, the same role my father thought should make me happy. I did not like the role, but I did my best to be a companion worth the investment.

I was uncomfortable with T.C. paying my tuition, but earning the money myself would probably have been more than I could have done. I was uncertain about my commitment to an academic career. Because he was willing to pay, I did not apply for scholarships. T.C. seemed fine with the arrangement, perhaps because it gave him a way to be part of my future. But I was uncomfortable about the level of indebtedness I felt in our relationship. I never talked about how I felt. Instead, I tried very hard to be the kind of companion I thought he wanted, to earn his love.

T.C. was so dispassionate, I never really knew if he loved me. He was often passive and distant. When I left for California, I thought we should contact each other often. Phoning each other signified to me a commitment to stay connected, involved in each other's lives across the two thousand miles that separated us. When I suggested frequent calls, T.C. mumbled something about the expense, so I waited for him to call me. He waited two weeks the first time. We rarely spoke more frequently than every week or two. He never wrote letters.

Through the years of our relationship, I relived repeatedly the confusions of my childhood, when I did not know if I was liked and wanted or merely tolerated because I did not understand the invitations I received. Whenever a conflict arose in our relationship, T.C. asked me what I wanted, so he could give it to me. I felt ungrateful being unhappy when he tried so hard to be good and nice. I was hurt by the long silences but never said so, and I never tried to call more often. Instead, I withdrew into my life in California.

I did not understand the lingering trauma of violence. T.C., I now think, controlled his emotional world by trying to be as good and kind as possible, so no one could blame him for conflict or be angry with him about anything, so no one else he loved would self-destruct.

T.C. believed he was helping me to be better by doing things for me. I wondered why I wasn't good enough as I was. I kept thinking that if I tried harder, T.C. would be more emotionally present to me. Instead, the distance between us grew, and the physical side of our relationship died. We were good companions, but we discussed little of emotional consequence. I could not ask for what I needed; I offered what I thought he wanted.

For years, I thought that T.C.'s detachment was the core problem in our relationship, but I think I may have been looking in the wrong direction. His emotional reserve allowed me to focus on what I thought was missing from him, rather than on my own emotional shield. I thought I did not know how he felt, but I was also unable to tell him how I felt.

If I had realized the emotional cost of his father's suicide, I might have understood that T.C. loved me as much as he could. I might have been more patient about my frustrations, more open about my own limitations in creating emotional intimacy. If I had been able to stop needing and admiring him, and instead simply understood him more, I might have been more helpful.

I did not grow up in a family that shared feelings. No one asked how I felt about living in the United States. I never spoke of the trauma I experienced in school. My mother and I never talked about my bewilderment or sense of loss. My father expected me to present myself to my family after my beatings as if nothing had happened, and, even if he hadn't forced me to come out of my room, my sense of personal dignity would have compelled me to hide my humiliation and anger. I refused to concede that what he did affected me.

I was accustomed to translating my vulnerabilities into cheerfulness and a veil of competence. My father encouraged my achievements, provided me with advice and ways to protect myself and to succeed, did things with me, and urged me to take risks. There was no place in our relationship for me to share my insecurities, fears, failures, sadness, and misgivings.

As my relationship with T.C. disintegrated, I invested more of my energies elsewhere. I worked as a part-time campus minister at Chapman College, where I was invited by my former professor, Fred Francis, to teach a course a semester in the religion department. I began to think I might make a career of teaching religion, if I survived my doctoral program. I was not certain I would finish.

During my course of study, I had recurring nightmares, mostly of threatened rapes. I dreamt of being pursued by danger—reflections, perhaps, of what it felt like to be an Asian American woman and feminist in theological graduate school. I had no minority professors. My feminist ideas were often ignored or belittled by the male students and professors, or received nervously. The anxieties of being so at odds with my environment showed up in my dreams, not in my conscious thoughts. Only later, when I discovered I was the first Asian American woman in the country to earn a doctorate in theology, did I realize how alone I was, what those dreams of danger might have meant.

Some of the most powerful dreams were of abused children. They were related to professional work I had begun doing with adolescents in 1974, just before leaving for Switzerland, which I resumed from 1978 to 1988 in Los Angeles. I worked as a volunteer in a summer camp program for high school students in California and Arizona. The National Conference of Christians and Jews (NCCJ) had created this human relations program, which was originally called Brotherhood, after the Watts riots in 1965. After many years of feminist agitation, Sisterhood was added to the name. I had joined the program to keep my activist work alive, to feed my soul.

Brotherhood/Sisterhood reshaped my life personally and theologically. The young people and colleagues I worked with haunted me. In the experiences of others, I felt echoes of my own life—my difficult relationship with Roy and my encounters with racism and

sexism. I struggled to move beyond my mask of competence and success, to work from places inside myself that made me feel more connected to what mattered to me, that were more loving in response to
other's pain. I struggled to take my life in my own hands. This struggle
forced me to live the theology I believed long before I could put it
into words.

My volunteer work for the NCCJ immersed me in the holiness of
life. I experienced the presence of a spirit that transforms life toward
greater loving and toward human thriving. I was changed by this presence. I began to explore my own pain and vulnerabilities, to connect
with people more honestly.

The program met at a retreat center above the valleys of Southern
California, nestled in the pine and live-oak covered slopes of the San
Gabriel Mountains. The weeklong June and August workshops focused on experiential ways of creating human understanding. This
focus was grounded in the belief that social change includes the transformation of the human heart. Over the years, the program took on
more social issues: homophobia, sexism, intimate violence, family
dysfunction, gangs, and addictions. As each issue was added, I had to
face my own attitudes and limitations in understanding; each issue
was a spiritual call to open my soul to the presence of others. I was
confronted with how my emotional shield limited my capacity to
hear well and to love generously. I learned to listen carefully to others
and to be challenged. Such openness was rarely easy.

At my third Brotherhood/Sisterhood week, in August 1979, the
forty staff members met together and got acquainted by practicing
exercises we would use with the youth. As we went around the circle,
I introduced myself as a feminist, an Asian American woman, and a
graduate student in religion. Across the circle was a new guy named
Jim who had a breezy, friendly air. When his turn came, he said, "I am
a social studies teacher, I play the guitar, and I like music." Then he
paused a minute and said, "And I guess I'm a masculinist," looking directly at me. The cold tone of his voice felt like a slap in the face.

I was dismayed to discover I had been paired with Jim as a co-facilitator of a small support group. As an experienced member of the
staff, I was supposed to guide Jim through his first camp. I could have
asked for a change, but I had too much pride to admit I didn't want to
work with him. I hoped he would ask for a change, but he didn't. We
were distantly polite as we prepared for our first group session.

At that meeting, we needed to explain some ground rules for re-spectful discussion. The week would be full of difficult, emotionally loaded issues; this exercise was important. Jim and I had to demon-strate how to self-disclose, how to communicate clearly, disagree, and maintain respect. We prepared a hypothetical situation as a role-play.

With our twelve high-school students seated in a circle, I was to begin. As I mentally rehearsed our planned dialogue, I stopped mo-mentarily to think. How could I demonstrate honest communication when I was pretending to like and work with him? How could I ori-ent him to the transformative work we had to do when I hid behind a screen? We were supposed to be models for the youth, but I knew they would see through phoniness in about three seconds. They would know I was being false. We would fail as staff. I did not want to betray the program.

In those few seconds, I changed my mind. I had to try a level of honesty I had never attempted before. Instead of enacting our imagi-nary scenario, I decided to tackle the truth. My mouth was dry and my heart was racing as I said, "When you introduced yourself as a masculinist at the staff meeting, I was really angry. I felt hurt that my commitment to justice for women that I work so hard for was belit-tled. You made it sound like I was silly to call myself a feminist. It felt like you were making fun of me. I wrote you off as a jerk."

It was Jim's turn to respond. He looked startled by what I had said. After a pause to think, he said, "When you called yourself a feminist, I got scared. Strong women scare me. I tend to be shy around women, and I don't think of myself as successful in relating to women. You seemed so confident. I figured you didn't like men. I called myself a masculinist to protect myself from you."

Suddenly, we were no longer adversaries. I could tell from the look in his eyes, the softening of his shoulders. We asked the group to discuss what had happened. They noticed the changes in body lan-guage, eye contact, and the shift of feelings.

After the group adjourned, Jim and I talked about our fears of each other. We saw that we both used bravado to cover our anxieties. I learned Jim was a man of sensitivity and depth. And I learned how to overcome my fear of self-disclosure, a lesson I would have to learn repeatedly.

Being a leader in this program forced me to move beyond my cheerful, confident American self. I felt compelled to do what I

hoped the youth would do. I had to be as honest as I could and practice a deeper listening, which encouraged others to share their honest
feelings. I discovered ways I was oblivious to the hurt in others. I was
ignorant about gay and lesbian issues, about the rates of depression and
suicide in homosexual youth, who had to struggle to affirm themselves in a society that made them invisible, ashamed, and targets of
contempt and hate.

I was not homophobic, but I was heterosexist. I fell easily into assumptions that someone was heterosexual unless they made a point of
coming out to me. I was oblivious to heterosexual privilege, the ease
of fitting in, of having my relationships be open and public, of having
my sexual identity an unquestioned norm that required no examina-
tion. Seeing that privilege helped me understand the difficulty white
men had perceiving and acknowledging their privilege.

Glen Poling, the director of community programs for the NCCJ,
was a gay man. He had been a third- or fourth-generation Salvation
Army preacher. In the early 1970s, in his twenties, he became estranged from his Iowan family and community because he came out
as a gay man. He had made a new life for himself in Los Angeles at the
NCCJ. He was committed to work against discrimination and violence, and his special assignments in the summer program were to
counsel gay, lesbian, and bisexual youth about questions of sexual
identity and to work with men on issues of sexism and sexual violence. One of the great losses in my life was his death of AIDS in 1991.

Glen had an exuberant, loving, tough-minded spirit. He was not
"nice"; he did not calm people's anxieties or fears by reassuring them.
Instead, he pushed them to face themselves. He pushed hard. He had
well-tuned radar for falseness. He took delight in the absurdities of
sixteen-year-olds whose pretenses to sophistication bordered on the
ridiculous. He was warmly, intelligently, emotionally present. He
gave exceptional bear hugs when he was happy. His sparkling blue
eyes narrowed into slits, nearly disappearing, when he laughed,
which he did often. He had a cap of thinning blond hair over a beautifully shaped head, a neat brown beard, and a small, trim, compact
body with a cute butt.

During the years Glen and I worked together, we had a habit of
talking late at night under the stars. We sat outside so he could smoke
his pipe, bundled in our parkas, which we needed in the mountain

night air. I could be uncertain, confused, hurt, and vulnerable with Glen. I asked his advice once about handling a member of the Asian American staff, a charismatic man who used the youth as a coterie of admirers with whom he vented his own pain instead of listening to and working with them. His narcissism frustrated me and stymied the work the rest of the staff wanted to do. I was inexperienced at confronting peers who failed in their responsibilities, and I tended to overreact. Glen encouraged me to describe the man's behavior to him, to act as a mirror, to explain what he had to change, and to remind him of his responsibilities. Glen made it clear I had the right to bring the man's behavior before the staff for discussion if he did not fulfill his obligations.

Glen and I shared the losses in our lives, my rupture from Japan, his departure from Iowa. We talked about his older brother's death in Vietnam and the effect of that war on my father. We shared mistakes we thought we made in our lives.

Glen's training as a minister meant he was more theologically educated than most of my conversation partners at camp. We talked at length about the Bible and religion, the theologies that interested us, the failure of the churches to include women, people of color, and gays and lesbians as equals. We struggled to discern how to live out a theology we believed gave life and hope. We dreamed of creating a church in Los Angeles that embodied our visions of inclusivity and justice.

I found a soulmate in Glen, and I followed his example whenever I had the courage to act similarly. His life's work was inseparably joined with his religious sensibilities. That joining meant he drew his motivations less from a political analysis of society and more from a deep well of love. He knew he was part of a long legacy of people who struggled and preached and prayed and dreamed of a world more whole, more loving, more merciful, more peaceful, more just. He lived at a time when churches rejected men like him, so he found another way, through NCCJ, to transform the world.

Glen transformed many lives. One moment occurred in August 1981. Three young black men, Joe, George, and Dan, the foster children of a white fundamentalist minister, were giving us trouble. Through the first three days of the week, they were virtually inseparable, closed, and defensive. Joe was the leader of the trio. He wore dark, mirror-finished sunglasses, even indoors. From the start of the week, he began loudly expressing his opinion that gays were sick and ought to be shot or locked up. The more staff and youth challenged him, the more vehement he became.

At one point, George and Dan approached me during a break. They asked me, "What do you call guys who like to have sex with other guys?" I replied, "I call them human beings."

"Naw, man, don't you call them a queer, or homo, or faggot, or somethin' like that?" George insisted. "No," I responded, "I don't think how people love each other should be labeled as bad. Human beings have a lot of ways we love each other. Love is good." "Huh," Dan said, and the two of them wandered off whispering to each other. I found the interrogation baffling.

On the fourth day of the week, the entire community of two hundred fifty met to discuss sexual violence and sexism. Young women told of being raped, either by members of their families or by strangers. Many listening were saddened and outraged by their stories. A dignified older woman, who had never used a word stronger than "darn" before, blurted out, "What the fuck is wrong with you men that you can do this to us!?" Tears were streaming down her face.

In the midst of this outrage and sorrow, Joe raised his hand. With his sunglasses on, Joe stood up and said with strong feeling, "I know how you feel. It's terrible what they done to you, and I know how you feel." His statement was met with considerable disbelief and derision. As the sounds of doubt rose, Joe shouted, "No, man, I know how you feel. I was raped myself."

The room went quiet in astonishment. He continued, "I know how you feel because I've been forced myself. I was raped." The silence lasted for nearly a minute. I wondered if his homophobia was based in this violation, in his rejection and projection of his pain and humiliation. I worried about our doubting of him and about how far we should push him to assess the meaning of that experience.

George stood up about six feet from Joe. In a soft voice, George said, "Joe, don't lie, not here, not now."

Joe turned to him and shouted, "I was raped! I was forced!" George raised his voice, "No way, man, don't lie. I know you lying!" Joe screamed back, "I was forced!"

George yelled over him, "No way! I know you lying! I saw you go in the toilet with that man. You begged him to let you suck his cock. I saw you suck his cock!"

Joe lunged at George. Two staff members stepped in and held them as they continued shouting. We listened in shock.

Across the meeting hall, Michael, a black staff member, bellowed in his booming bass voice, "Joe! Shut up and listen! You can't hide here. Shut up and listen!" George stopped. Joe continued to insist, "I was forced!"

Michael jumped up and down on the wooden floor, causing it to boom like a loud drum, in rhythm to his chant: "Joe, shut up and listen!"

Suddenly, Michael was the only one shouting. He stopped. Everyone sat frozen, unable to speak or move. Joe and George stopped struggling; the men holding them let go. I was trying to assess and to pick up the pieces of what had just exploded in our midst and to think of what to do next. No one spoke or moved. Even the facilitator was motionless. Someone had to act carefully, to take leadership.

Glen rose and turned toward Joe across the room. "Joe," Glen said, "do you remember what you said about how gays should be shot or locked up?"

Joe mumbled, "Yeah, but I don't believe that anymore." His voice rose, "If that's how you want to be, that's you and you can be like that. But I'm not like that, I'm not sick!"

"Joe," Glen responded, "what I hear you saying is that you think, if I am gay, I'm all right. That I am no less a human being and no less good."

"Yeah," Joe replied vehemently, "but I'm not like that—I'm not *sick!*"

Glen softened his voice to a whisper, "OK, Joe, I'm glad you think I'm all right." Slowly, deliberately, with emphasis, Glen said, "What I want you to know is that what you did was not bad or sick. You are all right. You are no less a human being . . . and you are *no less good.*"

In the pause that followed, two hundred forty-nine faces stared at Joe. Tears began to trickle from his sunglasses. He rushed abruptly toward the doors.

"Oh my God," I thought, "don't let him leave now. Don't let him run away."

Joe turned near the exit, stepped toward Glen, and collapsed into his arms, sobbing. With the unbearable tension in the room broken, we all began to cry—in relief, in sympathy, in joy, in sorrow. People began holding each other. Men held men, women held women, and men and women held each other in weeping huddles.

The next time we saw Joe, he had discarded his sunglasses, and his face glowed with an astonished happiness and surprised sweet shyness. Other youth praised his courage and told him repeatedly that he was OK. They thanked George for telling the truth and respecting the pain of those who had spoken. The survivors of rape were grateful he did not let Joe use their experiences as a shield to deny his own truth. Joe, George, and Dan became friends again. But instead of their previous closed, sour behavior, they smiled and interacted freely with others.

Follow-up to the meeting was intense. During the remaining days, Glen spent time with Joe, counseling him. Glen urged him not to leap at labels for himself and to pay attention to his feelings. He talked to Joe about how to survive his foster home, where homophobic religious ideas were forced on him and he was physically beaten. Glen gave Joe his phone number and offered to help him find support in his local community. He and other male staff worked with George and Dan to help them understand their own feelings and the ways they could support each other and Joe. The staff worked hard in our small groups to process feelings about sexual violence and homophobia. We also talked to each other about these feelings.

One of the insights that emerged from the discussions among the staff came from the men, who were pushed by Glen to confront their homophobia. Many of the men became aware of how much they withheld affection from other men and were afraid to make themselves open and vulnerable because of their homophobia. They were actually afraid of other men at a level they had never faced before, and it made them deeply lonely for their fathers, brothers, and each other. They associated physical touch and affection almost exclusively with sex.

In turning to women to meet their sexual and emotional needs, the men were unable to face questions about their own sexism. Being contemptuous and controlling of women allowed them to deny their emotional needs and vulnerabilities. If they acknowledged their need for control, they were afraid women would be angry with them and they would be cut off from the emotional support they depended upon from us.

The women on staff experienced the men's willingness to disclose what they had learned as an important act of solidarity with us. Whenever we worked with men who had possessed the courage to speak of their fears, we knew we worked with men who would not betray us when we were not present. Fighting sexism was no longer something they did for us; it was their issue too. We knew we could confront them with issues honestly and directly and be heard, and this new openness enabled us to be more forthcoming about other forms of oppression.

Lateral violence erupts when hate and trauma damage people's capacity to love themselves and one another. Joe and his foster brothers were projecting the denial, fear, and tensions in their group against gays and lesbians. In their foster home, they were taught fear and hate of homosexuals and punished with violence. The question they had asked me about what to call gays indicated that the two were struggling with what to think about Joe.

None of us really knew what happened in the restroom between Joe and the man he propositioned. We had his account and George's account side by side. Whatever happened there, Glen understood that Joe was struggling with complex sexual feelings and a self-hate that he projected as homophobia.

When Joe rose to speak at the group gathering, he was compelled by an internal sense of having been violated. This was an accurate intuition—vitriolic homophobia had taught him to hate and fear his own sexual feelings. These lessons in self-hate were a violation of him by others. George told Glen in private about what he had seen in the public toilet. As the only eyewitness, George believed he saw Joe willingly engage in a homosexual act. George felt the pressure of Joe's lie as a need to tell what he knew, so he broke ranks from the wall of silence the three had built. The integrity of his foster brother and a loving word from Glen set Joe free.

Glen was able to hear something deeper, something more important under the rhetoric of Joe's hate. Glen responded at that deeper level and opened life to a hard-earned grace, redeemed by acts of honesty and love. When Joe wept in Glen's arms, I knew something greater than all of us had entered that moment, something that was made possible by a community commitment to truth in its ambiguity and rawness. Love transformed the future that flowed from that moment. "You will know the truth, and the truth will make you free" (John 8:32).

In my many summers with this program, I learned how crucial presence and honesty were to loving, to living a spiritually rich life that integrated a commitment to justice with the care of souls. I learned to practice quiet discernment. I am not a patient person, but I learned to wait and watch when someone irritated me. I began to see myself and others as both distinct and connected. I learned to separate my inner life from the emotional needs of others. This distinction gave me ways to care about people different from me by listening to them above the noise of my own needs. I also developed greater courage. I began to speak up when something bothered me, when something seemed false, or when I felt manipulated.

The two issues about which I learned the most in NCCJ were the two that I struggled with in my doctoral program. I was on staff as an expert on both feminism and religion. Because I took leadership in these areas, I was thrust into a maelstrom that forced me to learn more than I could imagine about sexism, abuse, and theology. Later, these lessons would stand me in good stead as I struggled to construct a feminist Christian theology that did not fragment my soul, that gave me a life I could hold in my own hands.

In a group meeting in 1979 on sexism and violence, stories of rape and incest were told. Around the room, a few young women were being held by young men who were comforting them as they cried. Janice, a high-school psychologist, spoke. She turned to one of the young women. "Emily," she asked, "why are you crying in his arms?" Emily said she felt safe and that he cared about her.

"Don't you know"—Janice turned and swept her arm across the room—"don't all you girls know? When you turn to a man to protect you and make you feel safe, you give him the same power he has to rape you? How do you know the man who comforts you in public won't rape you in private? How do you know the man you love and marry won't turn on you and beat you? How many women get trapped in horrible relationships because they give their power up to be cared for by a man? How can you tell the difference between needy dependence and love? You can't get protection from someone who can turn that power against you, who has been trained to see himself as powerful by seeing you as weaker and needing his strength. You shouldn't give your own power away. You need to claim your own power as women, to trust yourselves and each other."

Silence. Then several of the young girls defended their male friends, saying they knew they would not hurt them. "But why do you need to lean on them?" Janice insisted, "Why don't you trust yourself and other women? What are you afraid of? Can't you claim your own power to defend yourself? Why be taken care of when you can be respected?"

Controversy raged all week about her description of the dangers and limits of benevolent paternalism. Some perceived Janice as anti-male and believed she was stereotyping all men as rapists. Others thought she was trying to fuel a war between men and women. Several young women began to discuss how they could support each other more, about what relationships with guys would be like if they were equal. The hornets' nest of feelings Janice stirred up buzzed without definitive resolution. But the questions she asked stayed with me, both personally and theologically.

My feminist analysis of human experience deepened every summer at Brotherhood/Sisterhood. The accounts of sexual violence never stopped, and they never ceased to stun me, despite hearing many stories. In the late 1970s, there was no public speaking or writing about the rape and violent abuse of children. I learned about them from survivors who taught me about the power of the human urge to heal and thrive and the crucial role of memory in the aftermath of violence.

Memory of abuse was, I came to understand, excruciatingly hard-earned. At a meeting at which women shared stories of rape and sexual abuse, a staff counselor, Alicia, suddenly doubled over as if she had been struck in the stomach. She bolted for the door and ran out.

Hours later, we found Alicia in the nurse's cabin under sedation. She was awake but her eyes were swollen. Her face looked ashen against her long dark hair. Slowly, in rambling fits and starts between jerky sobs, Alicia told us she had suddenly remembered being raped by a family friend when she was five. The memory had hit her like a physical blow.

That moment with Alicia was the first, but not the last time, I witnessed someone recover a memory of trauma. I did not know buried trauma could return in such an incapacitating way.

Alicia tried to tell us what happened. I had never before witnessed someone so close to psychic meltdown. But the next morning, Alicia had begun to put her traumatic memories into a narrative. It was as if she had had to take her own flesh into her teeth.

Alicia and other survivors in the program helped me understand that remembering violence requires a descent into hell. The terrifying feelings return, as if the flesh is torn again. Remembering requires reliving what happened before it can be retrieved and put into words. After the descent, the telling of truth about violence and abuse is possible when friends or other steady witnesses listen patiently until the story is told. The telling begins the recovery, the work of spirit to save.

This work of spirit also meant challenging explicit ideas about God. Sylvia, a slight, withdrawn fifteen-year-old, was in one of my small groups at camp. She had long, limp brown hair, pale freckled skin, and gray eyes. We hardly noticed her presence. She spoke only in reply to a direct question. We had learned she lived with her mother, a beautician, and her younger brother.

My co-facilitator, Ben, who was a therapist in private practice, wondered if we shouldn't send her home. One of our responsibilities was to assess the emotional stability of members of our group. Anyone who seemed too fragile or unstable for the demands of the program was sent home if staff made that recommendation. We decided to let her stay, but watched her carefully.

Midweek, we talked about our families. Members of the group spoke of alcoholism, divorce, and neglect. During the conversation, I sensed a small shift in Sylvia, an alertness that made her less invisible, a tension around her eyes, which began to fill with tears.

I asked Sylvia what she was feeling. Tears rolled down her cheeks. A young man across the circle gave her his bandanna. Sylvia wiped her eyes, took a deep breath, and spoke quietly as tears continued to stream down her face.

"It's my mom. She hits me. I don't know what to do. I'm supposed to clean up the breakfast dishes and cook dinner. Sometimes I don't have enough time to do everything before she gets home. Even if I get everything done, she still gets mad at me a lot of times.

"When she's mad, she beats me. She hits me with her fists or with her hairbrush. One time, she took the cord from a lamp and beat my legs with it until they were bleeding. I used to scream at her to stop, but it just made her hit me more. It's better if I'm just quiet and hold still. Last year, she grabbed my arm so hard she broke it. At the hospital, she told them I fell on the stairs. She said if I told what happened, she would take my brother and me to an orphanage and leave us there." As she spoke, Sylvia cupped her left arm with her right, as though it still hurt.

"I don't know what to do. She hits my brother too, but me mostly 'cause I'm bigger. I know she loves us. I don't know why she hits us. I try to be good so mom will leave us alone. I pray all the time that God will make her stop. He must be letting this happen to me because I need to go through it. I just wish I knew why." Those on her left and right put their arms around her as she wept.

When Sylvia was breathing more calmly, Ben took her hand and said, "Sylvia, your mother may love you, but it is wrong of her to hurt you. When she is hitting you, she is not loving you, she is taking out her own problems on you, which isn't right. You do not deserve to be hurt like that."

"Sylvia," I said, "God is not doing this to you. Your mother is making her own choice to hurt you. She is free to choose to do right or to do wrong. She is choosing herself to do wrong. God does not want you to be hurt. God's power is in love, not in hurting. I think your mother is acting in anger, not in love. I am sure she loves you, but love does not make people hurt each other. It is good that you pray to God, and I hope you keep praying. But you might have to do more than pray. I think God might want you to get some help. Is there someone—maybe a teacher or minister—who could help you?"

"I'm afraid to tell anyone because we might have to go to an orphanage." We let her think for a while about what to do.

Ben and I sat with Sylvia after the meeting and talked to her alone. She was not comfortable going to her minister or a teacher. One of the other staff facilitators, Esther, was a nurse at Sylvia's school. We asked Sylvia if we could tell Esther the problem. Sylvia said OK. Esther was glad to assist.

Esther and Sylvia made a plan. If the violence escalated, Esther would call the authorities and try to get the two placed in foster care.

Sylvia resisted the foster care part until the moment before she left to go home. I ached for her, so young and small and scared, faced with such horrible choices. I hope she survived and found healing.

I was haunted by Sylvia's conviction that God was letting her be hurt, the passivity and resignation it elicited from her. I heard such ideas from youth struggling with the violence in their lives, pain inflicted by the deliberate cruelty of their parents or others they loved. Believing in the benevolent protection of a powerful God, they interpreted violence as divine intent, pain for their own good. And the Christian tradition reinforced this impulse by upholding Jesus as a son who was willing to undergo horrible violence out of love for his father, in obedience to his father's will.

A RANT AGAINST LOUSY THEOLOGY

The intense weeklong NCCJ immersions into core social and religious questions haunted my intellectual work as I began my doctoral program. In college my core commitments to activism and to the church had coalesced. Now they threatened to split my soul apart because my feminist theological insights were challenging virtually every form of Christian theology I knew. I began to fear that there was no way for me to be a Christian and a feminist, if Christian meant believing the traditional doctrines about Jesus, doctrines I had come to believe were harmful. I signed up for a seminar on christology, doctrines about Jesus as Christ. I chose the topic for very personal reasons. I wanted to know if I could be a feminist and a Christian.

The seminar professor, Bernard Loomer, was retired and was substituting for my doctoral adviser on sabbatical. He had been my adviser's doctoral adviser at the University of Chicago Divinity School and, for many years, had been the dean there. He was short and built solid as a brick. He wore fine yellow or white sweaters that set off his white wispy hair and fair New England skin.

There were three students in the seminar. There was no way to hide behind numbers in the class, and Loomer was a masterful seminar leader. He had acute antennae for obfuscation and puffery, which he could squelch with a few penetrating questions. He appreciated probing, exploratory comments, and he expected us to venture into uncharted territory. Offering an idea in his presence was a great risk, but the reward for having a substantive thought was the glint of pleasure in his blue eyes and a small smile that touched his lips before he took another puff on his pipe and continued the conversation. The fact that he paused to contemplate a comment meant one had offered something weighty and worthy.

I spoke little in class that semester. It was my first semester in the doctoral program. My adviser was nervously supportive of my interest in feminism, but he was on sabbatical my first year. There was only one other woman in the doctoral program. She was not particularly friendly and gave little evidence of interest in feminist ideas. The professor of my seminar on Augustine was downright hostile to every feminist question I asked. I had no feminist intellectual companions.

None of the readings in Loomer's seminar addressed my questions about power, violence, and abuse, and none explained the life and death of Jesus in a way that made sense to me. The liberal theologians rejected the substitutionary atonement because it depicted God as less moral than human beings at our best. Their concern was with the picture of God that the atonement presented. Mine was with the victims of misused power, a perspective absent in liberal work. My intuitions about the problems with doctrines of Jesus weren't clear enough to venture for scrutiny, so I couldn't say what was wrong with what I read. Loomer aggravated my frustration by treating my feminist questions as if they were mildly irrelevant—all our readings were by white men. I struggled to stay engaged because I liked Loomer's teaching style, but I fumed inside about the lack of feminist ideas in our class discussions.

When the semester was over, I asked Loomer for an extension to write my paper. I was too angry and frustrated to write, though that was not the reason I gave him. I said I needed time to digest the material and reflect on it. Loomer said papers from incompletes were rarely any good because the material went cold. I explained that if he wanted a paper at all, it would have to be in a couple of months. He agreed.

I worried about what to write. Finally, I gave into my anger about the semester and wrote a feminist critique of most of the material in the class. My thirty pages of criticism concluded with feminist reflections about christology, power, and love. By the time I submitted the paper, I was taking another course from Loomer, an advanced seminar in process theology. I wondered what impact my paper would have on my grade in this second class, since I was sure I had failed the assignment. I had been too angry to care, but I was worried about my academic future if I did badly in another course with him.

Two weeks after I submitted the paper, Loomer made a two-hour appointment to talk to me about it. I braced myself for the worst. He had the paper on the table in front of him. I could see the first page had comments in the margins—a lot of them. He went through the paper, which he'd marked page by page. He told me where I had mentioned a good point and noted the places I had contradicted myself. It was the most thorough critique of my work I had ever received. I felt humiliated that I'd been so inconsistent and incoherent.

Toward the end, where I had put my own conclusions, he engaged me in a discussion of how I was using the concept of power and encouraged me to give more nuance to my analysis. Ninety minutes later, we reached the last page and on it was written an "A." I was astonished.

Loomer took his pipe out of his pocket, lit it, and said it was an excellent, provocative paper. Then he pushed it aside, looked directly at me and said, "What are you writing your dissertation on?"

"Interfaith dialogue, Christian–Buddhist," I answered.

"Why?" was his response.

"Because, my Japanese family is Buddhist, my American family is Christian, and I am interested in how the two might interact. It seems a more respectful approach to world religions than Christian missions, and John Cobb here at Claremont pioneered the dialogue approach. I am working with Cobb."

Loomer pointed to my paper with the stem of his pipe, tapping it as he spoke. "You need to do your dissertation on this topic."

"Why?" was my surprised reply.

"Because what you have to say is important. It has never been said before, and it is important you say it."

"But if I do a feminist dissertation, I won't be able to get a job. Hardly any of my professors take my feminist work seriously. I get graded down if I put anything feminist in my papers. I get told I can't think clearly because I am too angry or too polemical. All the advice I've gotten is to do the feminist work later, after my degree. Besides there aren't any experts on the faculty in feminist theology. It would be hard to put together a committee sympathetic to my work."

"It doesn't matter," Loomer looked directly at me, his blue eyes flashing. "What you have to say is important. It must be said. If you stay with that other topic, you'll get bored and not finish your degree." He tapped the paper with his pipe stem again. "You have enough emotional investment in this topic to carry you through the difficult writing process. You will finish, and it will be important work you do. This is the topic you must write on. Forget all that bad advice. Figure out how to do it. You need to do it."

I knew the value of anger from my activist work, but Loomer was the first professor who had responded supportively to my anger, who believed it carried an emotional passion that led to good intellectual work. I tried to keep my feminist anger under control. I picked my battles carefully. My rant against lousy theology for Loomer was the angriest I had ever dared to write.

I wrote milder feminist criticisms in my other classes, but this was the first encouraging response I had received. I felt a small rush of hope that maybe, if I had been able to persuade Loomer of the importance of the feminist challenge to Christianity, I might be able to persuade others. He was about as tough-minded a professor as I had had.

But I did not feel I could write on this question without risking my own soul. Radical white feminists tended to be anti-religion, but I had found in Christianity a historical and spiritual grounding for my activism that reached beyond myself and my particular issues to a long legacy of people who had struggled against oppression. Knowing that I belonged to such a legacy had broken my isolation, had given my life a sustainable commitment, and had led me into work that transformed my life. To walk away from that religious commitment for the sake of women's rights would be like cutting my heart in two. White feminists' views of liberation felt isolating, like the rest of my American life before I had put my activism together with a community and historical legacy. I was frightened by Loomer's advice because of where working on christology might take me.

I put aside his suggestion and focused on his process theology seminar. Twenty-two men and three women had enrolled, and it was the best seminar I had in graduate school. Long after class, we carried on our conversations at a local bar, where we ate happy-hour snacks for dinner. Loomer sometimes joined us.

We three women held our own in the class discussions. Rebecca

Parker, a seminary student, was new to me, but I liked the way her mind worked, and her comments in class made me want to get to know her. Most seminary students didn't take advanced doctoral seminars because they didn't have the intellectual training for them. She clearly had it. We began to talk often about process thought, aesthetics, and theology and became good friends. However, she was wary of my feminist passions. Our feminist work together would come after she left graduate school.

"OH, HONEY, NO!"

I found support for my feminist questions through a group of spiritual seekers who met every three weeks. We called ourselves "Sister Circle." We brought our feminist struggles to the group and processed our angers and hurts. We experimented with rituals, sometimes using goddess images and research on ancient matrilineal traditions or Wiccan resources from witches' wisdom. We found affirmations of women's power in these sources. If we could not find the rituals we needed, we created our own. We invented a ritual to protect ourselves from anti-feminist professors and employers. We wept together, purged pain, laughed, and danced. Through our rituals and friendships, we found new energy and hope for further struggle.

Through Sister Circle I met one of the most significant friends of my life, my first feminist intellectual companion. My friend Ann Appley told me about a remarkable feminist professor who lived at Pilgrim Place in Claremont, a retirement community for professionals who have worked for the church or for the academy teaching religion. Ann introduced me to Nelle Morton in October 1977, just after I began my doctoral program. When Nelle heard I was a new feminist Ph.D. student, she invited me over for coffee.

Mid-morning on a Tuesday, I made my way over to her cottage. Nelle retired after many years on the faculty of Drew University Theological School, where she had a distinguished career. She had begun her career in the Southern Presbyterian church as a civil rights worker, then she had become a feminist religion scholar. Her roots were deep in the hills of Tennessee. Her deep hearty voice was marked by the long vowels and rhythms of Appalachia. She wore a lock of her short white hair tied in a ribbon on top of her head, a cheerful, colorful comma above her substantial, imposing body. I loved her no-nonsense earthiness, directness, and irrepressible vivacity.

That first meeting, we sat on the patio in the autumn sun, and she served me Tennessee ham, fried with coffee, and a magnificent cup of French roast coffee. We got acquainted. I learned about her years at Drew and told her about my cross-cultural life.

I spent many hours with her, from September to May, during the four years I was in Claremont. We sat on her patio in warm weather. In winter we settled across the coffee table facing each other in the two loveseats in front of the fire. We talked about a host of feminist ideas—the latest feminist book she had read, what I was working on for a paper, a lecture she was writing, my problems with readings for classes, and the worst professors I encountered, as well as the good ones. Her weakening health prevented her from attending Sister Circle meetings; my reports of our activities delighted her. We found kinship in our Southern roots, Mississippi and Tennessee.

Once, I asked Nelle if she ever regretted never marrying or having children. I asked it as a general question about her life course because we were discussing marriage and its ambiguous impact on women. But behind my query was my struggle to love T.C. I rarely discussed our relationship with her, partly because it troubled me, though I couldn't say how, and partly because I was afraid to expose how dependent I was on the security I needed from him. I found it humiliating, as a feminist, to admit I needed a relationship that was so difficult for me. Nelle was the first woman I had known closely who chose a career. I wondered what it meant to have a career for a lifetime, instead of a marriage, and how it felt to make that choice.

Nelle's response came with a deep hearty laugh, "Oh, honey, NO! When I think about the boring life I'd have had and the boring person I probably would've become, I am glad I didn't marry. I've had such an exciting and interesting life. I wouldn't trade it for the world."

Graduate school was made immeasurably richer for my having such a fine intellectual and theological companion. I doubt I would have finished my doctorate without her support. She was a beacon of light for me in a sea of struggle.

Nelle was also a tough teacher. She pushed me to figure out how I could be a feminist and a Christian. She left Christianity during the years we had theological conversations. Nelle pushed me hard on why

I was staying. Some of our best conversations were about the anguish of being feminist and Christian. She thought it impossible to hold them together; I was determined to figure it out.

Her pushing motivated me eventually to take Bernie Loomer's advice and work on christology. The core questions for me were about Jesus. I wondered whether his life could be understood from a feminist perspective to free people to live whole and just lives. None of the traditional or liberal theologies were reasons to me to be Christian. But I was not willing to concede that the patriarchs could define Christianity for me and exclude me by their doctrines. I had chosen it as my own. I would not rip my soul asunder unless it was the only choice I had left.

After I left Claremont in 1981, I made regular trips to visit Nelle. She eventually moved to an assisted living apartment. I saw her last in early 1987 before she died; we discussed my dissertation, the way I had found to hold feminism and Christianity together. I told her that, when it was a book, I was going to dedicate it to her. She seemed pleased. Her name is there, in *Journeys by Heart*.

NO AND YES

As I worked on my dissertation, I struggled to find a theology that did justice to what I had learned in NCCJ and that would hold my life together, in my own hand. I had witnessed, over and over, in Brotherhood/Sisterhood the personal and interpersonal impact of larger social forces such as racism, homophobia, sexism, abuse, and addiction. Glen, Jim, Joe, Alicia, Sylvia and a host of others haunted me and forced me to struggle with the theological implications of what I knew psychologically, personally, and politically. I could not accept more traditional theologies without leaving the most important pieces of myself behind. Neither could I turn to feminist polemics, as if gender were the only oppression that mattered.

In college, the religious ideas of the Hebrew prophets, introduced to me by Willis Fisher, had united with my activism and fed my soul. Dr. Fisher helped me see my core commitments as whole and integrated. Feminist criticism and my work with NCCJ began to fragment that sense of wholeness.

My vague uneasiness about traditional Christian doctrines became more clearly defined as I witnessed their actual impact on human beings. I saw how religious ideas shaped human self-perceptions and responses to pain. Often, ideas I heard in graduate school directly conflicted with what I learned in NCCJ.

Once, in a graduate course in ethics, the professor gave a lecture on Reinhold Niebuhr's *Moral Man and Immoral Society.* Niebuhr said human beings were more moral in their private lives and relationships than they were when they organized power into social systems, that the worst evil emerged from these organized forms of behavior. I recalled the stories of rape and beating I had heard from adolescents at the hands of their own family members.

I knew that Niebuhr was mistaken. Violence was not a contrast between public and private behavior, but a continuum. As Adrienne Rich noted in *On Lies, Secrets, and Silence,* the family home is the most dangerous place in America for women. We are more likely to be assaulted or murdered there than on the streets. And the suicide rate is even higher than the murder rate.

Private and public violence cannot be separated. Alice Miller's *For Your Own Good,* a study of Adolf Hitler and the child-rearing practices of pre-Nazi Germany, convinced me that the private abuse of children was intimately related to socially organized evil.

Socially organized human institutions and movements can also do great good. The social pressures of groups sometimes help people be better—the church and college had pushed me to be a better person. NCCJ enabled many people to work more effectively for justice.

Child abuse and sexual violence had to be addressed by theological work because so much theology supported victimization. In the 1980s, research about child abuse was just beginning to appear. Reading the new work, I saw, with increasing clarity, how the Christian tradition had made holy the abuses of violent families in doctrines about God and Jesus. Public and private were united for me by the question of power and its uses and abuses. My theological analysis shifted from the centrality of gender to the dynamics of families and the construction of the human self.

I had witnessed abused youth idealizing their parents the way the Christian tradition idealized God. Abused children, because they are dependent on their caretakers' love, need to believe their parents are good. Love is as essential as food. Violence destroys the permeable membranes separating healthy selves in loving relationships and creates the intense emotional bonds of united, undifferentiated identities. Abused children are deeply bonded to perpetrators and will accept the blame for their abuse. To shield themselves from trauma, they minimize it. They call themselves bad. They believe they deserve the pain inflicted on them, rather than face the awful truth that their parents cannot be relied on. They give up on themselves, rather than accept the abyss of being emotionally abandoned.

Christianity presents God as the benevolent, all-powerful father, and human beings as sinful and helpless, replicating the model of the parent who is good, the child who is bad. We are supposed to be grateful for divine forgiveness and protection in the face of human disobedience and powerlessness. This gratefulness carries relief from the threat of horrible punishment which lurks behind God's benevolent image. When divine power is defined as control of sinfulness and evil, the response of many faithful people is to deny the tragedy of what happens to them, looking for a reason that God allows it. This system reinforces belief in the need for control and obedience, and fosters responses of guilt, relief, and schadenfreude. I could not see how these doctrines empowered people to affirm their own agency, to resist abuse, to take responsibility for ethical discernment, and to work for justice.

Power is structured as benevolent paternalism in Christianity. In examining the paternalistic structure of love in my own life, I saw the limits of such a view of love and power. Paternalism inhibits intimacy and maintains inappropriate forms of dependence. Adults are asked to surrender their lives passively and obediently in exchange for salvation.

Jesus is presented as the obedient son, accepting violence because his father wills it. The salvation offered by Jesus is gained by his sacrifice of himself to abuse. In other words, he accepts violence for the sake of his love for perpetrators of violence, whether it is God or sinful humanity. Defining love and relationship as obedience and sacrifice structures them in the terms of power and abuse.

But why would a loving being use violence to draw humanity closer to himself? Abuse creates intense emotional bonds, but they are the bonds of violated boundaries, of broken hearts. Why did God require a brutal sacrifice before he could love imperfect beings as themselves? Living, breathing, growing beings never reach perfection but change constantly, expanding their capacities to love. Brutality destroys love.

When control and love are confused, the faithful must believe even the most horrible and painful things are allowed or inflicted by God, that violence is supposed to happen, for the moral education of the victim or for a future reward. This confusion makes fear the primary motivation for love and a reward the ultimate value, rather than love itself. When love is not an intrinsic good, love comes to serve other purposes, such as control, which allows abuse to harm our capacities for loving.

Racism, sexism, intimate violence, and homophobia are abuses of power that are devastating to love. They prevent us from being fully present and alive. They diminish the presence of spirit by wrapping oppressor and oppressed, perpetrator and victim, together in emotional chains that force the air out of the spaces between them. These claustrophobic emotional chains of abuse and oppression can be mistaken for love because their emotional power to bind is fierce. But such chains suffocate the spirit, which breathes in the connecting spaces between us, in the place of freedom, care, and reciprocity. Without the spirit, two selves are fused into one, either of which can give up its self to the other. Neither will notice the spirit is missing. Selflessness becomes the model for love when the spirit is absent.

Violence fragments the self, creating selflessness, and it destroys love. The worst violence is abuse of children. Intimate violence injures human life at its most vulnerable. Its residues include impulses to self-harm, to violence against others, or to a vicarious fascination with violence. The emotional chains of abuse bind so tightly that they can isolate victims into an exclusive relationship with the violator. Possession of the other becomes an obsession.

When the Christian tradition represents Jesus' death as foreordained by God, as necessary to the divine plan for salvation, and as obediently accepted by Jesus the Son out of love for God the Father, God is made into a child abuser or a bystander to violence against his own child. The seal of abuse is placed on their relationship when they are made into a unity of being. If the two are one, Jesus can be selfless, can give himself totally to God, a willing lamb to slaughter. I thought of this system as cosmic child abuse.

I saw in Christianity's ideas about Jesus, a theology that made people passive and acquiescent in their own suffering, a legacy of abuse entrenched in doctrine. I could see that human beings were not led to trust their own wisdom, power, and capacities to love, but always to turn to another more powerful than they and to confuse the pain and emotional entrapment of abuse with love.

The spirit, the breathing space of love, allows us to discern when we have been violated, when our love for another has reached the limits of our ability to endure pain, when we cannot remain present. In claiming love as its highest ideal, Christian theology has misunderstood it. Love, I was convinced, was denied or lost through selflessness. Love for another requires self-knowledge and self-love. One cannot love without being open to change, and such openness shows internal strength, resiliency, presence to oneself. Love engages the self and its passions, instead of suppressing the self. I knew, from my own experience, that love is reduced when reciprocity and intimacy are absent. I preferred Audre Lorde's term, erotic power, as the alternative to the Christian use of agape—selfless love. Eros conveyed reciprocity in love, the yearning to be in another's presence, in the fullness of spirit, manifest in the power of love.

Love is most fully incarnate when human beings are present in many dimensions of themselves—physically, spiritually, emotionally, aesthetically, and intellectually present. Physical love is an important dimension of eros, a life-sustaining power that finds expression in many relationships. The love of flesh includes birth, care of the dying, nourishment of children, and tender affection, as well as sexual intimacy. The more present human beings can be to each other, as the fullest selves they can be, the more complete the love. Presence comes when vulnerability is acknowledged and valued, when respect for the other as separate is maintained.

Love is not without pain. Love involves change and to change involves risk. We face the limits of love in the finite circumstances of our lives, the experiences which have nurtured and wounded us. Love requires courage for risk-taking and self-possession, not self-sacrifice. The more we love, the more loss carves into our souls. Pain is the risk of loving, not the basis of love.

Love saves life. I believed it was possible to find this truth in Christianity, in a view of Jesus that bound him in love to others, that recognized the caring that inspired his commitment to resist an unjust empire and made him part of a long legacy of resistance and hope.

THE LAST TRY

In 1979, I suggested to T.C. that we marry. For seven years, I had loved him and lived with the fear he didn't really love me. I was trying hard to change things between us. I wanted him to love me. I thought that his agreement to marry would mean he did and that the security of such a commitment would allow us to build a better relationship. T.C. wasn't especially enthusiastic, but cooperated. We wed in April 1980 in the backyard of the house I rented near Claremont. My mother and her Japanese friends fixed the food for the reception and provided the flowers, music, and cake. After our honeymoon, T.C. returned to his job in Texas and I went back to Claremont.

A few weeks later, T.C.'s former doctoral adviser offered him a one-semester fall teaching appointment in California, which meant we could spend five or six months together. I still needed to spend another year in California because I had just accepted Loomer's challenge and changed dissertation topics. I had to prepare for doctoral exams in areas in which I had taken no courses as preparation.

When T.C. told me the news, I was thrilled and hopeful. I suggested I get an apartment between Claremont and his job in Pasadena. We would each have a twenty- to thirty-minute commute. I could live alone in the spring, take my exams, and move back to Texas to begin my dissertation.

T.C. said he'd thought he would get an apartment in Pasadena and visit me on weekends. This was the same pattern he established when we began our relationship, when I felt peripheral to his life, when I lived in uncertainty about his feelings for me.

We had this conversation by phone in late May 1980. I sat at the kitchen table, the receiver against my ear, staring out to the sunlit yard where the wedding had taken place just weeks before. I had looked forward to living together again. I was devastated that he did not want to. "Shit," I thought, "even when he could, he doesn't really want to live with me. It's been true all along that he didn't love me." I accepted his decision without protest. I was too hurt to say anything.

I made alternative plans. My friend Fran and I signed a lease on a two-bedroom townhouse together near Claremont. T.C. arrived at the end of the summer, intending to find a place in Pasadena. He never quite got around to it. He found a friend who allowed him to sleep over occasionally when an experiment ran long, but most nights he drove back forty-five minutes and stayed with me. The two of us were crammed into a small bedroom for the semester, where I studied for my exams. And Fran good-naturedly endured a roommate who had not been part of our plan.

I was unsettled and irritable. I told myself it was because T.C. and I were too crowded in the apartment. I could not admit how hurt I felt, how much I had withdrawn emotionally and did not want him close to me. When T.C. moved back to Texas in January, I came down with a cold that forced me into bed for two weeks. I had nightmares. Instead of studying, I started to explore my feelings. For the first time, I gained the courage to examine what was wrong between us.

My academic work helped me see our structures of power more clearly. Benevolent paternalism had been the bond between us from the beginning. When we first met, I was twenty-two and needed to feel safe and protected; I had great passions but little direction and needed an anchor. But as I took more of my life in my hand, his paternalism began to feel confining. Security eventually became less important to me than intimacy.

The honesty and vividness of relationships in NCCJ and my emotional distance from T.C. had become an acute contrast. I drew life from the former and felt miserable in the latter. I finally admitted this to myself. I also recognized that I acted paternalistically toward him by protecting him from my own intense feelings, believing he was too fragile to handle conflict.

I tried a number of times to convey to T.C. how unhappy I was, to push us toward a different way of relating. He resisted, probably because I presented my unhappiness in an accusatory way as frustration and anger, which he tried to appease. I was no longer able to be the kind of person I thought he wanted. I did not want to please him; I wanted honesty.

I lived in three interlocked dimensions: the abstract world of ideas that was my doctoral program, the public world of organizations where I focused my activist commitments, and the intimate world that composed my inner psychic life and my relationship with T.C. I had found it easier to work on the first two dimensions than the last, which created an increasing gap between the larger dimensions and the intimate one. I felt the gap as anguish. The anguish pushed me toward a greater investment in my doctoral work, activism, and the

NCCJ program. I was overcommitted to social and theological change and unable to resolve my relationship with T.C. The gap had grown too wide.

Awake in bed with my cold, I thought about my unhappiness: asleep, I dreamt the same scene many times, the end of our relationship:

I am driving in my red Datsun station wagon, the car I used to drive from Texas to California to be with T.C. The highway slopes gently downward in front of me, stretching for miles. I drive west, on the last open expanse of desert road before the drop into San Bernardino and the road to Claremont. It is midday under an azure desert sky; yellow sand and dark green Joshua trees flash by.

The snow-covered mountains of Cajon Pass rise before me and swallow the road. I look longingly at the peaks, holding my gaze far ahead. My eyes drift back down to the gray highway. A mile-long line of wrecked cars and trucks, piled into each other, lie at odd angles across every lane of the road. Bleeding bodies lie facedown on the asphalt, scattered among the green, silver, white, blue, yellow, and black vehicles. Everyone is dead.

I am desperate to get to the mountains. Suddenly my car becomes a child's red metal wagon. I sit in the bed of the toy, rolling down the highway, holding on to the long black handle. I pull back and down on the handle. The wagon rises slowly into the air and flies over the carnage, following the route of the highway. The hot desert wind rushes through my streaming hair as I lean over to look at the tragedy below me. I rise into the cool mountain air, pass over the peaks, and drop softly by the door of my townhouse near Claremont. I am free.

PART THREE

Epiphany
A Season of Illumination

CHAPTER 5

The Unblessed Child

Rebecca's Story

> It was you who took me from the womb;
> you who kept me safe on my mother's breast.
> On you I was cast from my birth,
> since my mother bore me you have been my God.
> Do not be far from me,
> For trouble is near and there is no one to help.
>
> Psalm 22:9–11

We crossed the threshold of the fifth century church, a brown husk of rough sandstone, like a seed cone fallen beneath the deep green pines on the shores of the Adriatic sea. Leaving the warm sunlight, we entered a dappled, cool interior. Our eyes adjusted and the brilliant, beautiful mosaics depicting biblical scenes came into focus. A numinous, vibrantly colorful world appeared—an intense blue sky, dolphins leaping, birds flying, deer running—abounding in joy. We stopped at the mosaic of Moses.

Moses stands in a field of emerald green. He is young, unbearded. Before him, the epiphany of God burns gold and red with flashes of orange. He has heard the voice, "Come no closer! Remove the sandals from your feet, for the place on which you are standing is holy ground" (Exodus 3:5), and is untying his sandal. Behind him, where he cannot see, the expanse of green is filled with small bushes aflame. The whole world is luminous, shimmering, burning with the presence of God.

Beside me, George took my hand. His presence brought happiness to my life. We had married that July 25, just after I left the Wallingford church. It was time for a fresh start. The congregation was doing well, and I wanted to turn my attention concertedly to theological writing, to renew a practice of reflection and study that was difficult to sustain in the immediate pulse of church life. Besides, I had a new love.

George, a symphony conductor and keyboardist, had been my friend since we first began playing music together in our teens. I'd always been drawn to his exuberance, his musical genius, his passion for beauty, his appetite for life, his outrageous humor. Long conversations, sitting before the fire at my home on rainy Seattle afternoons, deepened our connection.

When we married, I felt drenched in joy, as if I'd come through some ordeal and George took me in, fed me soup, fluffed the pillow under my head, and told me to close my eyes and sleep. Was I just tired from the work of the parish? I didn't think too hard about it. I took my ease. I'd come through a long night of grief and struggle and arrived in a place filled with light, beauty, music, and pleasure.

We traveled to Europe that summer—something I never imagined I as a girl from Hoquiam would do. George took me to cathedrals in Strasbourg and Laon, in Reims and Paris. We saw the pilgrim church at Vézelay, and the chateaux in the Loire valley. We rode the chair lifts to the tops of the Alps and hiked through the flower-filled meadows. We walked the night streets of Florence, and saw the tender faces of Fra Angelico's frescoes. At the end of the trip we came to Ravenna and entered the shimmering interiors, darkness lit with fire.

When the summer was over, the busy rhythm of rehearsal and concerts took over. Life was full of music and musicians, parties until the wee hours. In the upstairs of George's house, now my house as well, I unpacked my books and filled the shelves. A nest for thinking, at last.

I set to work writing. My friend Joanne Brown who was teaching at the local Lutheran college invited me to work with her on critiquing the doctrine of the atonement. We presented a lecture, "For God So Loved the World?," at an international conference on liberation theology. A collection of essays followed in which a chorus of women questioned the doctrine of the atonement and advocated religious ideas that assisted women to resist violence and recover from abuse.

Joanne and I were breaking new ground, but we were not alone. Our friend, Rita Nakashima Brock, had just published *Journeys by*

Heart. Academic meetings brought us together from time to time and we'd eagerly continue our conversations, catching up with one another's lives and the progress of our ideas.

The sense of being part of a movement was transforming my isolation. The inner anguish I'd struggled with had meaning beyond my own small life. The congregation had helped me understand love in new ways. Life with George blessed me with affection and the rich nourishment of art. Now I focused on writing, circling back into the inner life that was the source of my unrest.

But my work did not go well. Writing on obedience, self-sacrifice and surrender in Christian spirituality, I would repeatedly balk. Examining how these virtues fragment the wholeness of life and diminish freedom and passion, I found myself blocked by sadness and despair. Alone in my upstairs study, I'd stare at the computer screen, fighting tears.

I thought I'd survived divorce and recovered my life. I thought I'd fallen into the lap of luxury, married to a man I adored. But writing took me back to sorrow's sharp edge. Music was the thing to do. The cello, the world of rhythm and harmony and sound, was better than words. Rehearsing, giving concerts, and being the conductor's wife made a satisfying life. I let the theological work drift.

On Mother's Day that year, I was in the kitchen washing the dinner dishes with my mom. She turned to me and said, "I know that being a good wife to George is important to you, that you support him in his work, and that you would like to have children, if you can. But I want you to know your theological work is more important. Don't give it up. I have lived my life as my mother did, as a minister's wife and a mother. I have no regrets. I loved raising you children, and I believe in the church. But look at what it has been like for a brilliant intellectual woman like your grandmother to spend her life ironing sheets, cooking meals, helping out at the church. She's had to struggle with depression her whole life. Your grandmother and I have lived the life of wife and mother. This is what we've done. You can do something else. Write."

But I felt lost. Even with George's support and my mother's encouragement, I was too alone with the theological material I was struggling with. I asked the bishop for a new parish assignment, and spent the next two years as the minister of Vashon Island United

Methodist Church, a lively, well-functioning congregation on an island in Puget Sound, a ferry ride away from life with George.

The second fall I was on Vashon Island, a letter arrived in the mail,
inviting me to apply to be the president of Starr King School for the
Ministry, in Berkeley, California. The letter came out of the blue, arriving in the middle of the busy start up activities of fall, after the
weather had begun to turn crisp and the big leaf maple tree outside my
office window was a blaze of yellow. It was not easy to leave the Vashon church. We were just beginning to do some good work together
and I loved the people. But when Starr King made the offer, I accepted with excitement. Starr King was the Unitarian Universalist
school in Berkeley, part of the Graduate Theological Union, a con-
sortium of nine theological schools that worked together and with
the University of California at Berkeley. A rich, thriving intellectual
center, a first-rate theological library, scholars of religion abounding,
and a seminary with a progressive understanding of education—I
couldn't ask for more. It was 1989. No accredited theological school
in the United States or Canada had hired a woman as its permanent
head. I would be among the first.

I didn't know what this shift would mean for my marriage with
George. We had been divided between two households—one on the
island and one in the city. This would be more of the same only the
distance between Berkeley and Seattle was greater. We bought a spa-
cious old house in Oakland and kept a home-base in Seattle, where
most of George's work as a musician was centered. We took turns flying back and forth every few weeks.

My daily life became focused on the seminary and the challenges
before it: supporting students and faculty, attaining financial stability,
renovating the building, strengthening the school's progressive approach to education, sustaining denominational relationships, building the board of trustees into a strong body. Solving practical problems of institutional life occupied my interest and attention; working
with students was a joy. There was plenty to do. I'd work from the
crack of dawn until I fell exhausted into bed each night.

In the process of recruiting new trustees, I thought of Rita. Her
perspective as a theologian and an educator would be helpful to the
school. She accepted the invitation to serve on the board. The meetings, twice a year, gave us the occasion to continue our theological
conversations and deepen our friendship.

Starr King's approach to education involved individual attention to each student. Authenticity and wholeness were encouraged. Evasion and self-delusion were challenged. Students were trusted. The exercise of their agency and self-direction in charting their educational course was expected. The school avoided approaches to education that might disempower students, that might teach people to disregard their knowledge and experience of the world, in the service of ideals or agendas of the educator. In this atmosphere my own instincts for honesty in religious questions were welcome. And, later, when I would struggle to more fully face my own life, the school would prove hospitable to my searching spirit.

During my first year at Starr King, I was never in one place more than five days at a stretch. By midyear the second year, the pace was taking its toll. Life was fractured and frantic. Work dominated my energies. George and I had very little time together. I began to face that I was running away from something—from him, from intimate relationship? Why, I asked myself, was I driven to work all the time? Perhaps my sense of vocation was not a call from God. Perhaps it was a compulsion. I dressed my ambition up in the language of faithful dedication to a cause larger than myself. But my busy involvement with work was hiding something, and I was dimly aware that I was frightened in the context of marriage.

I had minimized the frightening aspects of my marriage. Once, early in my relationship with George, at an after-concert party that went into the early hours, the drinking had gone on for a long time. George, intoxicated, became enraged about something and threw a chair against the wall while he ranted. A friend turned to me and asked, "Are you checked out for this level?" I wasn't sure, but I said, "Sure." But something inside of me froze and leapt at the same time. I became surreptitiously obsessed with managing George's relationship to alcohol. When he was under the effects of alcohol—exuberant, angry or despondent—I became anxious and panicky. If I could just keep him from drinking too much, everything would be fine. The management of my panic and anxiety, through efforts to control and manage him, increasingly preoccupied me. I rode the ups and downs with him. I was alternately distressed and relieved, upset and appreciative. I was frightened for my life, then grateful to be alive. Drinking didn't do much for me—just made me sleepy. But I didn't need to drink. I'd found someone to do my drinking for me.

The good times helped me deny the craziness of our life—my craziness. But an undercurrent of fear flowed more and more wildly in me. The more fearful I was, the more I suppressed the fear, and the more estranged I became from myself and from George. I ignored that I was behaving obsessively just as I ignored the secrecy with which George conducted realms of his personal life, hidden from me. We silently agreed to keep silences between us. Drama, intrigue, and passion ran high, but I was numb.

Our house in Oakland was near Lake Merritt. One Saturday morning, a rare weekend when I was alone without work obligations, I walked to the lake. It was a pristine midwinter California morning. The sky was brilliantly clear. The air, cool. The sun, bright. The water was still as glass. Through the dark oaks, I looked across the mirror of water to Our Lady of Lourdes, an art deco church—white, blue and pink, its steeple rising into the sky. Behind it the Oakland hills rose, green and smoky blue. I stared blankly at the scene before my eyes. I noticed that I felt nothing. Nothing about the beauty before me inspired even a flicker of pleasure, resonance, or appreciation. I felt like a zombie, a person made of cardboard. A cold fire. I had become an absence. The thought came to me, "I cannot bear the beauty of the world." And then, "Something is wrong with my soul. I am in trouble. I need help."

Help was available. Friends watching me the next weekend, in a panicked state, trying to rescue George from a drama of dissipation, said to me, "Perhaps you are the one who needs help." I was offended but I recognized that what they said was true. They sent me to a group for people with family members affected by alcohol. Sitting on a cold folding chair in a dim church basement room I heard, "This program is not designed to help you fix someone else. This program is to help you get sane. Whatever your problems, there are those among us who have had them, too. There is no burden too heavy and no sorrow too great that it cannot be made better." So obsessed was I with what I regarded as someone else's problem, I had lost the habit of seeing myself. The faces of the people in the group startled me. The faces showed weariness and sorrow, completely unguarded. These were faces without masks. They looked like how my face felt to me, but this was a face that I would not show to anyone else. "These people are not ashamed," I observed with incredulity. I could not imagine being present in such an unguarded way, but I wanted to be. I kept coming back. I listened for many meetings. It would be a year before I would open my mouth to say anything more than my name.

The same week I called Sandi Hedlund, a therapist. I explained to her on the phone, "Look, I'm working all the time, but I think whatever is driving me to work so hard isn't as holy an ambition as I have believed. I keep dreaming over and over that I am still married to my first husband but he is leaving me for someone else. Something is wrong. I need help."

I met Sandi in her office. She greeted me kindly and let me talk for a while. Then she said, "You are telling me some pretty upsetting things, but you are smiling all the time. This week, whenever you feel yourself smiling, try putting your hands on your face." She showed me. "Touch your face and hold it until it relaxes a bit, and see if you can notice what shape your face might take if you weren't smiling."

The next week when I came back she asked, "What did you notice?"

"I noticed that under the smile I feel bad—angry, I think, and sad."

"When was the last time you got angry?"

"The last time I got angry?" I laughed. "I don't get angry. I don't think I've felt anger and expressed it since before I was twenty years old."

"Well, can you remember a time you expressed it?"

I thought for a minute. I did remember a time. "Yes. When I was five my family moved to a new town. I had a bedroom with two doors in the corner. One door opened into the kitchen, the other opened to the hall in front of the bathroom. I used to stand in the corner between the two doors and slam them, first one, then the other. I'd slam them as hard as a could. Hard enough to make the house shake. And I'd be crying and shouting. I was furious."

"What were you so mad about?" she asked, in a matter-of-fact tone of voice.

I was completely floored by her question. No one had ever asked me what I was mad about. I thought for a minute. "I was mad because we had moved and moving separated me from Frank. I didn't want to be separated from Frank. He was the man who lived around the corner from us. I was very upset at being taken away from him."

"Why?" She asked.

I stumbled to find the words. The ones that came to me felt like a child's words, but I said them out loud.

"He was my boyfriend."

Sandi looked at me calmly. She didn't say anything. She nodded in understanding. It seemed to be OK with her that I had been so mad. I felt pain flicker across my face. I wasn't smiling.

I'd reached out for help at just the moment everything began to crash. The next weekend, fortified with a sense of support from the group my friends had sent me to, and knowing that I had Sandi to talk to, I screwed up my courage and asked George who the other woman was in his life. Asked directly, he told me. "Are you serious about her?" I asked. "Yes," he said.

I could see that we weren't going to make it. It would be five more months before we would separate and a year before we would decide, sadly, to divorce. In the meantime, there would be hoping, wanting, and crying. There would be kindness to one another, remembered love, and long, close conversations. There would be efforts to do things differently. But there wouldn't be change.

In just a few weeks, I found myself at the old abyss. I began to cry at night, alone, uncontrollably. Something in the depth of my unhappiness startled me. It was true that I was grieving the probable loss of marriage with George, and I was fighting this loss. But my tears came from a deeper, older well. I began to recognize that the attachment to George was many things. Bonding with him, I had immersed myself in the world of art and music. Beauty graced my life and refreshed me with its intensity and wholeness. I could hardly bear losing this world George gave to me, along with the affection and warmth he showered on me. At the same time, I was drowning in an attachment that kept me preoccupied with drama and intensity. This preoccupation was a shield, a protection. Without George, I was sailing into the part of the sea where the map said, "Here lie monsters."

What, I asked myself, was I so frightened of? What was this edge of the world I felt I was falling off? When I asked this question, I drew a complete blank. No answer came. So, I prayed. "Dear God, tell me, what is wrong? Why do I feel like I am at the end of the world?" Still no answer came. I folded down onto my knees, curled over, head to

the ground, and prayed again. "I am willing to see it, whatever it is."
My mind felt like it was turned toward a solid, blank wall. I stayed still,
trying to listen, trying to feel, for a long time. Finally, the thought
came to me, "There is no language for this." Then an idea, "I will
paint it."

I got out paper and water colors. I let my mind remain empty of
all thought, all words. I painted.

The picture showed a garden. A row of sweet peas strung along a
fence and green beans strung between two poles. Next to the garden
was a house, with steps going up to a kitchen door. In front of the
steps was a man. In front of the man was a small child—me, in my
navy blue dress with red hearts, which my mother had sewn for me,
with bloomers to match. The man had no head. I couldn't paint his
face.

The next week I went to see Sandi. I was nervous. I said, "I need
to ask you a question."

"Go ahead," she replied.

"Can children have orgasms? Can a little girl have an orgasm?"

"Yes," Sandi said.

I showed her my watercolor. "This is Frank," I said. "This is his
garden and his house. These are the steps up to his kitchen door. He
was always working out in his garden. We kids would ride our tricy-
cles around the block. When we went by Frank's house he'd call to us.
We'd stop and he'd come over and talk to us. He liked kids. He was
nice to us. One day he said he'd show me his garden, if I'd come up
into the yard. He had sweet peas. They were so pretty. He cut some
and gave them to me. They were just for me, he said. He told me my
dress was pretty and that I could come visit any time.

"Sometimes I'd visit him with Tommy, the boy who lived next
door, and sometimes just I would visit him. We'd talk to him outside
in this garden. One day he said we should come into the house; he had
something for us to see.

"We went up the back steps, through the kitchen, into his dining
room. I remember there was an old sawdust-burning stove in the
room. Bay windows looked out over the garden. The floor was linoleum. He had a chair by the stove, and from behind the stove he
brought out this marvelous toy. It was a jumping jack.

"We sat down on the footstool in front of him in his chair. He stretched a long-armed paddle across his knee, held by his crossed legs. Then he brought the jumping jack out. Jack was suspended on the end of a long wire handle. Frank stood Jack on the paddle, out on his knee, holding him with the wire. Then he moved the paddle a bit, this way and that, and Jack danced.

"He was made from wood, painted black. His feet were red, his hands were white gloves, his face had big white eyes and a wide red smile, with fat lips. His feet went clack, clack, clickety-clack on the wooden paddle. I loved the sound most of all.

"When Tommy and I saw the jumping jack dance, we were enchanted. Frank said he made it. He carved it out of wood. He said, if I'd come back, he'd make me one. I said, 'Yes, please!'"

Later, remembering this, I would realize that the wooden doll Frank was manipulating was a black minstrel figure. This was among the first racialized images I encountered as a child. Only much later would I begin to understand that Frank's cruelty was racist, along with everything else. He racialized and sexualized his desire to humiliate and control. I would eventually have to unbind all of these cruel associations to know myself and others in freedom.

"I'm not sure what happened," I said to Sandi. "But telling you this memory, I feel terrible. A kind of horrible dread. A pain all over my body."

That week I decided to try to draw Frank's face. It bothered me that his face was blank in my watercolor. I got out the pastels and a good-sized sheet of rough paper and let my hands materialize the feeling of him from the blank sheet. After a while, a face emerged on the paper. I drew a red stake through his head. And underneath I carefully wrote his name:

ꓭꓵAꓘ⅃

I studied the drawing. Why had I written his name backwards? What did I feel looking at this face? I took pencil to paper and began to write words that held the feeling:

I am the mirror
Through which Frank becomes visible.
I stake his head into the accusation:

This is your name.
He breaks through green life
Cutting the tender shoot, new born.
He is not a gardener.
His sickle is old.
It stops the harvest.
Has my body given birth to anything
Except what he planted as a crime?

My own face, I felt, was the mirror image of Frank's face some-how. I decided to see if I could draw the face that was looking at Frank—the face that was mine, locked in an unbroken encounter with him. With pastels and the rough paper, I drew again. The child's face was round. Her cheeks were red with shame. Her throat was cov-ered with sharp red, yellow and blue lines of pain, extending down to her heart. Her big eyes were frozen wide open. Behind her, there was a forest of evergreen trees, like those that grew beyond our town of Hoquiam. Above the trees a great, silver moon rose—a canopy of protection.

Again, I studied my drawing, and with paper and pencil, tried to find the words that expressed what this picture held. I gave her a name: The Unblessed Child.

Her eyes see all the way into his
with a rage that will not let go
or turn into sorrow.
She is not blessed.
She is going to fight him
for a long time.

I took the pictures to Sandi. She contemplated them thoughtfully.

"At home, when you slammed the doors, you were angry about Frank."

"Yes," I said, "angry at being separated from him—and also in pain."

"What happened when you slammed the doors? How did your parents respond?"

"Oh," I said, "a terrible thing happened. I broke my mother's fa-vorite teapot. It was on the kitchen shelf, just outside my bedroom door. I slammed the door so hard the pot fell and crashed on the floor.

It was her favorite teapot. Cream colored, with a rooster painted on it. I can still see her in the kitchen, crying. I went and put my arms around her legs. I didn't want her to cry. It must have been terrible for her to have a child so angry and upset. And we lived in this miserable, tiny house—just half of a little duplex that was poorly built. The whole family seemed to be upset after we moved there.

"My father was very kind about this. He came and sat with me on my bed. He said that it was not good that I'd broken Mom's teapot, but I could buy her a new one and that would make things all right again. He would help me save my dimes until I had enough money, then we'd go to the five-and-ten-cent store and buy her a new one.

"I was relieved that I could do something to make it right. The day came when I had enough dimes. I picked out the fanciest teapot I could find—a glittering gold one, decorated with a lacy silver design. Mom still has it. She keeps it with her best china. I never thought it was quite as good as the cheerful one with the rooster on it, but she says she likes it.

"After that I think I stopped banging the doors. I felt terrible that my anger had caused harm. But I was still upset. I was having a difficult time 'going b.m.'—having a bowel movement. I became obsessively worried about this. Every morning, very early, while everyone else was still asleep, before going to the bathroom, I would get out of bed and creep upstairs to my parents' bedroom. There was a little room off their attic room that Dad had added to the house, where my little brother Ted slept in the crib. It seemed desperately important to me to perform the ritual of climbing the stairs as a prelude to going to the toilet. But I didn't want anyone to hear me or to know what I was doing. I can remember creeping up those stairs very slowly. Every little creak the wooden steps made terrified me. I was sure they would hear, wake up, and I would be in trouble. I felt that not being able to go b.m. was very bad. When I'd get to the toilet, I'd sit on it and try to push. But it felt like there was an enormous turd inside of me, too big to push out. If I could just be close enough to my parents there would be some magic in that, and I'd be able to push this thing out. Whatever was stuck inside of me felt like it was as big as my whole insides. I couldn't push it out.

"When it came time for me to start school, I didn't want to go. How was I going to go to school with this turd stuck inside of me?

What if they wouldn't let me sit for an hour on the toilet if I needed to? Then we had a summer hiking trip. I didn't want to go on the trip—because of this thing. I needed to be near a bathroom. There weren't any bathrooms in the mountains. I begged to stay home and was allowed to go stay with my grandparents during that time. I liked being with my grandparents. Grandma Ernst read me *Charlotte's Web* and my grandfather let me watch him shave, making funny faces with the shaving cream. I was six, I guess. But when the rest of the family came back from the hike, they'd had such a good time I felt bad. I was ashamed that my secret problem had kept me away from a fun time with my parents and brother and our friends the Gudger family from Hoquiam. I resolved to put the problem behind me, somehow."

"The physical problem with going to the bathroom was only one way I struggled with feeling that my body couldn't be trusted. I couldn't swallow, either. I got the mumps and was given medicine to swallow with a glass of water. This caused me no end of anxiety—I couldn't make my body do what everyone seemed to think was normal and easy. And I couldn't scream. My playmates loved to scream just for the fun of it, then laugh and laugh. They'd tell me to scream. But I couldn't. How did you make your body scream? This inability frightened me. What if something happened, like the house caught on fire, and I needed to scream for help but I couldn't? The inability to scream worried me terribly. Later, when I was twelve, I couldn't sleep. I'd lie in bed at night, in a panic, because I couldn't figure out how to make the transition from being awake to being asleep. How did a person do this? Walking home from school in the afternoon I'd begin to be anxious about the upcoming night. I would have to go to bed. I wouldn't be able to sleep. The anxiety was relentless.

"I solved the sleeping problem by reading *Man's Search for Meaning,* from my father's study. Viktor Frankl wrote about reverse psychology—accomplishing something you wanted to do by concentrating on not doing it. That at least was my childhood understanding of it, which was enough. 'I will lie here all night and not go to sleep,' I'd tell myself. 'I must not go to sleep. It is imperative that I stay awake.' By focusing all my willpower on staying awake, I would, of course, fall asleep. That I could accomplish some measure of control over my insomnia—even by this peculiar means—was a great relief to me. I was twelve."

Telling all this to Sandi, part of me felt these were just normal childhood stresses and anxieties. All children have worries and fears. But as modest as these struggles were, they had an underlying thread: physical anxiety over the trustworthy, basic operations of my body, combined with the feeling that I needed to be able to master my body, control it at will. Without this willful direction of my body, I was afraid something terrible was going to happen.

I knew that what I was telling and showing Sandi pointed to sexual abuse. I wasn't ignorant about the sexual abuse of children. As a parish minister, I'd counseled women struggling with depression who had been raped or molested. As a theological educator, I worked with women attending seminary who were survivors of sexual violence. They were seeking to integrate their personal experience of sexual violence with their commitment to be of assistance to others in a healthy way. Survivors often go into healing and helping professions. A study had shown that the number of women in seminary who had been sexually abused was well above the percentage in the general population. I'd served on the board of the Center for Sexual Abuse and Domestic Violence in Seattle. The center's director, Marie Fortune, was a ground-breaking educator around issues of sexual violence. My theological wrestling, preaching, and writing had their wellspring in my concern over the ways theology acculturates women to accept abuse.

But I didn't think sexual abuse was part of my own life history, and I balked at the thought. Still, I wanted to find out what the fragmented pieces of memory and feeling added up to. There was a picture here if only I could see how the scattered shards went together: my bodily anxiety; my submerged and controlled anger; my repeated bouts of grief and crying; my painful associations with Frank; my experience of intimate relationships in which I was not fully present and in which I ended up deeply wounded by my husband turning to someone else for sex, affection, and attention; my attachment to overwork; and my emotionally numbing preoccupation with drama, intrigue, and intoxication.

To the world I appeared successful and competent. As a seminary president, I was doing what many regarded as an excellent job in a difficult profession. As a public speaker, preacher, and teacher my work was appreciated and I had the positive regard of people I respected. I was far from perfect and didn't meet all the challenges of leadership with an equal measure of good sense or courage. But I was far from falling apart.

Inwardly, however, I was—and perhaps had been for a long time—in deep distress. The pattern I'd first become aware of in the parish ministry was becoming habitual: do my job by day, crash by night; function successfully in public, but in the more private realm of intimate relationship, fail. This split was probably not as clear-cut as I imagined. One trusted colleague said to me, "No one who knows anything about violence or suffering could look at you and think that you were untouched. It all shows in your eyes."

Sandi's patient presence, trust, and therapeutic wisdom guided me in assembling the mosaic. I never felt she presumed to know what the picture was—only that I was holding many broken shards in my hand. They needed to be pieced together for the sake of healing and wholeness.

She directed me in the use of non-verbal means to become more present to myself and to others: noticing the location of feelings in my body, creating and contemplating sand trays, drawing pictures, and performing simple rituals. Her calm, matter-of-fact style provided hospitable space for anything to be felt and said. Her straightforward questions and observations cut through the obfuscation of my rationalizations, denials, and intellectual theorization. Her compassion was implicit—never sentimental or dramatic. Nor did she overidentify. She was, simply, *present*.

That summer I went on a two-week, silent retreat. I returned to the Pacific Northwest, to the warm summer smell of sun on fir needles, the mud flats at low tide, the cry of the gulls, the deep forest. I stayed alone at our family's beach house on Puget Sound. I had set a task for myself: to allow all that I knew to assemble into a coherent picture—to see through, to see into, what I felt and knew. Every day I drew another picture using pastels on rough paper. I drew the way my hands felt; the way my throat, chest and heart felt; the way my womb and genitals felt. I drew the way my anger felt. I drew the way my sorrow at losing the marriage with George felt. Days of silence, while the tide came in and out again, in front of the house. At evening, across the water, the setting sun would strike the old, tall cedars turning them a golden green that seemed to ache with beauty. I remembered how Grandmother Ernst would always look across the water at twilight, the light on the cedars, and say, "Oh, this is my favorite time of day."

The quiet deepened around me. On the eighth day, I drew what it felt like in Frank's dining room. The picture showed a small child's body lying facedown across a man's lap. She is naked. His left hand pushes her down at the neck, pinning her hard. She is struggling. His right hand is between her legs.

I looked at the picture for a long time. Leaden. Pained. Sexually aroused.

"Orgasm will stop the pain," I thought to myself. I remembered how this phrase accompanied my adult experiences of sexual intimacy, like a mantra. Making love, feeling the pleasure grow warm, cherishing the sense of closeness to one I loved and desired, the moment would come when my presence of mind would slip into another zone that was painful, anguished, and desperate. I would be out of my mind with a longing for the pain to end. "Orgasm will stop the pain." At the moment of release, I would feel my inner consciousness break into a thousand pieces. Intimacy was obliteration. I had given these experiences a name: "white flashes" or "brain orgasm." As far as I knew everybody had them. This was what sex was: the annihilation of self-possession, the shattering of self, the ending of consciousness in an explosion of terrible light.

I was overcome with sadness noticing and remembering this. The men who had loved me had embraced this fragmentation. They had tried to hold this absence. But in loving me they became a cause of pain. In the most intimate experience of sexual connection their face and presence was obliterated by another's presence. The ghost of the abuser wore their face, filled their body filling mine. This was intolerable. They couldn't stay. They turned away.

I turned the picture over. "This isn't my life. This didn't happen. I'm making this up."

When I was a small child in Hoquiam, a friend of the family had given me a Raggedy Ann doll. My little brother Ted had been given the Raggedy Andy. I loved that doll and carried her with me when I went out into the neighborhood, venturing forth on my tricycle. I had her in my arms one afternoon when Frank invited me into his dining room to see how the jumping jack he was making for me was coming along.

"What is your doll's name?" he asked.

"Raggedy Ann," I said.

"Do you know what it says on her heart?" I knew. I knew that if you took off all her clothes there was a red heart painted on the muslin that was her soft torso. Inside the heart were words that said, "I love you." But there was something in Frank's tone of voice that I didn't like. So I said no. I lied to him.

"Well," he said, "It says something on her heart. You just have to lift up her dress and pull down her panties and you can see." I shook my head. "Go, ahead," he said. "Try it. Lift up her dress and look." I still hesitated, so he knelt down beside me and showed me how to lift up her dress and pull down her panties. He showed me the red heart and the words "I love you." He gave me back my doll. "Now you do it," he said. "You look." I dutifully obeyed. Pulling up her dress and tracing the red heart with my finger, feeling the paint on the cloth.

"What does it say on your heart if we lift up your dress?" Frank asked, still beside me. His hands around my waist. I felt his hands then, under my dress, tugging on my panties.

When I got out of there, I took Raggedy Ann home to our backyard. I found one of the clam-digging shovels and dug a hole in the garden. I buried her. I worked carefully to pat the dirt until it seemed to me she was thoroughly covered over. Later, we would move from that house. When we were packing up I went out to the garden to find her. Mom washed her in the washing machine for me—a touch annoyed that I'd left her out in the dirt and the rain. Raggedy Ann looked OK after that, but a little more raggedy. I remember trying to fix her face with some of Mom's lipstick to bring back her red smile and red cheeks. The lipstick wasn't too successful on the cloth and I felt I'd done something wrong. That wasn't as bad though as what I did to Raggedy Ann with a pencil. I'd take the sharp lead and push the pencil between her legs until I made a hole in the cloth. I had a hole there, and I thought Raggedy Ann should, too, though I winced performing this rough operation on her.

I took Raggedy Ann with me to our new house in Centralia and every move after that. I took her to my college dorm room and brought her with me when my young husband and I made our first home. I brought her with me to George's house and then to the California house. She was always with me, just as The Unblessed Child was always with me. I had tried hard to bury her, but the real task was to find or create a home where she could live.

I designed a test for myself. I would go back to Hoquiam. I would make a list of all the details that were set in my memory: Frank's house, its location, the dining room bay windows, the wooden steps from the garden up to the back kitchen door, the garden with its metal pipes planted in the ground to string lines for beans or sweet peas, the view from Frank's back yard of the roof of the church where my father served as minister, the chimney for the sawdust-burning stove. Though it was now nearly thirty-five years later, I'd find out if Frank still lived there. I'd see for myself how much I had made up. I'd test my recollection. This would tell me whether I should believe myself or dismiss my thoughts, memories and feelings.

The memories were painful and I was in a shaky state so I asked George to go with me. Out of long habit, I'd shared some of what I remembered of Frank with him. George was my confidant and friend and though there was strain between us I trusted that he cared about my well-being. Also, I'd thought my experience would help us make sense of some of the estrangement between us. We had agreed to a trial separation and were not seeing one another. But when I called him and asked him, he said of course he would come. I was grateful.

We drove to Hoquiam. Crossing the river from Aberdeen, I smelled the familiar salty and damp air, mixed with the smell of tide waters, creosote, and pulp-mill smoke. The white-and-gray clapboard houses with their storm porches lined the flat, straight streets. Fishing boats, with their complex nets of rigging, rocked in the river. Beyond the edge of town, the forested hills rose, misty above the yellow clay banks of the river. Though it was summer, the sky was a low, dull gray that glared with the light of the clouded sun. The grass yards were yellow and weedy. I hadn't been back for many years, but I remembered the turns of the street—this way, then that, and the United Methodist church came into view. We parked near the church and walked over to the parsonage. I thought we should say hello to the pastor and his family. After all I was his colleague in the ministry. I didn't want to get caught prowling around the neighborhood by someone who would recognize me and ask why I was there. It seemed better to make my presence known.

"Just passing through," I said, "thought I'd take a look at the old neighborhood."

"Good to see you. Nice to take the time, now and then, to remember the places we grew up. Take care."

We left the parsonage and began to walk around the block, following my memory of where Frank's house was. Coming around the corner, I saw the wooden stairs up to the kitchen door. My heart raced. I took George's arm and balked. "You've come all this way," he said, "don't turn back now." The stairs were on the wrong side of the house. My memory was that they were on the far side, not the near side. We walked on to the front of the house. To the right of the house was the side yard where the garden had been. There was just grass there now, but planted in the ground and standing like dead trees were the metal pipes spaced for stringing lines for green beans. We walked into the side yard. From the yard you could see across the back alley to the garage and then the roof of the church, at just the angle I'd drawn it. To our left the house stood, with its dining room bay window. Up above the window to the right was a round plate, painted over, covering where a stove pipe had once been.

Except for the steps being on the left not the right side of the house as you faced it from the street, everything was precisely as I had remembered.

We went to the front door and knocked. By the steps, a small child's tricycle was tipped over. A woman came to the door. I could see into the dining room, where she had a sewing project spread out on the table. She wore an apron. A yellow measuring tape hung around her neck and she had a needle and thread in her hand. We had interrupted her work.

I explained that I had grown up in the neighborhood and used to have a friend who lived in this house. Would she mind if we came in and looked around, for memory's sake? No, we couldn't come in. That would be an imposition. Maybe she knew him, I went on. He was an adult who liked to make friends with all the kids. "Frank," I said. "Oh," she said, "of course. You mean Frank————. He lived here with his two daughters. We bought the house from him— maybe ten years ago now. He moved down to the Oregon coast,

somewhere." Did she have a forwarding address? "Oh, no," she said.
"Maybe you could track down his daughters." Oregon City, she
thought. But she heard he died, a few years ago. She wished us well
and excused herself to get back to work. The door closed.

We walked away from the house. George could see I wasn't faring
too well. He put his arm around my shoulder as we walked away, and
said, "Listen, the important thing is this. He is dead, and you are
alive."

We got back to the car. I had a sudden impulse. "Wait here," I said
to George, "I'll be right back." There was an empty pint jar in the
back of the car. I grabbed it and raced back around the corner to
Frank's house. I looked quickly to see that no one was watching, then
I knelt down in the bushes by the front steps and a grabbed a handful
of the mossy, dank earth. I put it in the jar and screwed down the lid.
"I'm taking this from you," I said silently. "I'm taking your ground
because of everything you took from me."

Back in the car, George drove us out of town toward the coast. We
came to where the forest ended and the ocean began. The beach here
was deserted and wild, strewn with piles of driftwood logs. We
stopped and walked along in the sand for a while. I felt the salt air, the
damp, heard the gulls and terns as they dipped in the air and cried their
long and short calls. I took off my shoes and buried my feet in the
damp gritty sand.

At the end of the road we came to the Makah village, a poor huddle of unpainted buildings, dogs and barefoot kids playing in the dirt
roadway. The Indian men sat on the pier at the river's mouth, fishing.
Their faces were deeply weathered and their expression remained
motionless as they observed us, quietly. We had wandered onto their
land.

"They Speak by Silence," the Hoquiam artist, Elton Bennet, had
titled a silk-screen depiction of this coast. The Indians raised their
heads, acknowledging our presence. We nodded in silence before
turning the car around and heading back towards Seattle. I clutched
the small jar of reclaimed land in my hands.

As summer came to an end, I returned alone to Oakland. I set the jar
of earth from Frank's house on the edge of my drawing table and
placed the pictures I had drawn in the summer on the walls. I began a

life-sized drawing of a child, naked, running across the grass of Frank's garden, away from his house. Arms raised wide. Face stretched into a scream.

Sandi listened to what I had to tell. I could no longer deny that Frank had been a child molester—a seductive abuser who lured us into his house and isolated us to gratify his desires. Without the denial in place, without the shield of relationship with George, I fell into a state of terror. I knew that it wasn't happening now. That I wasn't a child now. That Frank was dead. That his hand wasn't in my cunt. That my neck wasn't pressed down under his grip. But it felt like it was happening now. For a period of several weeks I lived in a heightened state of fear. I felt like adrenaline was pumping through my body and wouldn't stop. I'd wake up in the morning and lie in bed, panic spreading through me. I did my best to keep breathing. Sandi arranged for me to spend a few days on retreat at Muir Beach, in a safe, comfortable space. She stayed nearby and worked with me several times during the day, with rest breaks in between. I began to calm down, to get the panic under control.

School started and the busy activities of teaching and administration filled my time again. I was still trying to work things out with George, but by the New Year it was clear we needed to let the marriage go.

In February I had a dream. I am riding on a roller coaster. Sandi is in the car behind me. At the top of the highest swell, with a huge dip opening before us, I announce to Sandi, "We are finished now. It's time to stop the roller coaster and get off." I told her the dream. I'd been in therapy for a year. "The dream either means we are done, or what is ahead is something that I want to avoid," I said to her. I was exhausted from the stress of uncontrollable fear, nightmares, intrusive flashbacks. The choice was mine. "I'd like to continue," I said. "Knowing hasn't set me free. I'm haunted by this past. There must be more healing that is possible. But how long will it take?"

"I don't know how long it will take," Sandi responded, "but I know more healing is possible."

I decided to tell my parents about what I remembered. I was home for a holiday at the beach house where they now lived in retirement. Sitting at the table after a meal, drinking coffee, I told them. My mother said, "I was always afraid something had happened to you. I was always worried. But you remember in Centralia when you were slamming the doors? Ted was hysterical all the time. I thought my two-year-old was mentally ill. He cried so much and couldn't be comforted. I was so worried about him, I don't think I paid very much attention to you."

Later I told Ted that I remembered Frank molesting me sexually. He said, "I don't remember much about Frank except he had that jumping jack toy." I hadn't mentioned the jumping jack to Ted in our conversation. "Yes, I remember it," I said. Ted continued, "I used to have the worst nightmares about that jumping jack, all while I was growing up. I'd dream I was locked in the bathroom and the jumping jack was huge, towering over me, trying to kill me. The dreams were awful! The same one, over and over again."

I vaguely remembered taking my baby brother over to Frank's house. Ted would have just been walking. He would have barely turned two when we moved from Hoquiam. How could he have remembered the jumping jack? What had he seen? What had Frank done to my little brother?

My father responded differently from my mother. He said, "I always thought you were just a happy, well-adjusted little girl. I can't imagine how terrible a man would have to feel to do what Frank did. The only child abuser that I've encountered was a man whose mind was destroyed in the war." He went on to talk about shell-shock and war trauma.

I pondered my parents' response. They listened respectfully to what I had to say. Neither of them said the things I'd feared they might, like "That couldn't possibly be true. How can you say such a thing!" They listened and they believed me. But their emotional response was subdued. They didn't throw their arms around me in comfort, sympathy and protection. That would have been out of character. Nor did they express outrage at Frank. In fact, my father expressed sympathy for whatever profound wounding might have led a man to behave abusively toward children. Mostly, they just took it in. Just as when I was a child, they silently absorbed the fury of me slamming doors. Was our whole family numb to pain? Was horror just to be absorbed and silently borne?

I began to think that Frank's abuse had done something not just to me, but to our whole family, to my brother Ted, and to all our relationships with each other. The parsonage in Hoquiam was where I fled to when I left Frank's house, but it was not a home in which the truth of my experience could be told or where I could find help.

I tried. I remember once running home from Frank's trying to find my father. He wasn't at the parsonage, so I went next door to the church. I went through the empty halls, the empty sanctuary, the darkened basement social hall, the classrooms, the church office, trying to find him. He was nowhere. I felt frantic in the church, looking everywhere for him.

After that I often had the same nightmare. I am in the basement hallway of the church. It is dark. I'm frightened, trying to find my father, but I can't find him. Then the fire extinguisher on the wall—a heavy, round brass cylinder—comes off the wall, onto the floor. It is rolling after me. It wants to crush me. I'm running down the hall. The fire extinguisher is alive with malice. It is going to crush me. Then I wake up.

As a child I adored my father. He was the kindest man I knew. On Sunday morning, in his black robe, leading the Sunday service, he was dignified and handsome. People looked to him for counsel and advice, and listened to what he had to say. His religion was practical, sane, intelligent, and modest. Neither grave nor sentimental, even as a child I felt it had strength and grandeur to it, as well as goodness. He never asked anything for himself, or imposed any judgments or punishments on his children. He believed love puts the other first, without fail. He regarded his children as geniuses to be treated with respect, trust, and praise. He taught us how to do things—from building boats to developing film in a homemade darkroom, to constructing a Morse code communication system, or running a printing press. It seemed to us that there was nothing our father did not understand and nothing that he did not know how to do. Sometimes at the dinner table we'd ask him to explain something to us. "Dad, how does the radio work?" And he'd tell us.

In the Hoquiam parsonage, when our father had a night off, our favorite game was to turn all the lights off in the house and play hide-and-seek with our parents. Mom would hide somewhere where we found her right off, then we'd all go looking for Dad. He would be nowhere to be found. Just when we'd start giving up, from somewhere in the darkness we would hear a long, low "Mooooo . . ." Mom would say, "There's a cow in the house!" We'd say, "No! It's Dad!" He would moo again in the darkness and we'd go off in all directions to find him. There was nothing better in my world than to catch my father in the dark and tumble into his arms, laughing "You aren't a cow!!" Unless it was to go hiking in the woods with my family. My parents loved the rainforest, beaches, and mountains of the Olympic peninsula where we lived. In the family photo collection there are pictures of me as a small girl—two or three years old—at the beach digging clams with my father. I am a round-cheeked, laughing girl. In photographs of mountain hiking trips I'm riding on his shoulders, the glee in my face perfectly radiant.

I loved my mother, too. At night, she would play the piano after we had gone to bed. Brahms, or Haydn, or Handel would drift up the stairs to where we were sleeping. The comfort of that sound, my sense of her presence floating in the music, held me safe across the threshold into sleep. She taught me to say the Lord's Prayer, to tie my shoes, to play the piano alongside her. She worked in the garden, in the kitchen, at the church. When I had the chicken pox she bought tiny Japanese parasols to cheer me up, made of painted pink, green, and yellow paper. As I grew older, I understood how smart she was. She was a thinker and a reader. Like my father, she related to her children as a teacher and guide, always interested in the exercise of our creativity and intelligence. She read out loud to us, holding us next to her on the couch, or around the campfire in summer. Her lively inflection filled the story with life. At the beach house in summer, we'd go for boat rides at twilight, sometimes fishing for silver salmon. Dad had built the twelve-foot wooden boat, with an inboard Briggs and Stratton engine. We'd putt-putt home in the dark, the water like glass, the running lights our only illumination, the houses along the shore glowing like lanterns hung in the trees. I'd sit in the back of the boat then, next to my mother, tucked inside her red car coat, with the old army blanket over our laps. Safe, warm, and happy.

The experience with Frank separated me from all this. I couldn't tell them what was happening to me. I couldn't express my distress and fear. I couldn't explain my rage. I couldn't ask for help.

My parents had taught us early to be self-reliant and to handle bad feelings with self-control. Once when I was five or six, I slipped while walking barefoot across a log. Just before I slipped my father had said, "Careful! You could get a sliver. Why don't you put on your shoes if you want to walk on the log?" The two-inch sliver had slid into the ball of my foot as he spoke. I was too ashamed to tell him. It was my fault that I'd gotten the sliver. I put my shoes on. In a few days, the foot was so swollen and sore I couldn't lace up my shoe, and I was having trouble walking. Stoic and ashamed, I tried to keep this pain hidden. It wasn't long before one of my parents noticed I was having trouble. Soon the shoe was off, a needle was sterilized, and my father's firm, steady hand was removing the sliver.

I treated the experience with Frank similarly. Slamming doors had hurt my mother and broken her teapot. I became deeply ashamed of the hurt and distress that had led to my temper tantrums. I silenced the pain and tried to take care of it myself, without getting caught. I didn't want my suffering to be imposed on anyone else in a way that injured them. I bore it in silence. I followed the example of my father who bore things in silence. Any pain or distress that might come to him, he absorbed. He never placed it back on anyone else. He took it in.

It was a Christ-like thing to do. Completely unselfish. I wanted to be good, like my father.

Frank exploited my desire to be good and reinforced it with threats of frightening punishment. "You want to be a good girl, don't you?" Of course I did. He told me that good girls don't tell about the things he did to me. Good is what my parents told me I was. If I wasn't good, I wouldn't be their girl—I would lose them, somehow. I kept quiet.

Frank told me what happened to girls who weren't good. Next door to the parsonage there was a family whose father wore a dark navy uniform and rode a motorcycle. Frank said, "If you tell your parents about the games we play, your father will have Jim come on his motorcycle, and he will arrest you. He will take you to jail. They will lock you up behind bars. They won't let your father or mother come to see you, and you won't have anything to eat."

I knew where the jail was. You could walk there from our house, passing the fire station, on the way towards the river where the fishing boats were docked. My father and I would walk to the river to see the boats sometimes. The jail was a stout stone building, with opaque, slit windows. It looked like a big box. I imagined the children locked up there, separated from their families, hungry.

Jim would come around from time to time during the day, wearing his blue uniform, with his shiny black boots and the big motorcycle. His children would run out to him when he rode up. All the kids in the neighborhood would gather round to see the motorcycle. Except me. I would hide from him.

Once, at the grocery store, I put a dime in the gum machine. I had learned a dime was worth ten pennies. I figured that meant I'd get ten penny gum balls from the machine. But it didn't work. The machine jammed. No gum balls came out at all. I was terrified. I was sure the store owner knew I was the one who had committed this crime—I'd done it in plain sight!

The next time Jim came to the neighborhood, I ran in the other direction. I hid on our storm porch, filled with anxiety. I peered out the crack in the door watching him at the curb with the kids. I was certain he was looking for me and that I was going to be arrested.

In this way, Frank's stories led me to fear the people who could have helped me. Frank was the one who was breaking a civil and a moral law. He was a criminal. But he persuaded me I was the criminal. I believed it to the core of my being.

I kept going back to Frank's house. There were things there that I wanted. I wanted the jumping jack toy he was making for me. It was never finished. "You'll have to come back another day. It's not done yet." He'd show me the wooden figure as he worked on it. The pieces were carved, but they weren't assembled yet. The pieces were assembled, but they weren't painted yet. But it wasn't just the jumping jack. Something in me responded to the emotional intensity and the attention. I became deeply attached to Frank and didn't want to be separated from him.

Years later, my mother told me that Frank did finish the jumping jack. He wrapped it up as a present and sent it home with me to open on Christmas. She said when I opened the box I pushed the jumping jack away, and wouldn't have anything to do with it. Nothing would persuade me to even look at the handmade toy. My reaction troubled her deeply, and she never forgot it, but she didn't know what to make of it. In retrospect, she grieves how little framework she had for understanding her child's silent terror.

Frank played other games that made me and Tommy laugh. He'd put black pieces of paper on his fingernails.

> Two little black birds, sitting on the hill,
> One named Jack, one named Jill.
> Fly away Jack, fly away Jill.

He'd swing his arms around behind his back, then out front again. The little black birds were gone. We'd laugh. "Make them come back!"

Come back Jack, come back Jill.

The birds would reappear to our delight. Sometimes he would make us guess which one would come back, Jack or Jill. The child who guessed right would be sent home, with a piece of candy. The one who guessed wrong had to stay, for a different game. In this way we were selected. We understood the rules and obeyed. I remember the feeling of being escorted to the front door by Frank, given a piece of candy, and shooed out—seeing Tommy sitting back inside the house still, looking frightened. And, I remember staying, when Tommy left. I felt dread as the front door closed behind him, and I was left alone with Frank.

I couldn't take my troubles home to my mother and father. Frank's threats had successfully separated me from them. Also, apart from occasional outbursts, I was already beginning to learn at home that a good person keeps quiet about pain and fear. She takes care of it herself.

Leaving Frank's house, physically in pain and emotionally overwhelmed, I'd run to my tricycle out on the lawn—the jet rocket. It was black with red plastic headlights and taillights, shaped to look like jets. I'd climb on the tricycle and ride as fast as I could. I'd pedal away from Frank's house and away from the parsonage, into the distant territory around on the back side of the block, where we weren't supposed to go alone. I'd pedal with all my might, round and round, furiously, until the trike was bumping and sailing over the sidewalk at a breakneck speed. I'd cycle all the way around the block, once, twice, three times. I'd feel the rush of the wind and exertion of my body, the jolts of the uneven sidewalk. I would make it go away. It didn't happen. It wasn't real. I felt the power in my body, the energy of riding as fast as I could. This circling had power. It was magic. It made Frank's hands on my body disappear. It purged the shame and fear. It erased the events, I was sure.

Then I could go home. Thus it was that hard work became the activity that maintained the separation between the two houses in whose interior spaces my sense of self was formed. At the parsonage,

I was The Blessed Child who had good parents. I hid my pain from them, lest I lose them. I strove, especially, to protect my father from pain by forming a self-image that reflected how he saw me: perfect. At Frank's house I was The Unblessed Child, stimulated by desires and wants, manipulated for his gratification, pleasured and pained. My inner self was severed into two. Nowhere was really home. Home was the jet rocket, riding at breakneck speed.

When I became an adult and married for the first time, the intimate sphere of life with my husband was haunted by both these houses from my past. I thought of myself as good and loving. I knew what a good person does. She lives for the other, unselfishly. Her own needs and wants are irrelevant to love. She bears pain silently. The theology of liberal Protestantism blessed this way of life in a hymn.

> Be still my soul,
> the Lord is on thy side,
> bear patiently,
> the cross of grief and pain.

My theological education reinforced it. My devotion to the ministry and to church life made me a housekeeper in the home of goodness. But this self was partial. At home, The Unblessed Child showed up in bed. Making love, my consciousness fractured. I couldn't maintain self-possession. All the magic circling in the world hadn't excised from my body the physical feeling of terror and overwhelm. Consciousness couldn't hold it. Sex was annihilation.

For a number of years, I considered this experience in sex to be some kind of spontaneous mystical experience. The same "white flashes" could be induced by a pattern of meditation, I discovered, though without the tinge of terror. I became interested in the mystics of Western and Eastern Christianity—searching for companionship. In the late '60s and early '70s popular culture was exploding with interest in altered states, induced by drugs or meditative techniques imported to the West from Hindu and Buddhist tradition. Like many, I found Tibetan and Zen Buddhism, as represented in a few notable teachers who had come to the West, especially attractive. Perhaps in these traditions there was a context for my experience to make sense, I thought. And I considered converting—Protestant-style—to Buddhism.

But something held me back. I read Augustine's *Confessions* and was deeply moved by the quality of self-disclosure that Augustine presented in his confessions addressed to God. "Almighty God, unto whom all hearts are open, all desires known, and from whom no secrets are hid . . ." We had said this collect every Sunday morning at my father's church. Augustine's life was laid open before this God, in an intimacy of address and trust that made my mouth water. I desired just such a relationship. "Our hearts are restless until they rest in Thee," he wrote. The details of Augustine's theology, which have proved problematic in so many ways, were irrelevant to me at that point in time. It was his candor before God. It was his witness to a relationship in which no secrets were hid. It was the presence of a "Thou" before whom the "I" was free that awakened my longing. Something in me believed that such a "Thou" existed.

> As the deer longs for flowing streams,
>   so my soul longs for you, O God. (Psalm 42:1)

It was then that I made a conscious choice to make my home in the household of biblical faith, to live within the sphere of theistic imagination. Christianity became not only my inherited faith but my chosen faith. Augustine had converted me.

I did not regard Christianity as an exclusive choice. I felt there was *sufficient,* not exclusive, truth in Christianity. Besides I reasoned that though I might "convert" to Buddhism, my unconscious was Christian. I sensed it might take a lifetime to work out the way my soul had been configured, for better or for worse, within a Christian culture.

My effort to bring to language all that was held in the cells of my body was not over. There were more rooms in Frank's house. The abuse hadn't stopped in the dining room. Frank had taken me further into the house, and more had happened there. I knew this. But I didn't want to open the bedroom door and see. I didn't want to let this knowledge speak.

The ending of my marriage to George had left me unprotected from the inner anguish of my life. I had neither the warmth of George's love to shelter me, nor my preoccupation with his life to distract me. Personal crisis had ensued. It felt like more than I could endure without intimate support. I was lonesome for company, affection, and romance. I accepted without self-reproach that I needed a hand to hold.

David came into my life about this time. Mutual friends introduced us to one another. The friends knew that I was single again and that David was a good person. They thought we would like each other. We did.

David offered his hand and I was glad of it. There was kindness in his brown eyes. He knew first-hand that recovery from personal trauma was possible. He enjoyed simple pleasures—camping in the wilderness, reading well-written prose, going to a baseball game to cheer unabashedly for the home team. A gifted law teacher and writer, David had never married. But now at midlife the possibility of a committed relationship held strong appeal for him. I was worried that I was not as ready as he to enter into a serious relationship, and told him so. But my need for companionship was stronger than the inner voice that woke me in the night reminding me that a new relationship might be premature.

I trusted David's ability to be present to trauma and shame, and told him my story, showing him the drawings that had helped me piece together my past. He was a compassionate witness who didn't run away appalled; he could be present to pain. I felt I could be at home with him, without hiding. "We're only as sick as our secrets," was one of the maxims David lived by. He wasn't interested in helping me hide from my own secrets. He knew health was in the opposite direction.

We spent hours hiking in the green hills of northern California the spring we met. It had rained hard that winter, after seven years of drought. The wildflowers, multi-colored and fragile, were abundant. We wandered through oak groves and the dark sanctuaries of the redwood forest. It was a welcome return to love. Before the year was over, we decided to live together.

I knew that until I had faced and integrated all that had happened to me, my past was going to haunt the present in a way that disrupted love. I needed to go further in therapy. Until I could be present to myself fully, I wasn't going to be able to fully offer my presence to another. Nothing but the desire to love authentically and fully was strong enough to motivate my turning again to the rooms of the house I feared.

I was painfully aware that I wasn't there yet, despite my hopes and my willingness to open myself again to love. Sexual intimacy felt freer to me than it ever had before, but I wasn't free. Lying in bed at night, the moments of pleasure and closeness invariably ushered me back to the place of terror. I'd talk to the ghost now. "Leave me alone, go away, you don't belong here." But the coldness, anxiety, and dread took hold of me. I felt split, possessed, haunted, captive to a fear that I couldn't exorcize by calling its name.

David's affection was a mercy. He'd wrap me in a lullaby, singing in a warm and steady voice while he held me. The simplicity and directness of this kindness helped me make it through the hard nights. But the haunting that held me didn't yield to affection or to willpower. I tried prayer, but God seemed powerless to free me. One night, responding to my anguish, David said, "Try praying. I'll pray with you if you want."

"No," I said. "God is not any help. I've asked."

David said, "Your God is not helping you with this?"

"No," I said, angry and frustrated.

"Well, then," David said, "this is California. Get another God."

I laughed. David's suggestion reminded me that I had the power to choose the God I would worship. I had sought a "Thou" before whom no secrets were hid. In this search, along with other feminist theologians, I'd deconstructed God the Omnipotent, God the Divine Child Abuser, God the King. I'd reconstructed God as Goddess, as Spirit of Life, as Source from Whom All Blessings Flow, as Love at the Heart of Life. I'd addressed her in new words in liturgy and song. I'd tried not talking to her at all, reverencing the reality that finally we do not know any name for the ultimate beyond "I am who I am." But in all this I had not deconstructed God as Frank.

This was the force of the abuser in my life. He occupied the place of God. It was his presence, his will, his actions that ruled my life. I had no other god before him. My spirit bowed down to him. I accepted that I was who he said I was. His spirit filled my life.

I began to think of my struggle as a struggle with idolatry. The relationship I had with Frank was an unholy alliance, a bond that still hadn't been broken. The obeisance I rendered to him was unholy worship. To be free from idolatry would require a different relationship at the core of my life—a relationship that wasn't one of possession, obedience, and terror; a relationship in which I did not bow down to the demands of self-abnegation and the dictates of fear. The "Thou" I needed was more than the "Thou" before whom no secret was hid. It was also the "Thou" before whom no self-destructive service was required—a "Thou" of mercy and freedom. I had to face that at the core of my being I did not believe such mercy or such freedom existed. I only *really believed* in Frank.

I decided that I would doubt my certainty that there was no mercy. I would consider the possibility that I was wrong to believe that life was inescapably defined by cruelty and abuse. I became a skeptic in relationship to my own despair. But the path ahead was still long.

With support at home and with Sandi's presence to help me stay steady, I crossed through the passage from the dining room at Frank's to the bedroom. I faced what I felt and remembered from the deepest interior of the house:

I can see him standing over me. I am lying on the bed. To my left is the yellow-golden light of the pulled-down shade. He is at the foot of the iron bedstead, standing. He is in his undershirt. He takes off his belt. He unzips his pants. He shows me his thing. He climbs on top of me. The belt is across my chest. I am pinned down. He tells me to hold my legs tight together. He pushes between my legs. He sends me to the bathroom to clean up. Be a good girl. Wash yourself.

This did not only happen one time. This isn't the only thing that happened.

I am lying on the bed. To my left is the yellow-golden light of the pulled-down shade. He is at the foot of the iron bedstead, standing. He is in his undershirt. He takes off his belt. He unzips his pants. He shows me his thing. He climbs on top of me. He is over my face. The thing is in my face. I can't breathe. My throat is blocked. I can't breathe. My mouth is aching. I can't breathe. I am going to die.

"I left her there for dead," I said to Sandi. "I got out of that room somehow, but I left her there on the bed. Left her for dead. She's still there, in that room."

I drew a picture of the child left for dead. She is blue. There is a cock in her mouth. Her eyes are closed. Red tears drop from her eyes. Around her head, a golden light circles her.

I can see Frank's face over my face. I can see what he wants from me. He wants my terror. He wants me to be terrified. It is my abject terror he wants to possess and control. Then I remember the worst thing that happened. In those moments, face to face with his desire for me to be terrified, I looked at his face and I saw a man in cruel, anguished, need.

I see his face. It is full of pain. I feel as if he is trying to get back his own face. As if, by forcing my face to wear the face of terror, I will be the mirror in which he will be restored to himself. He isn't looking at me. He is looking through me. He is looking at himself. In the presence of such pain, my heart awakes in compassion.

That was the intensity of the bond. The glue was compassion. I couldn't turn away from this face holding mine in terror without turning away from the compassion I felt. I let the gaze hold. I let myself be locked into another's need for release from pain.

In an essay on anger, Audre Lorde writes of the work of learning to train one's anger—to hone its energy to be used for life not against it. I believe the same must be done with compassion. One must hone the capacity to feel another's need for release from pain and not turn from that feeling but offer one's presence to the other. Empathetic connection to another is not necessarily life-giving or life-saving. The empathetic bond can hold a human being captive to another's unjust demand. Our ability to *feel for another* can become an unholy bond in which the other's obligation to *feel for himself,* or *feel for herself,* is ignored. This was Frank's crime. He could not or did not feel for himself. He required me to feel for him. My mistake was to accept this assignment. A child's heart is not honed to know how to use its empathy for pain.

Both our capacity for connection and our capacity for separation have to be cultivated into responses that are life-giving and life-sustaining. The power to hold and the power to let go, to connect and to disconnect, each of these powers can be used for good or for ill. Ethical maturity learns the difference and knows the right time for each. Neither power can be valorized as an absolute good without risking harm.

For centuries, Christian theology imagined God's supremacy as a supremacy of separateness. Karl Barth described God's relationship to the world like a tangent to a circle. Christ is the one point of contact between the earthly and the divine. God's freedom was his impassability—his ability to be unaffected by the world. God's radical otherness remains a strong tenet of much theology. These theologies have been rightly criticized for supporting the ascendancy of patriarchal values of dispassion and independence. In the twentieth century, the theological pendulum swung the other way. Theology described a God who could feel—a relational, connected, empathetic God, who suffers with us. God's love for us was expressed in his union with Jesus in experiencing abandonment and pain. But this theology has sometimes valorized empathetic union without distinguishing it from abuse.

Forty years after having been raped as a child, I reread Jürgen Moltmann's *The Crucified God: The Cross of Christ as the Foundation and Criticism of Christian Theology* and found myself shaking. The interaction he describes between God and Jesus felt horribly familiar to me—a merging of father and son, named love, in which the father inflicts violence on the child and then feels it as if he were the one suffering, he the one dying. "God suffered in Jesus, God himself died in Jesus for us. God is on the cross of Jesus 'for us'." Then, through this cathexis—this undifferentiated connection which is simultaneously the extreme of human estrangement—the way is prepared for resurrection. Life is saved. "The cross of the Son divides God from God to the utmost degree of enmity and distinction. The resurrection of the Son abandoned by God unites God with God in the most intimate fellowship."

This is what the abuser does. He requires the other to feel pain and then imagines the other is himself. He finds life by externalizing his pain and then embracing the one he tortures. Christian theology has described God as engaged in precisely this kind of transaction. And in doing so it has erased both the suffering of victims and the crime of perpetrators. The Roman Empire—whose agenda was exploitation, backed up with terror, when needed—is erased and is replaced by God the loving father. The man of sorrows is erased and is replaced by the obedient child indistinguishable from the father.

Love is neither transcendence nor undifferentiated union. Love is the wisdom of life that knows when connection can heal and when separation will make life flourish. Love is the capacity to use the powers of holding on and letting go in the service of life. Love is capable of detachment as well as empathy, differentiation as well as union, hierarchy as well as mutuality. Love is the guardian of powers. Love directs the use of specific powers, in response to particular circumstances, for the sake of creating, sustaining, or healing life. In every situation, love asks, "What will serve life?" This means human love comes from a growing wisdom about life itself. If one wants to love, it is life that one must seek to fully know. To love is to choose life.

To survive the painful experience of Frank's sadistic abuse I constructed an intricate set of internal walls within my self. On one side of the thickest dividing wall lived my well-adjusted self: competent, kind, high-achieving, creative, thoughtful—my father's daughter. On the other side lived The Unblessed Child and the child left for dead, in an inner series of rooms more and more carefully closed and sealed. The girl on the tricycle had the key. She's the one who locked Frank's house away through the magic of furious work. She moved between the two houses, organizing things so as to keep them apart, for the sake of saving herself and preserving her family. In doing this she was trying especially to protect her father from the truth of her life. She was determined to be the girl he wanted her to be: good and happy; not the girl she was: shamed, hurt, and afraid.

My strategies were particular to me and perhaps show the creativity with which I as a small child made use of the materials at hand to survive. The religious values and ideas of liberal Protestantism, so faithfully embodied in my parents' lives, were admirably suited to compartmentalizing myself. The good self thrives by internally entombing the aspects of life and feeling that do not fit. Self-sacrifice easily becomes internal closure. Had my parents been able to see and understand what was happening to me, I know that in their love for me they would have come to my rescue. But as my mother said to me later, "It is so terrible that we didn't see what was happening to you. In those days nobody talked about sexual abuse of children. We didn't imagine that such a thing really happened."

The internal silences I created replicated the public silences. What my community could not name it could not see. And what the community could not see, I could not integrate. My religious community, most of all, could not see violence against children because it could not name clearly the violence that happened to Jesus. Even liberal Protestantism called Jesus' death on the cross an example of love that disciples were to imitate.

> "Are ye able," said the master, "to be crucified with me?"
> "Yea" the sturdy dreamers answered,

"To the death we follow thee.
Lord, we are able, our spirits are thine,
Re-mold and make us like thee divine,
Thy guiding radiance above us shall be,
A beacon to life, to love and loyalty."

I sang this hymn throughout my childhood with sincere passion. Its valor guided the construction of my interior world. Love and loyalty were preserved through my internalized ability to be crucified. Unfortunately, this also meant I internalized the ability to crucify.

The divided houses had to come down for me to survive in a fuller way. The way I had structured and organized my internal life did not, finally, succeed in fostering love. The repeated loss of intimate relationship showed me that too much of my life was closed away and unreachable. Those I sought to love found themselves left out in the cold. They felt their love didn't penetrate. When George and I were divorcing he said to me, with pain, "I tried so hard to love you. I wanted to love you. But I couldn't get over the wall inside of you." David and I would stay together for six years, but my good self offered little hospitality to the full range of human emotion, especially my own, and certainly that of others. And my wounded self distressed David deeply, touching on unresolved aspects of his own life.

Because I wanted to love and to be loved—the most elemental human desire—I took on the task of dismantling my internal home. Doors were unsealed that had been closed. Long shut rooms were entered. As my well-constructed home started to come down, chaos erupted.

It happened one Saturday afternoon, when David and I were living together. I'd been away from home for most of the week, at a denominational gathering. I was tired. My responsibilities as a seminary president were weighing especially heavily. The therapy work with Sandi had entered the most painful place of recollection. I'd given up my art therapy room at home, assuring David that it was more important that he have the space to use as a study. In the midst of this stress, I did something that hurt David. It doesn't too much matter now what it was, just that it hurt him. He told me that he was hurt. I argued with him. "How could this have hurt you? I didn't mean to hurt you! It was just a little thing!" But it wasn't. It *had* hurt him. He wanted me to understand that what I had done had upset him, had grieved him, had made him feel badly about himself. I would hear none of it. I felt he was wrong to be hurt. He shouldn't feel hurt. It was his fault he felt hurt. He shouldn't ask me to take responsibility for him feeling hurt. I dumped on him all the messages I had repeatedly delivered internally to The Unblessed Child. David resisted my barrage. He told me my defensiveness was an avoidance, a denial. He confronted me with my unwillingness to see my part in him being hurt.

My denial broke, then, and I saw myself. I saw that, indeed, I had acted in a way that had harmed him. I was appalled and deeply ashamed. I said I was sorry. He asked me to try and make right the harm I had caused. But I had no idea what to do. I felt panic. I just wanted him to stop being unhappy with me. So I continued to say, "I'm sorry, I'm sorry!" The argument ended there. Him hurt and me sorry. We'd talk about it later, when we calmed down.

But I couldn't calm down. I went to the kitchen to be by myself. My sense of shame was relentless. How could I have behaved so thoughtlessly? I could not bear the thought that I had hurt someone I loved. There seemed to be no way to make it right. The damage was done. I began to cry, enraged with myself. Then this rage cracked open inside me into a clear message about what to do. The abuser had to be killed. No amount of punishment would be enough. I went to the knife drawer and selected the bread knife, remembering how my parents had given me this knife for my birthday. With my right hand, I pressed the serrated knife against the flesh of my inner left forearm. I felt the bite of its tiny teeth. Then I pulled. I hadn't cut very deeply. So I did it again, pressing harder. I began a third cut, when I heard a voice, over my left shoulder, sharp as a bell. "No. Stop." I stopped. No one was there—but the voice recalled me to my senses. I began to calm down. I washed my arm with soap and water. The cuts were bleeding, red and angry. I bound up the arm with a gauze bandage and tape. The bleeding stopped. I went to the bedroom and found a long-sleeved shirt that would hide the slices in my arm.

That evening David and I went to a fund-raiser for the school. It was my task to greet people, express words of appreciation for their support, and make a speech celebrating our honored guest. It was a lovely evening—festive and warm. There were beautiful flowers, delicious food, and good people to be with. I hid my self-injury from David and from all my friends and colleagues. But, that night at home, I wanted David to know. I had frightened myself. Though I had struggled with suicidal impulses through the years, I had never experienced the loss of control that had happened to me that afternoon.

When I told David he was deeply concerned and alarmed. He encouraged me to call Sandi, then and there. I was reluctant to do that. I didn't want to bother her at eleven o'clock on Saturday night. After all, I was all right. I wasn't bleeding to death. The wounds had closed. But, I promised I would call first thing in the morning.

I called Sandi. She talked with me and helped me see that if I felt the impulse to hurt myself, and doing so created release, I needed a way to channel these feelings that wouldn't cause physical harm. She told me if I felt this way again, I should fill the sink with cold water and ice and put my arms in. "It will hurt a lot," she said. "And then there will be a physical release." That would be better than cutting myself. She made me promise that before I cut myself again, I would call her.

It was helpful that the therapist didn't react to my self-destructive impulse by saying, "Oh my God, you can't do that to yourself!! You must not!" Such a response would have asked me either to intensify my internal systems of self-discipline; or would have required me to turn myself over to someone else who could take care of me, because I was a danger to myself. Neither of these things would have helped me. The one would have reinforced an internal mechanism of willful control that was stifling my life. The other would have reinforced a tendency to give my power away to others, instead of exercising my power of self-direction and choice. What I needed was a stronger core, a centered self who was supportive of my well-being rather than destructive of it. The voice in me that said, "No, stop," needed to move from left field to center.

It would take time. It was as if my internal house had always held this destructive, violent person, and now she was out in the open. The target of her punishing rage was, above all, me.

Her fury was not easy to live with. Morning after morning I would wake up feeling, "I want to die." The feeling was like a liquid that oozed through me, a numbing drug. Sometimes, the only way I could get to sleep at night was to imagine, in slow motion, a deep surgical cut down the center of my body.

I tell this now, still with some shame, but I want to be an honest reporter about the depth of struggle involved for survivors of childhood sexual abuse. No two stories are identical, either in the circumstances of violation, or in the resources for survival that children employ. But my experience was not atypical. While I was working most intensively on remembering and integrating my own life experience, I intentionally avoided reading psychological and therapeutic literature about child abuse. I chose to relate to my own experience as a primary text. Secondary texts, I felt, might cloud an already difficult internal perception. Subsequently, reading the literature, I discovered that suicidal feelings and actions are typical. My experience, if anything, was mild in comparison with those who repeatedly mutilate themselves to release the body's pain or force the body to speak. And I have lived to tell of this period in my life, while others have died by their own hand. In fact, more people die by suicide in the United States than by homicide. Self-inflicted violence is more common than other-directed violence.

It was no longer clear to me whether I was fighting Frank or fighting myself. The abuser was inside me. But it was clear that if I could not find a way to get free from the impulse to injure myself that Frank was going to win. I was determined that this would not happen.

When Sandi looked at the cuts on my arm she observed that there was clearly a healthy human being in me who was planning to stay around. There was enough strength in me to deal with the dangerous side of myself. I hadn't cut in a place that would have damaged a tendon or opened an artery. I laughed. "So, I wanted to kill myself, but I didn't want to mess up my ability to play the cello—that would have been going too far!"

Music had saved my life more than once. As a small child, trying to sleep at night after coming home from Frank's, it was the sound of my mother at the piano that had kept me connected to her beyond the severing that Frank's violence imposed. The music she played was rich and complex, its harmonies painful then joyful, its rhythms slow with sorrow, or dancing with exuberance. Listening, I felt there was a world that could hold me, hold all of us. Music made this world of grace tangible.

She taught me to read music even before I learned to read letters and words. During primary school, I would run home from church sometimes and sit at the piano in the living room, slowly playing the canon "Dona Nobis Pacem." I imagined this music had the power to make peace in the world. I would construct fantastic melodramas in my head. The train would be bearing down on the maiden in distress tied to the rails. At the last moment, the hero would arrive. He would sing "Dona Nobis Pacem," and the train would stop. Life would be saved.

At age twelve I heard a recording of Pablo Casals playing the Bach unaccompanied cello suites. Listening, I felt pure lust. After that I wanted one thing above all else in life: to be able to make those sounds and play that music. As a teenager, learning to play the cello provided focus to my life. While adolescence brought its own crises of development, music held me. I couldn't find the physical pathway to being sexual without fear; but I could put my whole self—spirit and body—into playing the cello.

Music provided the experience of integration—heart, mind, body, and soul, anguish and joy—that I found nowhere else. There was no way I was going to cut the tendon to my left hand.

A sacrament, the old theologies say, is an outward and visible sign of an inward and spiritual grace. A sacrament is a tangible experience of salvation, the salving of wounds, the arrival of wholeness. Felt, tasted, seen, and known with the body in sacramental form, grace is preserved as a possibility to be more fully realized in one's inner being and one's relationships. The sacrament of music made audible to me a world in which all could be felt, in a body of wholeness. When I'd married George, I was reaching for the blessing of this wholeness, seeking Orpheus, the god of music who could descend to the underworld and rescue his love from imprisonment.

The challenge for me, as for many survivors of abuse, was to find a way beyond the *possibility* of healing and wholeness to its actual realization. Facing the horrors of the past was not enough. The violence was *in* me. In my body. In my impulses. In how I had constructed my internal domain.

A dream image captured the dilemma.

I am bent over, sobbing. My hands pull against my face in anguish. There is something gagging my mouth. I reach into my throat and grab hold of something round and slippery and begin to pull. It is the end of a thick, slick, white gelatinous cord. At first I think it is snot, but it is more than that. It is like a rope of kelp—the seaweed that grows in forests just off shore. I pull on the rope of congealed snot-stuff. I want to get it out of my throat. I pull and pull. It slides out, one foot, two feet, three feet. I keep pulling. It is a massive coil of stuff inside me. I keep pulling. Soon there is a whole pile outside my body. I keep yanking and pulling, and then it jerks to a stop. It is stuck. I tug and the slippery, thick cord breaks somewhere down inside my body. The broken end springs free and spills out of my mouth. I am filled with despair and dread. There is more inside me, and I can't reach it now.

It was midspring, 1997. Suddenly I felt I simply could not go on. The suicidal despair had continued to haunt my days and nights. I repeatedly lost control and was overwhelmed with the desire to hurt myself. The sink full of ice water had become a routine to still the self-directed rage. On at least one occasion, I again grabbed a knife and fiercely sliced my arm. David was hanging in there with me, urging me to take care of myself, and to draw on the resources around me for help and healing. But the strain on our relationship was severe. My self-destructive impulses resonated painfully with difficult memories from David's past. We struggled to hold our relationship together, but the force of past injuries was eroding the bonds of connection between us.

I wanted silence. I wanted stillness. I wanted a sanatorium, or a retreat. I had to get out of where I was. I called the chair of the school's board of trustees, Arliss Ungar, and said, "I need to take a break from the school." "When?" she asked. "Before the semester is over." "How long?" she asked. "Ten days—maybe two weeks," I said. "The school will be fine," she said. "We'll take care of things. Arrange to go at the end of this week." An AWOL seminary president didn't seem like a good thing to me, but the leadership of the school believed that work shouldn't take precedence over spiritual or physical needs. Arliss didn't ask me to explain. She acted in support of my well-being without hesitation and without question. So did my faculty colleagues.

I left everything. I got in the car and drove north to the City of Ten Thousand Buddhas. I'd called the head of the university there, who was a friend of our school. "I need to take refuge," I said. "Of course," she said. "We will make a place for you." "What is the fee for a person to make a private retreat there?" "Fee?" she said. "We do not charge a fee. Make a donation if you would like."

One of the Buddhist teachers escorted me to a tiny cottage in the woods. "This is your space. What else do you need?"

"I need silence. I need to not talk to anyone."

"No problem," she said. "Here." She handed me a small, worn, plastic badge, in Chinese. The Chinese was translated in parentheses, "Not talking."

I grinned. "You are used to people not talking here?"

"Of course," she replied. "You are welcome to eat with the community of monks. The food is simple. Just rice, vegetables and tofu. They eat one meal a day, at midday. The meal is in silence. The men and women eat in separate sections. You can eat with the women."

I nodded.

"You are also welcome to participate in the rituals of the community, if you like. But there is no expectation. The sutras are chanted in the Hall of the Ten Thousand Buddhas at three o'clock in the morning, then there is an hour of bowing, followed by an hour of silent sitting in meditation, then an hour of reading and commentary on the sutras. Then people go about their day's work. At midday there are prayers. At six in the evening, there is the evening sutra recitation, followed by instruction, and the evening meditation."

I went into the little cottage and spread out the things I had brought with me: all of the drawings I had made since beginning therapy; drawing paper, pastels, ink, colored pencils, watercolors. I brought the cello in from the car, and set up the music stand, with Bach's cello suites opened to the G major suite. I got out photographs I had brought of everyone I loved and arranged them on a small altar. My mother and father, my brothers Howard and Ted, my grandmother Ernst, biting into a strawberry. David, grinning in the cockpit of a Cessna 172, the plane he loved to fly. A photograph of the students, faculty and staff of the school taken on the first day of school that fall. I set out the picture of myself at four years old, astride my black rocket tricycle, looking tough, and another picture of myself as a baby in my grandfather Ernst's arms, with my young, handsome parents standing on either side, taken on the day of my baptism, in front of the parsonage in Hoquiam. I also set at the altar the jar of dirt I had stolen from Frank's yard on my journey back there, and my Raggedy Ann doll.

I placed on the altar a tall votive candle that I'd bought at the Mexican grocery just outside the entry gate to the City of Ten Thousand Buddhas. It only cost a dollar. On the front was a stained-glass picture of an angel guiding two small children across a raging torrent of water. I lit the candle and went outside for a walk.

The City of Ten Thousand Buddhas is a city of ten directions. This means it is a Buddhist community in which all pathways into the pure land cross. These pathways include education, service, hospitality, ordinary work, ritual, and meditation. There was a hall for the repose of the ancestors and a hall for the healing of the sick and those in distress. The Bodhisattva Kuan Yin—the woman of infinite compassion—sat at the center.

The city had been created from the abandoned buildings of a former state hospital for the insane. It was out in the country, east of Ukiah, in a northern California valley among the lush coastal hills. It was early spring. The new grass was tall, tender, bright green. The grounds were going wild with overgrown trees. The fields were blooming with daffodils and tulips run riot. Peacocks lived there— harbingers of the pure land. Some were all white. Others, emerald green, scarlet, and blue. Their fanned tails shimmered like a pond of jewels. A hill rose behind the buildings where one could walk through pine woods along the edge of a vineyard. In the distance, the hills rose more steeply, dark blue against the clear blue of the spring sky.

I took deep breaths of the cool air and went back to the cottage. I began to draw. Over the course of ten days of silence, I made a series of drawings in which I pictured my body being cut open. Inside the length of my torso was an old, huge, gray penis around which my body had grown like a tree grows around a stone. Using pastels, colored pencils and watercolors as my "surgical tools," I removed the old penis from the inside of my body, cutting all the blood vessels that had grown like roots around it. An empty cavity was left. The patient looked like she might die on the operating table. I took needle and deep red thread and sewed through the paper to sew her body back together.

Every afternoon I walked for hours through the fields and forest that went on for miles beyond the City of Ten Thousand Buddhas. The day the penis was removed and the cavity lay open I walked the farthest, venturing across fields, then up into the hills, following a stream. In late afternoon, far away from any visible human activity, I came to a grove where the warm sun slanted through the oaks and dappled the grass alongside the water. I stopped. I lay down in the tall sweet grass for a while, feeling the warm earth under me. "Earth, heal me," I said. Then I rose, took off all my clothes, and waded into the water. A small cascade of white water crashed over the rocks and swirled into a still pool. I crouched down, feeling the cold water rush around me. Then I moved my feet forward into the soft mud on the bottom of the pool. Slowly, I turned and lay down in the water, letting my whole body sink beneath the surface to rest on the mud. I relaxed the muscles holding up my head and the water closed over my face, cool and still, lapping quietly. In a few moments, I jumped up—it was too cold to bear for long.

I felt at peace. I smiled to the sky and the trees, to the green pasture and the still waters. "Surely goodness and mercy will follow me all the days of my life."

That evening, as every evening, the community's ritual involved an hour of chanting and bowing, concluding with a walking meditation accompanied by drums, gongs, and bells. The ritual was in Chinese, but I could follow the translation. After several days, I began to get a feeling for what was happening. Every evening, a symbolic meal was set on the altar. Offerings of fruits, beautifully arranged, were placed there, along with bowls of water, with flower petals floating in them. This meal was to offer strength and nourishment to the travelers who were nearing the pure land—the land of ultimate bliss, in which the cycles of death and rebirth ended in a place of beauty and pleasure. Prayers were said at this symbolic table, that all souls might be reborn in the pure land. Then, the hungry ghosts were prayed for—those wandering, bound in confusion and pain. At that point in the ritual, one of the priests took some of the food from the altar and carried it outside the sanctuary. He placed it among the stones of the garden, for the hungry ghosts—that they might be assisted, as well as for those inside the sanctuary, to find their way to the pure land.

At the end of ten days of silence, drawing, walking, and ritual I was ready to leave. The ritual I had performed had released Frank from my body. I could feel the interior spaces of my being freed from the endless cord of his invasive presence. I felt raw, hollowed out, and growing stronger. Years before, when I had aborted the pregnancy, I had vowed to my unborn child that if he or she could not live, I would. I would not allow two lives to be lost. When my body was freed from Frank's, I fulfilled the vow to my unborn child. I found a way to live.

It was pouring rain as I prepared to go. I disassembled the altar and loaded the car. Just before driving through the gates to leave, I realized what I should do. I stopped the car and found the jar filled with dirt from Frank's yard. I had held on to this jar for five years. It had come to seem more and more like Frank's ashes—the presence of the dead man who haunted me. I took the jar, walked to the rhododendrons blooming in the garden, and dumped Frank's soil out onto the ground, while the pouring rain soaked me to the bones. I threw the glass jar away in the garbage can on the way out. The City of Ten Thousand Buddhas could take care of one more hungry ghost. Every day the monks put food in the garden to help all the ghosts bound in misery and pain find their way home. I happily turned the job of taking care of Frank over to them and brushed the dirt off my hands.

After this, Sandi told me we would have to find a way to go back into that bedroom at Frank's house so that the child left for dead was not left alone in Frank's house. We worked on this in therapy, but I couldn't cross that threshold again. She'd invite me to place ourselves there imaginatively, along with the girl on the tricycle who had gotten out of the house alive. Our task was to enter through the bedroom door, and go in to comfort and help the child left for dead. But the place was too terrible to me.

I understood the point of the therapeutic move. The split between the tough little girl who survived by running away and the child left for dead needed to be healed. As long as part of me was left there, in Frank's house, I wasn't going to be whole. I was settling for a piece of me to be abandoned eternally to the abuser.

Finally, one day, during a therapy session, Sandi used a rapid eye movement technique with me—a therapeutic process used with people suffering from post-traumatic stress syndrome. The process involves the physical movement of the eyes back and forth, and then a guided descent to a place of painful memory, with the presence of the therapist. This process often works to unblock traumatic experiences. I was willing to try it.

During the guided descent, I re-approached the dreaded room.

This time, I moved across the threshold. I was on that bed again. I was feeling the terror again. I swallowed hard, going again into that place of not being able to breathe, believing that I was going to die. Then I saw that my mother and grandmother were there with me. They could see what Frank was doing. Their sight was powerful. They would not let him get away with it. I felt comforted and strengthened by their presence. Then, with slow dawning, I felt the space encompassed with a great love that held me and confronted Frank. It was a force-field of presence that encompassed Frank as well. I knew that even if Frank killed me, nothing would separate me from this presence. I would be taken up into all embracing arms.

Tears came to my eyes as I returned to the present time and said to Sandi with amazement, "The child left for dead—she is the part of me who has experienced God! She knows there is a power that can stop Frank, and that, even if Frank succeeds, this power is greater than him and will still hold her and preserve her. She is my faith. She is the one who has never given up. She is the one who has been able to preach all these years, when I have been able to say from some place deep inside of me that there was grace at work in life that would see us through. She has always been with me. Her knowledge has never left me. She is the reason that people tell me that I am luminous or radiant, sometimes—something I have never understood. The luminous moon has sheltered me all along. But, shit, it makes me angry that this is how I came to know God."

"No one," Sandi said, "should have to come to know God this way. What happened to you meant God had to tip his—or her—hand. A child shouldn't have to be confronted with all the power of heaven—it is too much to take in. The Bible is full of places that make clear that seeing God is too much for most of us. The prophets beg to be saved from this vision."

"I'm with them," I said, "but, still, it is better to know."

I went back to the City of Ten Thousand Buddhas two years later to work on this book. Rita and I had been telling each other our stories for twenty years. Our respective theological thinking had evolved as each of us did our work with students, parishioners, and youth. We each had come to deeply value the power of caring community and to respect the difficult task of restoring wholeness and repairing the human capacity for ethical relationship when it has been disrupted by war, racism, homophobia, sexism, or the intimate violations of physical and sexual abuse. We believed that religious language and ritual were critically important in people's ability to name their life experience and negotiate it in ways that would lead to recovery and wellbeing, even in the midst of the complex ambiguities and conflicts of life. We felt the incompleteness of personal healing that ignored the larger social contexts that create cycles of human violence.

At the same time, we knew that the larger social ills we each were dedicated to combating did not only exist "out there." The violence of the world infected our souls, everyone's soul, we thought. A dedicated life must be both a life of active participation in the world and sustained attention to the inner soul-work necessary to become as free as possible from internalized violence.

We said to one another that to live is to be haunted by presence, presence that will not let us rest easy with violence, presence that will not let us become numb to pain, presence that will not let us close ourselves off from our deepest knowing. To be present to life is to be transparent to life-giving grace in many forms, within and surrounding us, even when we are faced with life-threatening violence.

We had decided to write a book exploring these themes. I spent a week at the City of Ten Thousand Buddhas doing research. I took countless notes, reading particularly in the field of biblical studies. At the end of the week, I sent Rita an e-mail summarizing the research. I said it wouldn't be enough to write a book that criticized everything that was wrong with how Christianity spoke about Jesus' crucifixion. We were going to have to find a way to say something about what *saved life* if we were convinced, and we were, that no one was saved by the execution of Jesus. In reflecting on my experience in therapy I concluded my e-mail with the following:

> When I was raped as a child, there was a moment that I have been able to remember in which I was quite sure I was going to die—and perhaps I was, in fact, close to being killed.
>
> I was being orally raped. I couldn't breathe. I was just a small child! Four years old. And the weight of the man on top of me was crushing. In that moment I knew that there was a Presence with me that was "stronger" than the rapist and that could encompass my terror. This Presence had a quality of unbounded compassion for me and unbreakable

connection to me, an encompassing embrace of me and for that matter, of the man raping me. I understood that if I died, I would somehow still be with this Presence, this Presence would "take me up," this Presence was "greater than" death, and "greater than" the power of the man who was raping me.

This Presence could not stop the man from killing me, if he chose to. And, at the same time, it *could* stop him. Because, I knew, if he noticed it he *would* be stopped. He would not be able to continue. You couldn't. It was clear to me. You *couldn't* be aware of this Presence and do what the man was doing to me. He only could do it by not noticing, not knowing. So, this Presence *did* have the power to save me from death and there is a way in which I believe it did. The man did stop short of killing me, and I think it was because some part of him could not ultimately deny the knowledge that he was raping God. Not that I was God, obviously, but that the Presence was there and in raping me he was going against the Presence.

The man was stopped by the Presence, that's what I believe. The Presence saved my life. But he might not have been stopped. He could have killed me. Molesters do kill. The Nazis did kill. Batterers do kill spouses and children. I know that had he killed me, it would have been because he completely denied the Presence. Such denial is entirely possible and happens all the time.

One thing my own experience shows is that extreme danger can be revelatory. Near-death experiences tend to be, apparently. And this was a violent near-death experience. But it still offends me when the murder of Jesus is lauded as revelatory of God's presence—and I'm not sure why. I think it is the pious suggestion that such experiences are, therefore, a blessing. If I hadn't been raped as a child, I wouldn't have experienced the blessing of this divine revelation.

Shit.

I would gladly turn the blessing over to anyone who is willing to live with the curses that have accompanied that violation. And it also troubles me that people would think that God's presence shows up in extremities and emergencies but isn't available all the rest of the time. Somehow that lets those untouched by violence off the hook from the call to reverence the presence of God in all of life; or, it says that only those who have suffered terrible violation have access to knowledge of God. This is an awful idea.

So, if you find me arguing against the theological notion that Jesus' execution is a revelatory gift, you'll understand why. Jesus didn't have to die for us to know that God is present. He didn't have to rise from the

dead for us to know that God's creative power is greater than death. Judaism already affirmed all this, knew all this. Furthermore, *nobody* has to
suffer for God to be made known to us.

As Rita and I talked about this we observed that such awareness of
presence can be fleeting, dimly perceived, jumbled, and intermittent.
Violence can fracture this knowing. It can destroy the numinous
quality of life, as truly as it can place in clear terms the light of presence. We can be so violated that we lose the luminosity in ourselves,
our aliveness scattered to coals and ashes, fragments of broken fire.
We can live in the muddy ashes of a life without presence, dissolve
into the critical acids of self-hatred, or burrow deep into the confines
of that which we can rationally control. Without some glow in the
night, life fades, presence is diminished.

The devastation varies—racial violence, hate crimes, war, rape,
political torture, economic exploitation, state terrorism, emotional
and physical abuse—but all involve the denial of presence. This denial
may be distributed differently, and resisted differently, in various contexts. There is no universal strategy by which the deeds of evil are resisted and life has a chance of being restored. There are only the records of how human beings have recovered and sustained presence,
what Gandhi called "satyagraha," or soul force, what the Gospel of
John calls eternal life or life abundant. Sometimes, we have even accomplished restoration.

Whatever restoration we find comes always with the legacy of the
harm done to us. Nothing erases violence, but, sometimes, the power
of presence gets us through, literally saves us to live on, to heal, to
work for justice.

Even before I began to recover memories of having been sexually
molested I had decided to stop taking communion. I remember one
Sunday sitting in the back of the church when the words of the communion liturgy were being read. An overwhelming feeling came over
me that I had to get out of the sanctuary. The place felt dangerous.
The idea that the sacrifice of somebody was a good idea, to be praised,
suddenly felt directly threatening to me.

It wasn't until several years later that I consciously understood that
I had been treated as a sacrifice—asked to give my life to a man who

needed to make me suffer so he could find release for his suffering. Not participating in communion was an important step. It helped clear a space in my head in which I could face my own life history. I had to get away from the idea of sacrifice as a good thing in order to end the splitting of myself into the part that knew and the part that didn't know.

I also had to find a community of truth. When friends sent me to a support group for people struggling with their response to the effects of alcohol on those they loved, I found a place of unmasked human presence.

Because that group was one in which people didn't hide, I began to learn not to hide. It took me a long time, but I gradually began to tell the truth about my life. It was like learning to speak all over again. The habits of hiding and denying were so old, I didn't know how to speak except in a way that was a kind of lie. I didn't know how to say, "I hurt. I am afraid." I only knew how to say, "I'm fine. Nothing is wrong. Everything is great."

One night a man in the group talked about his efforts to make amends to his children. He was sober now, but during years when he'd been drinking, he had sexually abused his daughters. He spoke with simple honesty about his own past behavior. His sorrow was evident, but he was neither self-pitying nor asking for pity. He had caused his own children great harm. He wasn't asking for forgiveness or understanding. He didn't expect his children to be able to forgive him, but knew that whether they did or didn't was their business, not his. What he was doing was telling the truth, not hiding from himself, from God, from his fellow human beings, or—most important of all—from his children. That's all.

The circle we were sitting in was small. Maybe there were seven of us at the meeting. It was as intimate as a family sitting around the dinner table. Almost as intimate as the setting long ago when I was four years old and Frank had told me to be a good girl and come with him into the bedroom because he had something nice for me in there. That was a lie. And it was a lie at church when the liturgy said it was good that Jesus died on the cross. And my presence at my own family's dinner table had been a lie when I pretended that I was fine, that we were all fine.

But this was the truth. Plain and simple. The man had done irreparable damage, and he knew he'd done it. He admitted he'd done it. He was in grief because he'd done it, and he knew that the damage couldn't be undone by him. He had caused harm he couldn't repair. And it was to people he loved.

At first, I wanted to flee from the group. I was sitting knee-to-knee with a sexual abuser. But then I remembered that he and I were there for the same reason. We were trying to recover from living a lie, living under the weight of denials, splits, avoidance, absence. We were there for each other, all of us in the group, and we told the truth about our lives because telling the truth restored us to the human community. It brought us back from the dead. It was a way of showing up. Of coming back, alive. It made us free.

Not long after that meeting, I was at a worship service. Communion was to be observed. I was preparing to make a quiet exit during one of the hymns, but decided to stay. I knew the worship leader and trusted her. We were sitting in the round in a small chapel. We could see one another's faces in the candle light. Words were spoken that told of Jesus' crucifixion. It was a narrative of lamentation and grief, not praise and thanksgiving. Prayers were offered for victims of violence and abuse, all those who suffer in body, mind, and spirit. Then bread and wine were offered to any who wished, as a sign that there is nourishment for the suffering, comfort for the grieving, and hope that someday all people will gather at one table in peace.

My consciousness slipped into another realm. I felt the presence of Frank. I could see him in the circle across from me. The bread and cup were passed to him. He ate and drank. Then the elements came to me. I ate the bread and drank from the cup. Somewhere deep inside me a noise that had been roaring for years became silent. An old ache, like a stone, began to fall. I returned to normal consciousness. Around me were the quiet voices of familiar friends. I knew that in the end, all there is, is mercy. The promise was true. Weeping may endure for the night, but joy comes in the morning.

CHAPTER 6

The Feast of Epiphany

Rita's Story

> The Lord is my shepherd, I shall not want.
> He makes me lie down in green pastures;
> he leads me beside the still waters;
> he restores my soul.
> Surely goodness and mercy shall follow me
> all the days of my life.
>
> Psalm 23:1–3a, 6a

I stepped out of my sweats into the crisp night air and slid into the velvety lake. In the fall, after the East Texas summer warmed the water, I'd swim in the moonlight, a shimmer on the placid mirror of water. In the deeper middle, the silkiness cooled and chilled me enough to force me back to shore, into my sweats, and home for a hot shower.

The piney woods of Texas have small lakes, forests, rolling hills, and soft sandy soil the color of ripe apricots. On midsummer nights, the exuberant bellowings of bullfrogs echo across the water surfaces, sounding boards that carry the competing croaks for miles. Fireflies glow in the underbrush around the ponds, as if the stars danced in joy to this ancient amphibious mating ritual.

Unpaved roads cut the woods. During the day, trucks stir up dust as they visit oil derricks to collect their sticky black treasure. The sandy back roads were a great jogging surface.

I had left Claremont in August 1981 to teach at a small black college in rural East Texas. I had never lived in a place so isolated. It was beautiful. I rented a condo in a resort community twelve miles from the college. In summer the resort swelled into a bustling vacation site. Few, however, lived there year-round.

I enjoyed the privacy of my retreat. Many mornings, I drank coffee on the deck, listened to the jays and watched the lake, which was just visible through the trees and the dun-colored condos. With little to do for entertainment and no friends yet to speak of, I started jogging.

After a day of teaching, I'd lace up my Avias and set off on the sandy trails. My shoes made a puff-puff whisper to accompany my breathing and thoughts. At mile four on my six-mile run, I'd turn onto a long stretch of rural highway that angled west and drifted very slowly downhill. At the turn, I'd start a mile sprint, pulled forward by the golden light at day's end, shining off the trees and road surface. I'd speed into the orange orb of sun as if it would swallow me in its glow. My body and soul breathed light, swallowing it in great gulps of joy.

T.C. was a five-hour drive away. When I arrived in Texas that fall, I had just ended a brief affair. The intensity of it made me painfully aware of the emotional emptiness of my marriage. When my lover and I parted, I felt bereft of light and dishonest betraying T.C. My first few months in Texas, T.C. and I spent weekends either at my place or his. These were times of anguish, as I sought to ease myself out of our marriage. I was startled by how fiercely T.C. tried to hold on and saddened by the intensity of his emotion when mine was gone. Eventually, I filed for divorce.

As my life in Texas took shape, I got to know some interesting colleagues, though feminists were scarce in rural East Texas, even at the college. My regular lunch companions were Parkey, a Disciples minister and a development officer at the college, and Pritchy, the chair of the department of education, both native Texans. We frequented a local diner that served hot lunch specials like chicken fried steak and meatloaf.

UNLIKELY LOVE

Pritchy quickly became more than a lunch companion. He was as different from T.C. as I could imagine. T.C. had been a scientist who dressed in jeans and T-shirts for the lab and surrendered his thinning, unruly hair occasionally to an indifferent haircut. His shoes were scruffy, and he had a vaguely rumpled air. The only suit T.C. owned was the light blue one he bought for our wedding.

Pritchy favored charcoal gray, navy, or chocolate French-cut designer jackets in cashmere, merino, or silk. The close cut emphasized his tall, lanky frame. His khaki, navy, or gray slacks had knife sharp creases, and he preferred glove-soft tasseled loafers of Italian leather in black or brown. The cuff links on his laundered shirts matched the tack on his silk ties. Even when Pritchy sported jeans and cowboy boots, he wore a starched shirt. His jeans were pressed with front creases, and the only T-shirts he wore were underwear. He had blue eyes, a neatly clipped salt-and-pepper beard, and dark brown, thick, wavy, well-styled hair, with a touch of gray. His words were marked by the long, flat vowels of native Texans, and he spoke in the husky voice of a heavy smoker.

Pritchy's sneakers were the least worn item in his closet. He avoided most activities that required "exertion." While he was a good dancer and liked an occasional walk, Pritchy's main form of exercise was alternately lifting a coffee cup and a cigarette to his lips while holding the newspaper.

He was eleven years older than I and divorced. His younger son, Parc, ten, lived with his wife; Derek, sixteen, lived with him. Between his career as a high-school English teacher and a college professor, Pritchy worked as a hairdresser. He left public school teaching when one of his favorite Hispanic students came home from Vietnam with no legs and proudly showed him the small medal he'd won. He couldn't stand the sorrow of such waste, and he decided he preferred to cut hair rather than watch the boys he educated come home in body bags. But eventually, styling hair bored him, so he went back to school for a doctorate in education.

Pritchy's research focused on ethnic minorities, long before it was a trend, which made him unusual for a white male in the field of education. He had learned to care about racial justice because of Thomas Jefferson Johnson, a black fellow student. They met in 1959, when they attended summer graduate school at the University of Texas. T. J. was a French teacher in a segregated high school in Abilene, Texas. Pritchy was chagrined that T. J.'s vocabulary far exceeded his and that T. J.'s French was fluent. Pritchy felt far less sophisticated and intelligent than the first black man he came to know well.

As their friendship developed, T. J. asked him to join a regular, weekly protest line attempting to integrate a movie theater in Austin. Pritchy describes his political awakening:

> One night policemen leaped from trucks, swinging their nightsticks. I had never seen policemen swing nightsticks as they plunged into a panicked crowd, hitting men and women in their stomachs and heads. I was

terrified by the shrieks and cries from the . . . protesters and even more terrified by the blood that was being splattered on me as the police hit people, coming closer and closer to me where I was pinned by the crowd against the building. I could see that these uniformed men were not just trying to break up a protest. They wanted to kill us. It was that night that I realized for the first time, that police . . . were there to preserve a racist social order, not to protect protesters who were exercising their Constitutional right to assemble peacefully.★

Pritchy and T.J. were not the usual students who attended UT Austin in 1959. T.J. was black. Pritchy had grown up "poor white trash," raised on a farm by a strong mother and a dissipated, philandering father. Pritchy understood what being an underdog meant and spent his academic career researching minority education.

He invited me over for dinner the first time I met him. He had an attractive house decorated in matched shades of blue. Oil paintings hung on the walls. The central, free-standing fireplace dominated the living room and behind its stone back was a peaked-ceiling dining room, ringed by lush plants, with a wall of glass that looked onto a large deck. I appreciated his ability to create a home, his attention to physical things and to beauty. Pritchy cooked a standard Texas meal: steak, baked potatoes, corn on the cob, and an iceberg lettuce salad. As we talked over dinner, I got a taste of his humor as we joked about the pretentiousness of the college's administrators.

Pritchy took delight in the ridiculousness of life, including his own. His son Derek was a fundamentalist and very involved with his Southern Baptist church; Parc followed his brother's lead. Pritchy, of course, was an atheist—reading Bertrand Russell in college had convinced him there was no God. Such ironies amused him. He figured his boys would outgrow their adolescent religious rebellion eventually.

He had a wonderful, uproarious laugh, and his sense of fun was unpredictable. One Friday, during a rare winter blizzard, we decided to see a movie in Tyler, forty minutes away, the nearest theater. As the more seasoned winter driver, I took the wheel. We skidded our way through the thickly falling snow, and Pritchy invented outrageous stories of the fate that would befall us for our foolhardiness. We

★G. Pritchy Smith "Who Shall Have the Moral Courage to Heal Racism in America?" *Multicultural Education,* Spring 1998: 4–10.

laughed the whole way to Tyler and back, driving through a foot of unplowed snow.

Pritchy had few defensive boundaries or fears; he was direct and honest. If he was uncertain or nervous about something, he said so, and we talked about it. Pritchy included me unselfconsciously in the details of his life, inviting me to his place, introducing me to his sons. I met Derek on my first visit to the house and Parc the first weekend he visited.

The four of us went camping and tubing on the San Marcos River, visited Six Flags, and engaged in other activities one does with boys that age. I attended two seasons of high-school basketball games because Derek was a starting varsity player. His sons and I developed our own relationship around religion.

The boys' earnest religious quality echoed a sensibility in their father that lay under his cynicism. His openness kept Pritchy from succumbing to a world-weariness that sometimes weighed him down. He had a large heart, a capacity for pleasure, generosity, and joy that made life with him lively and emotionally satisfying.

Unlike T.C. and other liberal white men I had known, Pritchy held no illusions about being a good person. Instead of trying to keep me happy, Pritchy was honest about his feelings and limitations. I knew that he had had many sexual dalliances while married, which worried me as a feminist. I wondered if he saw women as sexual objects, if he was habitually covert. His descriptions of his liaisons indicated that he took sensual and aesthetic pleasure in women and enjoyed pleasing them, so I decided to withhold judgment. I was intrigued by his openness about his behavior. I trusted his lack of pretense. He didn't present himself as the kind of man a feminist might like. On the other hand, he was attentive, generous, and thoughtful. I enjoyed being with him, despite my misgivings about his profligate past and double standards.

When his wife divorced him, she received custody of both boys. But Derek had chosen to live with him, which pleased Pritchy enormously. He bitterly resented his wife having an affair and hated her new husband. When I noted the inconsistency of his double standard about marital faithfulness, he insisted women and men did not engage in sex for the same reasons, and it was more serious for a woman to stray. "Who, then," I inquired, "were all those women who happily fucked you in one-night stands?" I didn't think it was fair of him to hold women to a standard of behavior he was unwilling to live up to himself.

When we began to spend more time together and our emotional bonds deepened, Pritchy asked me what the rules of our relationship were to be. I was brought up short by this bald-faced question. I didn't think about love in terms of rules.

I wanted to be honest. I struggled to explain my apprehensions about both of us seeing other people without the other knowing. I knew that I didn't want to repeat my betrayal of T.C. I was unwilling to be in such pain again. My affair had not only distanced me from T.C., but also immersed me in self-reproach and despair. I did not want to hate myself or to be deceiving or deceived. He asked me point-blank how I would feel about him being with other women.

"Scared," I said, "my gut churns when I think about it. But being kept in the dark about it would be worse. I'd feel betrayed and angry. If you're going to have sex with other women, I want to know so I can make choices for my life based on what's really going on. I don't know if I'd stay in this relationship, but I want to decide on knowing, not on ignorance. I'm more likely to walk out if you lie to me than if you screw someone else. But if there are to be any rules about this, they apply to us both. No double standards." My answer brought him up short. He decided he preferred to try monogamy, rather than risk my being intimate with others.

Pritchy was emotionally open, which helped me to live more completely out of the self I had discovered at NCCJ. If I was angry, frightened, or hurt, I said so. Feelings flowed—we occasionally argued openly. The emotional intensity was a welcome change from T.C.'s obsequiousness.

I flourished in the open, passionate, affectionate atmosphere of our life together. For the first time in an intimate relationship, I felt safe enough to talk about fears and pain. I discovered the power of physical intimacy grounded in emotional connection. I knew love without doubt.

Eighteen months into our relationship, I was fired from the college for insubordination. I went out of town to a feminist meeting they had tried to prevent me from attending. I collected unemployment and moved in with Pritchy to save money.

My termination made Pritchy's association with me difficult. The college treated him as if he were harboring a fugitive. The college was indifferent to academic protocols and policies and didn't give tenure. He started looking for other jobs, but senior positions were hard to find for a white male who worked in minority education. We worried about what might happen to him.

I fluctuated between anger at the college and despair that the time, money, and energy I had invested in a doctoral program might have been wasted. Teaching jobs for a minority female doctoral student, and a feminist at that, were scarce. I sent my vita to every school that advertised a position in my field.

In April 1983, after a woman resigned late in the semester, Valparaiso University flew me to Indiana for an interview. The dean offered me a two-year position. I accepted. In August Pritch and I packed up a rented truck, and I drove north.

I missed Pritchy terribly. We wrote long letters every day and talked several times a week. I spent the first half of that year in Valparaiso profoundly lonely, but lonely in a way different from how I felt living with T.C.

The moral quality of my relationship with T.C. was goodness, but his goodness confined me. In trying to live up to it, I could not face the troubling parts of myself I needed to know. I kept hidden what hurt me, what kept me alienated from him and myself. I felt I would never be good enough for him to love me; I was afraid of being discovered. I was lonely for myself, for T.C., and for the warmth of intimacy and love.

The moral quality of my relationship with Pritchy was honesty. In the emotional storms of our life together, I found the courage to expose much I had learned to hide, to work through my anger because he refused to capitulate to me. Pritchy answered back with an emotional intensity that created a deep passion and connection in our life together. I could ask for what I wanted, and be clear about my limits. I learned to trust honesty, to forgive hurts, and to admit failures. Our separation deprived me of that daily warmth. I was lonely for his presence.

THE DISCOVERY

The call came in early September 1983. My sister Jo Ann said quietly, "Mom is in a coma, and the doctors think she won't last long. I think you'd better come home now." I wondered what to do. Classes were to start that coming week.

I called my department chair and explained. He suggested I begin my classes a week later. I caught the first flight from Chicago to Los Angeles the next day. Jo Ann picked me up at the airport in the smoggy fall heat of Southern California. We drove up Cajon Pass to Barstow across the searing desert vistas.

When I arrived at her bedside, my mother drifted into semi-consciousness, not opening her eyes, but trembling and stirring. Jo Ann said firmly, "Mom, Rita's here. Can you hear me? Rita's here now." My mother nodded her quivering head and slipped back into a coma.

Jo Ann showed me a letter taped on the wall opposite the bed. My mother had looked at it whenever she awoke. I sent it when she had entered the hospital for the last time. In it, I thanked her for being a wonderful mother and said I loved her.

I had difficulty writing the letter. It felt only partially true, even vaguely dishonest. I didn't mention my sense of abandonment. I felt I had thanked her excessively and falsely—an act of rudeness in Japan. Now, as she lay dying, I thought it was all right. It had made her happy, maybe eased her departure. Only later would I know how much she had done for me, and how much I would believe what I wrote, living into its truth.

I took a turn at my mother's side the next morning so Jo and Ray could shower and change. The soap operas were suspended for the appearance of Jean Kirkpatrick at the UN to protest a Soviet attack on a Korean civilian jet. Her gravelly, angry words split the silence, covering the sound of my mother's shallow, labored breathing. I held her cool, flaccid hand.

My mother's body was ravaged by cancer that took half her face, part of her spine, and, finally, most of her lungs. I wanted to release her spirit from the torment of that body. With steady, measured deep breaths, I imagined my mother's spirit leaving her body and entering me through our hands. Her only movement was the slow, barely perceptible lifting and falling of her chest.

Jo and Ray returned. We watched Ayako through the early afternoon. Her breaths grew intermittent, her passing marked by soft, sad sighs. Her doctor and I stood at the foot of the bed, Jo and Ray on either side. Finally, after several minutes, we knew she had taken her last breath. The doctor asked if we wanted her on a respirator. "No," we said. "Let her go." She died at 4 P.M.

We waited for her Japanese friends to arrive. They maintained a steady stream of visitors to her bedside every evening, keeping her company, taking turns in small groups. Around half past four, we heard five of them coming down the hall to her room. My sister told them she had died. They wept at the news.

One of them brought a letter from Hideko in Hawaii, a neighbor who had been my mother's good friend for years. The group gathered around my mother's body and read the letter to her. Hideko wrote that she hoped my mother would be able to join her soon for a walk on the beach. The women wept, then sang my mother's favorite Japanese folk songs and hymns.

Music had bound them together at celebrations. My mother had been an important member of their community of immigrant women. She had held dinners, taught Japanese Sunday school, and organized a booth at an annual food fair that raised money for foreign exchange students. She and her friends took pride in raising the most money every year with their teriyaki chicken wings and stuffed fried wontons.

As I watched them at Ayako's bedside, I realized she was more a person to them than she was to me. She was my mother, but I never knew her as a friend. I felt sad about the distances between us and grateful she had had good friends.

The next morning, the stark desert sunlight spilled through the window across my mother's leaf green bedspread. Jo, Ray, and I sat in her bedroom looking for the plot number for her burial. Jo held a gray metal box that contained packets of important papers and said, "I know the number is in here because I saw it a couple of months ago when I looked in this box. It's with the mortuary papers." She passed each of us a manilla envelope to inspect. Mine was faded with age and a little frayed. I opened the packet, removed a sheet, and unfolded it.

At the top of the page was printed: ADOPTION PAPERS FOR RITA NAKASHIMA. I wondered who she could be. Her first name was identical to mine, but her last name was my mother's maiden name. Below the name, these words:

Date: September 15, 1958
Birth Mother: Ayako Nakashima

Adopted Father: Roy Grady Brock
Child: Rita Nakashima
Birthplace: Fukuoka, Japan

I was looking at my own adoption papers. As the information slowly sank in, I blurted, "I'm adopted!"

Jo looked up and said, "WHAT?"

"I'm adopted! Look!" I handed her the paper.

"Oh my God," she said, "you *are* adopted!" Ray had the same astonished response. Jo swore that the envelope of papers had not been in the box before. My mother put them there within the past two months.

Why had my mother done such a thing? Why leave me with devastating news she knew I would find only after she was gone? She could have called me or told me many times when I visited her. Was she afraid I would reject Roy altogether, or be angry with her? After all these years, why did I need to know at all?

"I always thought *I* was adopted!" said my large, hazel-eyed, auburn-haired sister. "You looked like mom, so until Ray was born, and looked like me, I thought I was adopted." At five-foot-four, I was two inches taller than my mother and had her coloring: black hair, brown eyes, olive skin. Jo was taller and looked white, except for her almond-shaped eyes, which I lacked. She and Ray tended toward corpulence, like Roy, while my mother was slight.

It never occurred to me I might be adopted. Certainly, my size and coloring made me my mother's child, and, unlike Jo, I had memories of Japan, but I thought my freckles made me enough Roy's daughter that I never doubted him. Now, at thirty-three years of age, I discovered that I was my father's stepchild, a half-sibling to Jo and Ray. My parents had always called me Rita Brock, which wasn't legal until my adoption in 1958. The meaning of my life shifted, like a house that moved off its hidden foundation, exposing the old stones underneath.

"Who was my birth father?" I wondered. None of the papers in the metal box told us; we pored over each one, hoping for clues. Bob and Blossom Allen, friends of my parents, would be at the funeral. Bob had been a medic and had met Blossom, a Japanese nurse like my mother, when they had worked with my parents at the U.S. military hospital in Fukuoka. I decided to ask them.

In bed that night, I lay thinking. I floated in my own time capsule, trying to understand how I had been born. Did my birth father know I existed? Had he rejected me? Was I really half white?

Being half-white had always felt strange to me, an identity I was supposed to feel and know, but couldn't quite grasp. I didn't look 100 percent Japanese and probably wasn't half-black. Hispanic? But what were the odds of a Japanese woman, in postwar Japan, meeting an Hispanic man? No, I thought, not Hispanic, but what? Filipino?

After the memorial service, in my mother's backyard, I sat across the picnic table from Bob and Blossom. During a pause in the conversation, I said "I have an odd question for you." They glanced at each other, puzzled. I rushed on, "Do you know who my father was?"

They looked surprised. "Your mother didn't tell you?" Bob asked.

"No."

"Well, we know Ayako always meant to tell you. We don't remember your father's name. But he was a nice man, a small, wiry medic in the U.S. Army." Bob paused a minute to think. "His name was Rodriguez, Mario or something. He was Puerto Rican. His tour of duty ran out so he had to leave your mom."

"Yes," added Blossom, "I know she meant to tell you. I'm surprised she never told you. I'm sorry we can't remember more. It was a long time ago."

"I knew I wasn't white!" I was flooded with relief.

Bob looked startled at my vehemence and said, as if to comfort me, "Well, Puerto Ricans are Caucasian."

I let it go. Maybe he thought I was offended at not being white. My ambivalence about believing I was half-white was difficult to explain. It had to do with the mismatch between the way I was treated because of my appearance and genes that neither protected me from racism nor felt like a recognizable identity. But my dilemma was clarified. It was reassuring to know at least that much—that how I felt and looked matched who I was. But it was not enough. Who, beyond being a Puerto Rican soldier, was my father?

I had always wanted a Japanese middle name. Rita Brock gave no indication of my ethnicity. When I had mentioned my problems with it to Sister Circle, they had suggested I add a Japanese name. Something in me resisted. I wanted my Japanese name to mean a relationship, something given to me for a reason. I decided to wait for the right name to find me. Now I knew: Nakashima had been my legal last name for my first eight years. I retrieved it. I had a Japanese name.

A week after boarding the plane to Los Angeles, I returned to Valparaiso with my life in turmoil. My mother died. My father was a stepfather. I had a different father I had never met.

My life was cleaved into pieces. I could not hold it together. I taught my classes in a state of numbness, barely able to function. Wednesday evening, I took a shower, sat on my futon naked, and lit candles in the dark bedroom. I sang, over and over, a Sister Circle song as I held myself and rocked, "All shall be well, all shall be well, all manner of things shall be well." I sang it as a dirge.

I needed to speak to my mother, to tell her I was angry about how she told me about my father, to tell her how much I would miss her. I began a letter to her in the candlelight. As I wrote in fits and starts, I sobbed. Finally, an hour later, I lay back on the futon, hot and exhausted, tears leaking from my eyes.

As I stared at the flickering candle flames, I felt a breeze come from the hallway where no breeze could be. I looked toward the door and, in the semi-darkness, I saw my mother in her young, cancer-free body. She floated into the room naked, parallel to the floor. She came to a halt about four-feet over my body, hovering above me. Her eyes met mine. "It will be all right," she said. Her legs lowered from her hips slowly until our toes met. Her toes were warm. Her body slipped into mine, and I felt a warm calm enter me.

I took another shower, went to bed, slept soundly, and awakened feeling fresh and alive.

I do not know what I think of life after death. I do not live with the thought of what will come after I have died. If a conscious personal life transcends my physical body, I am prepared to discern what to do when that time comes.

For those who remain, staying alive is hard-earned when frost kills out of season. My mother was barely fifty-five. I lost someone I loved at the core of my being. Though I knew she would die, I was not prepared to lose her, especially now that she was the only source of knowledge about my father. After her death, sadness smothered me; my core was ashes.

Mourning cut through my attempt to carry on with daily life as if I were the same. Pain lanced the sadness and freed me. Life would go on, not as before, but it would go on. This I knew. I knew with certainty that there is life after death for those who remain. Grief brought me back to life.

I have no explanation for what happened when I saw my mother: I was not asleep—I was awake with my eyes open. I felt the breeze; I heard her voice; I felt her toes touch mine; I felt warmed. Perhaps the intensity of my grief caused me to hallucinate, but that is too easy and dismissive an explanation for what I experienced. My soul was restored to peace and life. I do not know if grief alone can generate such grace, such fire.

I spent my earliest years with people for whom spirits of the dead are ordinary appearances, summoned in morning rituals to bring protection, comfort, and good luck. The dead provide a legacy of presence that folds tragedy into the ongoing world of relationships among the living—life as a ceaseless chain of being. My mother's spirit linked me to that legacy.

THE EPIPHANY

I plunged into a demanding teaching schedule and focused on getting through the semester. I was supported from afar by Pritchy. I resolved to search for my birth father when I had a break the following summer. I would begin my inquiries through my congressman and Department of the Army records.

I had a metal box of papers I took from my mother's bedroom, stuffed with envelopes, old records of school reports, citizenship papers, and travel documents. In one packet, I found correspondence between my father and the Immigration and Naturalization Service that traced the saga of our sojourn in Okinawa and Roy's repeated attempts to clear me for entry into the United States. Included were the letter from Senator John Stennis and the affidavit Roy signed.

Jo called around Halloween with the news that she'd found another box of old papers; inside was a thin ricepaper document in Japanese. Her voice carried the excitement and intrigue of a half-formed discovery, "Right in the middle of this paper are the words—in English!—'Clemente Morales Torres.' I think it's your birth certificate, and Clemente is your father!"

Around Thanksgiving Jo called again. "I was looking through another box of Mom's stuff. I found a really old address book. I've never seen it before, but it has a lot of Japanese addresses in it. Inside I found the names of Miguel and Maria Morales Torres. Their address is Box 51C, Dorado, Puerto Rico. Maybe they're relatives of Clemente's, like a brother and sister or his parents."

My response was shocked silence. When I finally spoke, I blurted, "Dorado!?! I'm going there after Christmas this year! I was invited to a theological conference last February. Pritchy's going with me, after we do Christmas in Texas with Parc and Derek. I can't believe you have an address in Dorado! I made plans before I had any idea I had a personal connection to Puerto Rico."

I sent a return-receipt letter addressed to Clemente Morales Torres at the Dorado address. I explained the circumstances that indicated he might be my father and asked if I could meet him. No return receipt arrived. I left for Texas with the mysteries unresolved. Who was my father? Why had he been a secret? Was he unaware he had a daughter? Was he ashamed he had me? Would he be angry that I'd looked for him? Was he alive? Would he be in Dorado? Who were Miguel and Maria?

I attended the conference impatiently. Pritch spent the time lounging on the beach and playing detective. He asked several of the hotel staff how to locate Clemente in Dorado. None of them knew him, but they had suggestions for finding him. We arranged a ride into town the moment the conference ended.

A waiter at the hotel had suggested an old, well-established restaurant in town where Clemente might be known. The hotel van deposited us on Dorado's main street in front of the restaurant. We went inside and asked a waiter if he knew Clemente Morales Torres. No, he told us, but the cook might. The waiter disappeared into the kitchen. A young man appeared who said, "I know his brother Miguel; just a minute." He left the restaurant. While Pritch and I stood near the entrance wondering what to do next, the waiter reappeared with a short, dapper-looking man in a panama hat, a young woman holding his arm.

"This is his cousin Elauterio from New Jersey," the waiter said. Elauterio explained he didn't speak English, so his niece from Dorado was going to translate. I asked if he knew Clemente Morales Torres. "Yes, he's my cousin," Elauterio replied in English.

"How old is he," I asked.

"About fifty-five."

"Was he in Japan during the occupation?"

"Yes."

"I think he might be my father."

With a thoughtful nod, Elauterio said matter-of-factly, "Yes, I think so."

Before I could respond to Elauterio, the cook returned breathless with a piece of paper. "His brother Miguel is not in his store, but he will be home after four o'clock, so call the number on this paper then."

Elauterio took the paper and interjected, "I take you to his house, come on."

Pritch and I followed Elauterio and his niece to the sunbaked street and into a grocery store on the corner. An older man stood behind the counter. "This, your uncle Ernesto," Elauterio declared. Ernesto and I shook hands, though both of us looked bewildered. Then Pritch and I were hurried out behind the store to Elauterio's white Toyota.

As Pritch and I sat in the back seat, I had a fleeting thought. "What if they are setting us up to mug us?" I had traveled all over the world, and I knew American tourists were targets for scams. It was not a particularly prudent move for Pritch and me to turn ourselves over to strangers who went along with everything I said. I expected the hunt for my father to be difficult and, thus far, it seemed suspiciously easy. But my curiosity and hope overrode my cautions. I decided Pritch and I were bigger than Elauterio and his niece, so, if they tried anything, we could probably handle it.

We roared about a mile to the edge of town, to an area of white walls with a security gate. Elauterio said something in Spanish to the guard, who waived us in. We sped down the block and turned into the driveway of a large white stucco house with wrought iron grillwork over the windows, doorways, and patio entrances. A middle-aged, pleasant-looking woman with short black hair hosed the driveway. She walked over to Elauterio's window and listened to his explanation. She looked at me in the back seat. For an awkward moment we stared at each other. Pritch interjected, "We think Clemente might be her father."

The woman's reply in English was prosaic, "I think so. I'm your aunt Rosa. Why don't you come in the house?"

As we exited the back seat, a yellow Toyota screeched to a halt at the curb behind us. A woman leapt out and ran up the driveway, her long curly black hair streaming behind her. She grabbed me in a tight hug, and sobbed. "Our prayers are answered! You've come! Praise the Lord, our prayers are answered!"

I pulled back astounded, "You know about me?"

"YES, of *course!!!* I'm your aunt Vilma! We've been praying for you to come!"

I thought, "Who is this strange hysterical woman and why is she sobbing? How could she be my aunt? How did she get here so fast? What is going on here?"

Pritchy interjected, "What was her mother's maiden name?"

"Nakashima, Ayako Nakashima—SEE!!" As she answered, Vilma yanked a wallet out of her purse. She flipped it open to a plastic pocket and held it up. My eyes focused on my baby picture. My mother had mounted the same one in a family album. My heart raced as I processed what this photo meant.

"Oh my God!," I said, "You *are* the right family!"

"YES, of course!!!" Vilma shouted and hugged me again, *"We've been praying for you to come!"*

Rosa, the wife of my father's younger brother Miguel, herded us into the house. Waves of people began to arrive, cousins, aunts, and uncles. Word spread by phone that the "Japan-niece" had arrived. Vilma explained that Clemente drove a taxicab in Manhattan and wouldn't be home until morning. She left him a message, "Found your daughter Rita, call me."

According to Vilma, Clemente lived with my mother until I was six months old. After he was sent to Korea, my mother corresponded with my Puerto Rican family for another two years. Hence, the baby photo. Vilma and Carmen, the youngest of eleven, were still living at home when I was born. They had kept the letters and photos my mother mailed to that old Dorado address. They were deeply attached to me and my mother and sad that she died before they met her.

Prolonged pandemonium ensued as more and more relatives arrived and wanted to hear the story of my life. Finally, Vilma announced, "You have to meet your grandparents."

"They are still alive?" I was astonished.

"Yes, your grandfather is eighty-three and has prayed every night before he slept that he would not die before he saw his first grandchild," Vilma teared up as she said this. "He lives near San Juan, a half-hour away. Your grandmother is also alive, but she has hardening of the arteries and can't remember very much. We will take you there. We will call and tell them we are coming."

A fleet of Toyotas drove the ocean shore road to Levittown on the edge of San Juan. We arrived at a small lime green stucco house trimmed with the wrought iron found on Puerto Rican houses. At the door, an old, short, leathery brown-skinned man with thin gray hair and thick glasses greeted us. "This is your abuelo Miguel," Vilma said quietly, "He cannot see well, but I told him who you are." Abuelo Miguel took me in a tight embrace and wept quietly for several min-utes.

When he let me go, Vilma took us inside and sat us down on the couch in the living room. After we were settled, she led a tiny, stooped, gray-haired, freckled old woman to me, "This is your abuela Maria. She is senile, so she thinks you are your mother." Abuela Ma-ria's eyes held a vague, faraway lost look, as if she couldn't quite focus them. I thought, "At least she's tracking the right story. She's just a generation behind." Abuela Maria beamed at me with a huge, nearly toothless smile, and said something in Spanish, which was accompa-nied by a powerful garlic breath.

I sat between my grandparents on the couch, each holding one of my hands. Everyone talked excitedly in Spanish. I couldn't under-stand anything. I felt bewildered and swallowed by something I could not comprehend, a ferocity of emotion I did not share.

Vilma disappeared down a hall. In a few minutes, she emerged from the back of the house with the mirror off a dresser. "See," she said, "this is the mirror of your grandmother. She was so sure you would come that she did not pray. She put your pictures on this mirror and looked at them every day so she would not forget you." In a ring around the mirror were dozens of my baby pictures, from birth to age two, copies of the same photos my mother had in her albums.

I like to think God might be like this: a presence whom we have never seen—perhaps do not know exists—but who has loved us from the beginning. Who puts, on a mirror, images of us at our most tender and vulnerable and wants us to be well, to thrive, and to be protected from harm. I like to imagine God with her wrinkled, freckled face peering at us, remembering us, loving us, hoping for us, embracing us with a twinkling gaze of joy and concern, without our ever needing to know. God's presence in that moment was my grandmother's smiling face welcoming me home from far away.

I realized I belonged to people who had embraced me without question, without ever knowing me personally. They simply accepted that I existed and that they should care about me. I felt as if a huge sea of love surrounded me. The love was enormous and amorphous, untied to me personally, yet able to encompass me when I appeared.

Looking at those photographs on the dresser mirror, I had a glimpse of life so much larger than my own, I could not comprehend it. I sensed that no matter what happened, a discernable, enlivening, creative presence underlying all things embraced me and wished me well. I had known it only faintly, with deep doubts. Yet I had trusted it beyond all reason, in the same way I trusted that moment of grief when my mother came to me and brought me a renewed life. I live without certainty of the existence of that presence. Trying to grasp it is like staring directly at an object in the dark—it disappears. Turning away puts it dimly into my peripheral vision. In unexpected moments, I feel that presence at the edges of my consciousness, sustaining my life.

I have felt this presence, always, from as early as I have memories, a watchful, caring, calm presence, like a soft breeze. It opens me to the natural world, it hovers in my dreams, and it appears in intimate moments of care. I have known it in love and physical intimacy and in aloneness. I have felt it in moments of ritual and worship. I know no other thing called spirit except this presence that has bound me to so much life. "Surely goodness and mercy shall follow me all the days of my life."

Somehow, my life is marked by this legacy of presence, people who wished me well without ever knowing me. And this is how I can speak of God: a presence gradually unfolded by life in its richness and tragedies, its devastating losses and its abundance; a power calling us into a fullness of living; a passion for life, for good and ill; an unquenchable fire at the core of life, glimpsed in light and shadows.

My Puerto Rican family prayed for me all those years. I was touched by their faithfulness to my well-being and by their welcome. Their love and the commitment of my parents marked my life. Even when I was forced to cross cultures and endure racist hostility and even when I was frightened or despairing, I knew these things would not destroy me. That confidence was not part of my mask of competence and achievement, but something deeper and quieter. Even at those moments, and there were many, when I felt utterly alone and frightened, some other part of me said I would be all right.

But the story of my life and family is also marked by failure. Clemente failed to remain in touch with my mother and me. The U.S. military deliberately forced us apart. Until he converted to Evangelical Protestantism late in his life, my grandfather was unfaithful in his marriage and violent toward my grandmother and his children. That legacy of violence marks them all, from the failure to keep commitments to the vicissitudes of psychological instability. Roy failed to understand the effects of his violence on me. My parents failed to tell me the truth about my life before they died, so I am left with an aching void where questions swirl without answers. Pieces of my life will never be put together. There is much I will never know. There is truth that will never be reclaimed, sadness and loss unassuaged.

After I met my grandparents, the entourage of relatives escorted me to the home of my Aunt Delia and her husband Modesto. They insisted Pritchy and I cancel our room at the hotel the next day and stay with them. Vilma and Carmen delivered us back to the hotel around midnight, exhilarated and exhausted.

They came for us at ten the next morning. They told me to call Clemente collect in New York. He and I talked for an hour as he cried and told me how much I meant to him, how he had to leave my mother and me, and how he had intended to write to us. He promised to visit me as soon as I got home.

I had wondered and puzzled for four months about who this man might be, afraid to hope for very much, certain I would be disappointed. I never thought he would be waiting for thirty-three years, longing for me to be back in his life. He said he considered hiring a detective to find me, not to meet me, but just so he could see that I was all right. He was afraid if he tried to meet me, it might ruin my life. I was touched by his concern, but everything felt unreal, like a dream from which I would awaken. I felt odd talking to a stranger about my family and life, a man who had intense feelings for me while I had little for him. I felt dazed as Pritch and I checked out and walked to the car with our bags.

For our few remaining days in Puerto Rico, Vilma and Carmen planned a grand tour for us. It began in Dorado with a stop at a large abandoned house on risers at the edge of the sea, on Industria Street # 37, Box 51C, my grandparents' old house. The letter I sent was still in the mailbox, unopened, unclaimed, a small, searching missive of longing and hope. I put it in my purse.

We drove south one day to the dry side of the island, boarded a boat after dark under a new moon and saw tiny phosphorescent creatures light up the sea like shooting stars. A trail of sparkling diamonds marked our wake and outlined the fish swimming below the surface. When we scooped water, the stars in the sky had fallen into the liquid cupped in our palms, tiny sparkles captured for a moment by our astonished wonder.

The next day we went to the rain forest and hiked its lush trails of green foliage and babbling waters. A sixteen-year-old daughter of my uncle Ernesto joined us for the hike. Vilma led the way; we followed, with Pritchy bringing up the rear. At a resting point on a steep part of the trail, I waited for Pritch on a bench overlooking a small waterfall. He sat, "Yup, you definitely belong to this family. I've been watching all of you climb ahead of me, and you all have the same ass."

Our last night in Puerto Rico was the Feast of Epiphany. Delia and Modesto roasted a pig in the backyard, and traditional Puerto Rican food emerged from the kitchen on huge heaped platters. A mariachi band played. I danced with my grandfather, with my uncles, with Pritchy, and with cousins. We celebrated into the wee hours, and I was the guest of honor.

The next morning Vilma and Carmen took us to the airport. They extracted a promise that I would visit again soon. On the plane ride to Dallas, Pritch and I relived the highlights of the week. Neither of us could digest all that had happened: the coincidence of being in Dorado, of walking unaware into the waiting arms of my family, of being the sudden answer to thirty-three years of prayer, and the feelings of my relatives, their unflagging hope and wild joy. The season of Epiphany had overtaken us all.

MEETING CLEMENTE

I returned to Indiana to start the spring semester and waited for Clemente, but he never quite got around to coming. I had looked forward to his visit. I felt a taste of my mother's disappointment. Three months later, I had to attend a meeting in New York, so I arranged to spend a couple of days with him. He met me at the airport.

As I stepped out of the end of the jetway, a short, gray-haired man waited for me. He held a picture in his hand and walked toward me. We looked into each other's eyes. I could see I had his eyes.

I stared into a stranger's face; yet it was so like my own. I wondered what the resemblance meant, where it would lead us. His gaze was sad, tentative, and hopeful. Mine was guarded, cloaked in the disappointment of wanting a father who loved me, but having one who did not keep his commitments. His eyes filled with tears. The truth sank in. He really was my birth father.

"Rita?" he asked. I nodded. He hugged me and wept.

It was an anticlimactic meeting for me, subdued in comparison to my reception in Puerto Rico and dampened by my disappointment in his broken promise. It was hard to see where this meeting would lead us.

Clemente drove me to an apartment in Queens, the home of his fourth wife Beatrice. He took me on a tour of Manhattan in his yellow cab and told me about his life. He was alternately dispassionately realistic and vividly hyperbolic. On the G.I. Bill, he attended law school at the University of Wisconsin, Madison, where he'd met his first wife, whom he described as a superstitious German Catholic. He said she tried to run over him with a car. My father is an atheist, so the match may have been doomed from the start. He left her and their four children after fifteen years of an emotionally volatile marriage and went back to Puerto Rico.

While he practiced criminal law in San Juan, he married two beautiful women in succession. Not believing in "concupiscence," he felt he had to marry them. A decade after arriving home, divorced from his third wife, he sold his practice and moved to New York.

He quit law after he had to defend a man accused of molesting his mentally disabled daughter. The girl was required to testify. When she took the stand, she began screaming as soon as she saw her father. He was acquitted because she was unable to speak. Clemente sold his practice the next day to a guy down the hall. He decided to find work that did not give him nightmares.

He and Beatrice met in Manhattan and married. Beatrice joined us for dinner in an Argentine restaurant famous for its tango music. I liked her instantly. She was from Colombia, and was beautiful, warm, and gracious. During dinner, my father left for the toilet.

When we were alone, Beatrice said, "I want you to know I will not be staying with your father a long time. When we met, I was a mother of three children, raising them myself. I was doing OK. Now there is only my son at home. He is fifteen. Clemente is a good father to him, so I will let him stay until my son goes to college. But Clemente is not a good husband. When we first met, we talked a lot and went dancing. Now, he doesn't talk to me or do much with me. I did not marry to be taken care of, I married to have a companion and to have love. Your father is not very good at either one. I tell you this because I want you to know that even if I ask your father to leave my house, you will always be welcome. My house is your house any time you want to come. You will always be part of my family.

"On our first date, in this restaurant, your father told me the story of his lost daughter. He cried. I fell in love with him because of your story and his love for you. I thought he could love others too. But he has been a disappointment as a husband. He seems better suited to be a father, even of a daughter he does not know."

The hope of finding me seemed to have consumed Clemente's emotional imagination. I felt far too ordinary to warrant such intense emotions, especially when I could not return them. Over the years, we have slowly and intermittently gotten to know each other a little, but it is not an easy relationship for me. We have so little to talk about.

I do not know how much of his inability to make commitments and to keep faith with his children is part of being in the Korean War for two years, or part of his upbringing in a violent family, or part of the gender expectations of his culture. His younger brother Miguel has a stable life with his wife Rosa. His oldest sister has had more misery and instability than one life ever ought to have. He is not the only one of his brothers to have fathered a child without keeping a commitment to the child and mother. I was just the first in this generation.

THE BEST WAY TO KEEP A SECRET

Just before Christmas of 1984, Pritchy and I loaded his blue Datsun station wagon with three overstuffed suitcases, pressed shirts on hangers, and a large box of gifts, and headed from Hawkins, Texas, to the Tombigbee River in Mississippi. I put together a photo album of our

Puerto Rican adventure, and we drove from Texas with a pile of books to read out loud.

I did not know how my Southern relatives would take the news that Roy was not my birth father. I had not been to Amory since I was sixteen. I looked forward to the visit.

For Christmas dinner, Annie Pearl, Roy's older sister, and her daughters Betty Jo and Linda Faye, fixed a Southern feast. As we sat on the front porch finishing our slices of pecan pie and the gourmet coffee Pritch and I had brought as a gift, I announced there was some information I needed to share. After I told the story of finding my family in Dorado, Annie Pearl looked at me in amazement and said, "You didn't know you was adopted?"

"No," I said, puzzled at her question.

"We all knew you was adopted and wadn't Grady's chile; you didn't know?" she replied. She always called my father by his hated middle name. When I shook my head, she explained, "Grady told us he and your daddy was buddies. We thought they was friends. Grady said he promised your daddy he would take care o' you and your mama if anything happened to your daddy in Korea. Grady told us your daddy was killed there. To keep his promise, Grady said he had to marry Ayako so he could take care o' you."

I told her the facts: that my fathers did not know each other, that Clemente was alive, and that I had never been told that Roy was not my birth father.

"We all knew you was adopted, but since your daddy was dead, I guess we figured there wadn't any point in talking about him. Ain't that a curiosity? All this time you visited us when you was little, and then you lived here, but no one ever told you, you was adopted. If that don't beat all." Annie Pearl reflected on this a moment and then said, "That just goes to prove—if you want to keep a secret, you tell everyone and don't tell 'em it's a secret and they won't talk about it!" Pritchy's uproarious laugh set us all off til we couldn't breathe.

Roy's family had loved and accepted a Japanese child and her mother in the immediate aftermath of World War II. In six years of summer visits and a year in 1962 and 1963, when my mother, Jo, Ray, and I lived there, I never suspected I was not directly related to them. My cousins and I squabbled and played, stole melons and carrots from the garden, swam in the creek, and ate Mr. Bob's hamburgers together

as if we had always done those things. Even in my most unhappy moments, I felt part of this clan. They had not hesitated to embrace me.

My father's favorite cousin, Virginia Ann, and her family were less
clear about the details of my birth, but they also vaguely remembered
something about a father. It had not been important to them. I was
Grady and Ayako's daughter and that was all that mattered. They enjoyed the story and pictures of my Puerto Rican adventure, especially
Robert, her brother, who appreciated my zany, exuberant relatives. I
had had a crush on Robert for years. He and Pritchy traded jokes and
barbs at dinner. Pritch loved the earthiness and warmth of the whole
Brock clan. He called them "real country." They reminded him of
folks from his roots in Dublin, Texas.

On the drive back to Texas, we began to untangle some of what
happened in Puerto Rico. I think I functioned as a cipher for the
Puerto Rican family, a way of avoiding the reality of violence that
was a fact of life with my grandfather, a way Clemente could hold on
to hope after the trauma of war without living in the present. Vilma
and Carmen, as the youngest, were deeply invested in my well-being
from the beginning. It was as though they believed, if their prayers
could keep me well and bring me home, they would have evidence of
something beyond life in a violent home.

I was not immune to these feelings myself. Finding my family in
Puerto Rico gave me respite from the memories of my estrangement
from Roy. Remembering how Roy had tried to beat me, I was comforted to know that somewhere, without my knowledge, others had
loved me and prayed for me all those years. I felt as if their love and
concern had been part of my ability to resist violence and survive.
Learning that Roy and I were not biologically connected created a reassuring distance that confirmed the decision I had made to leave, to
separate myself from his control. I felt glad I had another father, as
flawed as he was. And I felt a new clarity about my bi-racial identity. I
flew home to Columbia, Missouri, to begin the second semester of a
new job.

Eight months after our trip to Mississippi, Pritch said he wanted to
move to Columbia to be with me. He was ready to quit his career,
having despaired at finding another job. He was sure that I was the
only thing in his life that made him happy. His cynicism and world-
weariness had taken over, and he was desperately lonely. His increas-

ing emotional dependency frightened me. My paltry instructor's salary could not support us, and I did not know how to make him happy and pursue a career when he wanted to stop working and spend more time with me. I felt pushed away by his intense neediness—it panicked me to take on such responsibility for another.

I knew it would hurt him, but I told him I wanted to date other men. I needed some breathing space in our relationship. After several months of anguished letters and calls, we finally called it quits. Pritch found a great job in Florida later, and we've remained friends.

Three years after Pritch and I broke up, Parc sent me his high school graduation announcement. In his thank you note for the gift I sent, he said, "Don't tell Dad, but I'm sorry you broke up. You were my favorite of all his girlfriends." A real charmer, just like his dad.

MY FATHER RECLAIMED

The winter of 1987, I sat in my dining room at the end of the day, looking at the snow falling on the street. Jo Ann and I were on the phone discussing family matters.

Roy's military career came up. I mentioned I thought Vietnam had really done him in. Jo Ann said, "Maybe, but then there was that time in a Nazi prison."

"What prison?" I asked.

"You know, the one he was in during the war."

"No," I said, "I don't know."

"He never told you?" my sister was incredulous.

"No."

"Oh well, he lied about his age to join the army at the beginning of World War II. He had barely turned twenty when he was sent to North Africa in 1943. He got injured and captured. They put him in a German POW camp. When the war ended, he was sent to Walter Reed Army Hospital for electroshock treatments. I guess he came home in pretty bad shape. He shook a lot. Aunt Pearl didn't know what to do with him. Virginia Ann's family took care of him for two years. Are you sure Dad didn't tell you about this?"

"No, I remember he used to tell war stories to his friends who came over to play poker on Friday nights. He described battles he fought in, but the stories kept changing, so I thought he was a liar. I assumed he made up those stories to impress his friends. I never remember any stories about North Africa. They were mostly about France."

"Maybe he made things up because he couldn't remember much. I think electroshock messes up your memory. He told me about the prison and the time he spent at Virginia Ann's. I think he would sit in a chair and shake uncontrollably sometimes. He couldn't do much except sit. He didn't act normal for about two years. I think he was in that prison a long time."

"That's odd," I said. "He never said much to me about his time in World War II. He told me about Vietnam while he was there. He told me stories of the war, like the time he ran through a minefield carrying his commanding officer who was wounded. He told me about the time he did an emergency appendectomy in the field because there wasn't a doctor around. In the tapes he sent home, he would tell me not to tell Mom the stories because he didn't want to worry her.

"And he told me lots of stories about the sixteen-year-old Vietnamese guide he worked with. She translated for him. He ran the medical aide station at the camp, and he left his medics in charge while he followed her out into the countryside. She took him into the hills where her people lived so he could give them medicines and medical care. He said he got into trouble every now and then for giving away military medical supplies, but he did it anyway. Since he had saved his commanding officer's life, the guy didn't do much about his insubordination. Dad thought his guide was amazing. She was smart, brave, and committed to saving her people. I think he admired her a lot. She was shot and killed just before he came back."

"He never talked about Vietnam to me," Jo Ann noted.

"Well," I replied, "he never talked about it with me after he got back, either, just while he was there. He asked me to erase the tapes he sent after I heard them. I recorded my messages back to him on the same tapes so Mom wouldn't find them lying around. He was horrible after he got back, so we didn't talk about much at all."

I hung up the phone and was washed in waves of sadness. The man I knew as my father was greater than my unflattering judgments of him. He had hidden the brokenness of his early adult years with stories of heroism. We both masked pain and tragedy. We lacked a mutual language of vulnerability.

His veil of secrets became visible to me. The grief that was absent at his death in 1976 suddenly poured out. I wept looking out the window as snowflakes fell silently across the glow of streetlights.

I grieved for the father who had been my childhood friend, my adolescent confidant, my most committed supporter, for the father who had believed in me and encouraged me to take risks, who had been a decent, caring human being. The anger in me cooled, and the flesh of bronze I had carried for so long dissolved. In their place came a longing for him, a sorrow that he was gone, and a reassessment of his life. I began to see that, given all that he had lived through, he had been a good father to me. He had kept his commitments to my mother and me.

My father was lucky to have had a family like Virginia Ann's. Her mother Laura's epilepsy gave them knowledge of seizures, of how to continue with ordinary life while caring for someone who could not function. They lived with passion, humor, intelligence, and zest. The flow of ordinary life and loving people who treated Roy in humane ways eventually brought him back. No wonder he was so attached to them.

These are the moments of grace in a life broken by violence: attentive care and the steady witness of those who did not shrink in the face of trauma. This grace restored my father's soul. There is no gratitude large enough to match the generosity of such love, except to try to live in a similar way for others.

After my father decided to reapply for military service, he was sent to occupied Japan. He had an eighth-grade education and a damaged psyche, and the paternalistic care of military life may have been his best option. But the military was an odd career for him. He hated the compliance needed to advance in rank and refused to do anything for a promotion. I had learned a deep skepticism of authority from him. He was moved up only once—to staff sergeant. He had been at one rank so long, the Army advanced him for time served.

The three years our family lived in Landstuhl, Germany, from 1963 to 1966, my father refused to leave the base. We took an occasional afternoon drive to see the countryside in spring or fall, but no amount of cajoling could make him take us to see the great German cities, museums, or ancient ruins nearby. I loved touring with my classes. I judged him a stodgy stick-in-the-mud and xenophobic American. It never occurred to me there might be a deeper reason for his aversion to Germans.

At every opportunity I misjudged his behavior and drew the most ungenerous conclusions about him. I was grateful to have come to a moment when I could see his life more clearly and to acknowledge the goodness in him, but my gratitude was weighed with sadness. My reassessment of his life came a decade after his death, when it was too late to restore our broken relationship and heal old wounds. And my life had been turned upside down by the knowledge that he was not my birth father. He conferred grace on someone else's daughter.

AT LAST

In the spring of 1987, I submitted a dissertation draft at the end of my third and last extension of time to complete the doctoral degree. I could have taken a leave of absence, but I feared that if I stopped paying my tuition fee, I would lose my goad to finish. Given the series of upheavals, revelations, deaths, personal crises, and major job changes in my life from 1976 to 1986, I sometimes wonder how I managed to survive, much less finish a dissertation. Throughout this time, friends in various parts of the country would ask me, "Is it done yet?" Their prodding helped. I would have been too chagrined not to complete it.

I defended the dissertation in late spring 1987 and was awarded my Ph.D. in January 1988. My graduation ceremony in May 1988 was the first major event of my life since the discovery of my Puerto Rican family. I invited them to come. Clemente bought me the hood. Beatrice helped me find the fabric for my doctoral robe in the New York garment district where she worked. Jo, who once had made theater costumes, designed and sewed a beautiful doctoral gown. My Norwegian grad school skiing companion, Dagfinn, helped me make the arrangements for a party.

Vilma's husband, Johannes, came with their three sons, Frankie, Johnny, and Jimmy, who were attending college in Fresno. Clemente flew in from New York. Friends from Southern California cheered when I walked across the stage, especially a contingent from my favorite church in Los Angeles, All Peoples Christian Church.

The next day, Clemente and I drove out to Hemet to meet Bob and Blossom, the couple at my mother's funeral who had first told me about my Puerto Rican father. We realized that Bob and Blossom had my father confused with his friend Ramos, who had stayed in Japan and befriended my mother and me after Clemente left. We spent the afternoon in a warm glow of memories.

On our last day in Southern California, Clemente asked me to take him to my mother's grave in Barstow. On the way, Clemente asked me to stop at a florist where he bought two potted magenta azaleas. We made the long, slow climb up Cajon Pass, the last time I took that road. We rose slowly out of the brown haze of San Bernardino and turned around the bend at the crest. The azure desert sky expanded before us.

Roy and Ayako's graves were shaded by a tree that was much larger now than it was the last time I was at the site. Clemente took one of the azaleas out of the car and set it next to Roy's grave. "Thank you for taking such good care of my daughter," he whispered. He took the other azalea and placed it next to my mother's grave. He bowed his head silently and did not speak for a very long time. There were tears in his eyes when he looked up. We took photos standing by the flowers and headstones.

After lunch we headed back to Los Angeles. The Joshua trees whipped by; we crossed the Mojave River with its patch of bright green trees; the highway disappeared into the mountains of Cajon Pass in front of us; and then we dropped into the brown air of the Los Angeles basin, headed for the airport and our respective flights home.

A PICTURE OF MY LIFE

Sorting through an old box of photos in the summer of 2000, I found one of my family taken by Dagfinn at my graduation party. We are sitting on a long couch: Johannes, Frankie, Johnny, Jimmy, and Clemente. We are in colors of beige, brown, and white, each of us with brown eyes and dark hair. I am sitting half on Clemente's lap and half on the arm of the couch and smiling. For a moment, I relive the relief and celebration of that time.

Tears spring to my eyes. It is the wrong picture. It is not the picture I want to remember. The picture I imagine is different. I am standing in my doctoral gown with diploma in hand. The gown is unzipped in front; you can see a slice of my red dress. My red shoes show up sharply against the grass where I stand. I am standing with Roy to my left and Ayako to my right, their arms around me as they are turned a little toward me. Jo Ann and Ray flank them on either side. Roy is wearing his dark brown suit with white shirt, his brown shoes polished military bright. Ayako is in her lilac Easter dress and white pumps, in colors too bright for a Japanese matron, in colors I remember her liking when I was a child. Just behind me, their hands on my shoulders, stand Denver, Joy, and Lillian Clark. Surrounding us are Nelle, Pritchy, and all the friends who attended the party. Everyone is smiling jubilantly. My parents look proud and pleased.

After seventeen years of amazement, after retelling the story of my Puerto Rican family many times, after seventeen years of carrying this new family in my heart, and after seventeen years of getting acquainted with Clemente, I realize my sense of loss. I feel as though something was taken from me when I was split between two fathers. The picture of my life has taken on disjunctures and aching absences. It is as if someone had cut and removed sections of the picture and taped it back together. It is not the life I remember. Roy is the only father I knew as a child, the one who encouraged my passions and sense of adventure, who committed himself to me and made sure I would thrive.

That Roy made mistakes does not remove all he did for me; I had great luck in having a father like him. This is a letter he sent to me dated the eighth of April, 1972, just after my mother's first cancer surgery and just before I was due to arrive in Japan.

> Dear Sis,
>
> This letter should reach you in Hong Kong, the largest brothel of the far east. There are a lot of things to see and hear, but I am damned if I know how to tell you what to see.
>
> Rita, Mother is doing wonderful. I am sorry we missed ports with letters. I know you were worried. Sis, I was the one who made the decision not to notify you immediately when Mother had her operation. So if you must have someone to be mad at, let it be me. But remember I *love* you and I had my reasons.
>
> Your birthday is soon. Twenty-two years old. Where did the years go? Man how time flies when you get in the late years. One thing I can say Sis, I have seen all the places I wanted to see and done all the things I wanted to do. I regret some things I did but if it was to do over again I probably would do it the same way. It has been a fast life, very full. I always had to do things in a hurry because there was a new place to see, another war to be fought. Death was always right around the corner. I could not make close friends because tomorrow they might be dead and it hurt too bad to lose a friend, so I was a loner. Oh, I had my love affairs, too many really. Sis, they were always deep meaningful relationships with human

beings that had compassion. Some I only needed to talk to. Others I needed to express my love and to receive their love. I never in my life went to a whorehouse just to have intercourse. That was never my problem. I never let a pair of hot pants get the upper hand of my better judgment. It was never cheap with me. I had to take all precaution to see that there was no baby left behind. This I could not stand. And VD was always a worry.

Rita, all I am trying to say is I am human. I have lived. I loved every minute of it and I know by the way you write that you are in love with life. Your description of your trip in Africa and your words from Ceylon said it all. I feel like you finally understand people and love them for both their weaknesses and their strengths.

Skinny dipping? Does this word still have the same meaning? You were allowed to swim in the nude? If so, you are getting pretty *brave*. I thought I was the only one in the family who liked to sleep and swim in the nude.

Rita, since your mother has had her operation, we are even closer together than before. The strong love we had is now on the surface and it is wonderful. It makes you want to live.

Rita, what I am going to ask now, I would like an answer on, if possible, right after you leave Japan, the place of your birth and the place I came to know you. Since Christmas, I have been changing inside. Now even more I feel this change. I want our relationship to change from father daughter, this still yes, but now less so. I want to put it on a higher plane than before. My feelings about what you are doing should not be a major factor. I want to express love toward you so strong that it will work its way back to you. I could not explain what I wanted our relationship to be at Christmas time because I did not know. Now I do.

Now that you have had a love affair and you felt you wanted to tell me, it makes me believe you are now a mature woman who has the mind and heart of a 22-year-old woman. The love you had with G. is not the kind I and your mother have. Our love is so kind we can discuss our opinions without pushing them down each other's throat. I want this with you. I promise I will listen and make comments only when you ask. Will you do this? I want to be able to grab and hug and kiss you both as my daughter and a 22-year-old friend, without you thinking he is a dirty old man. I want to be jubilant about being alive, not suppress it. I want you at times to be able to sit and make small talk. I want you to be able to come to our bedroom like you used to sit and talk about life aspirations. Your mother would love this too. Think about this. Give me a chance. I do hope it is yes.

Love, your dad, Roy.

We never discussed this letter. I went on to graduate school and Switzerland with his question unanswered. I regret not reaching out to him when I could, and when he asked me to. I didn't give him a chance. The loss is mine.

I wondered how much of my ambivalence about being white was connected to my feelings about Roy. The American black/white racial divide forces those of us with more than one racial identity to choose only one. Nonetheless, I found it easy to claim being both Hispanic and Asian—they fell on one side of that divide. I was reluctant to acknowledge I also had a white part of me. White stood for supremacy, for the source of racial oppression I experienced, and for my troubled relationship to Roy. But now, the exposed foundations of my life revealed stones of three different hues. Their mortar is love.

Ji-chan knew the human heart well. His assessment of Roy was accurate. Roy was a responsible person. He had a good heart. He took good care of my mother and me.

And still, and yet, the picture I imagine is not enough to capture what I feel. To complete the photo, I want Ba-chan and Ji-chan, stooped with age, to stand with me. Aunt Shizue and Uncle Katsume near them. Virginia Ann and Annie Pearl with their clans. Also Clemente, Vilma, Carmen, Miguel, and Maria, for they, too, are part of my life now. They loved me far longer than I have known them. They will, now, always be a part of my life, which has long been sustained by a collection of people from three cultures, languages, and places— a vast communion of saints.

> Therefore, since we are surrounded by so great a cloud of witnesses, let us also lay aside every weight and the sin that clings so closely, and let us run with perseverance the race that is set before us. (Hebrews 12:1)

> Set me as a seal upon your heart,
> as a seal upon your arm;
> for love is as strong as death,
> passion fierce as the grave.
> Its flashes are flashes of fire,
> a raging flame.
> Many waters cannot quench love,
> neither can floods drown it.
> If one offered for love all the wealth of his house,
> it would be utterly scorned.
>
> Song of Songs 8:6–7

We have sifted the inheritance of pain and violence that has marked our lives and embraced the kindness watching for us, this side the ground. In our efforts to cleave to life, we have found the presence of God.

Violence destroys life. The mother murdered by her husband did not return. Her four young children grew up without her presence, and the loss will echo throughout their lives. Violence bleeds through a lifetime. Nothing will return life to a time when violence was absent. There is no pristine life, no spring in which winter is fully past. Cold lingers in the blossoms and the fruit and threatens over and over to kill the tree.

Presence burns fiercely, but Presence cannot override the decisions of perpetrators of violence. It is a human act to stay the hand of violence. Life is ours to choose.

It is a human act to heal the aftermath of violence. Healing is neither a solitary nor simple journey. There is a synergy to grace. The shattered person must respond to what love offers: connection that will be reliable and care that will not violate the fragile membranes of the self. The wounded soul retains the power to say yes or no to grace.

Through extremities of experience, God is with us. The riveting force of searing pain, the knife edge of grief or loss—these moments reveal God perhaps more vividly than any other experience. They also hide God. When Rebecca lacked the means to stop violation, she protected herself by encasing knowledge of both trauma and Presence in a shroud. Though Presence was starkly revealed to her in the midst of terror, Presence was forgotten. For over three decades, Rebecca was cut off from an abiding awareness of Presence. This loss of memory threatened her life; she wished to die. She turned violence on herself.

Recovery can be impossible. Legacies of violence bequeath the isolation of the lone sufferer, the denial of pain, acts of rage against others, the acid of cynicism, fragmentation of the soul, the inertia of passivity and despair, and the wish to die. The journey back to self and God can be a descent into hell, even when we have the support of friends and family. Many cannot make the descent and live half-lives. Others descend, fragment completely, and never return. They cannot respond, even to the most tender of mercies.

When systems trap us in violence, they betray us. Jesus has been betrayed by his own tradition. A military empire murdered him. His life and work were not furthered by his death. His execution ruptured his community. Its scattered ashes were difficult to restore to fire.

His followers sought to recover. They experienced the presence of God in their grief. In the garden weeping, Mary saw her teacher in the guise of a gardener. Talking with a stranger on the road, two disciples felt their hearts burn within them and discovered death was not the end. Mourning brought them to a moment of awareness of the dead, a moment that came as surprise, as unexpected grace.

The dead provide a legacy of Presence that folds tragedy into living—existence as a ceaseless chain of being. Jesus' spirit linked his followers to that legacy. They did not let their movement die. Risking the cost, they refused to acquiesce to the legacy of violence. They remembered the legacy of Presence.

But Western Christianity claims we are saved by the execution, that violence and terror reveal the grace of God. This claim isolates Jesus, as violence isolates its victims. When the victims of violence are made singular, solitary, unprecedented in their pain, the power of violence remains.

Jesus' death was not unique. The torture inflicted on Jesus had been visited on many. It continues in the world, masked by the words "virtuous suffering" and "self-sacrificing love."

We cannot say what would have happened if Jesus had not been murdered, but unjust, violent death is traumatizing. His community retained the scars and limitations of those who survive violence. Christianity bears the marks of unresolved trauma. Jesus' resurrection and the continuation of his movement are not triumphs, but a glimpse of the power of survival, of the embers that survive the deluge.

To know that the presence of God endures through violence is to know life holds more than its destruction. The power of life is strong. Salvation is sometimes possible.

Salvation begins with the courage of witnesses whose gaze is steady. Steady witnesses neither flee in horror to hide their eyes, nor console with sweet words, "It isn't all that bad. Something good is intended by this." Violence is illuminated by insistent exposure. Steady witnesses end the hidden life of violence by bringing it to public attention. They help to restore souls fragmented by violence. They accompany the journey to healing.

When Lyle came home from World War II, Maxine was a steady witness. She provided presence for him to return to life. Roy had a family of steady witnesses when he returned to Mississippi after being a prisoner of war. Both of these men, through caring human presence, returned to life after the devastation of war. Both of them went on to give generous assistance to others.

Sandi was a steady witness who helped Rebecca to remember the terror and anguish that haunted an unblessed child and to rediscover that Presence had been with her from the beginning. Family, friends, and community sustained her on the journey to healing. Remembering ended Rebecca's isolation; and she began to integrate her life.

Salvation requires love. Fainthearted love, idealized love, impatient love cannot walk in the valley of the shadow of death. Healing love touches the hidden wounds of violation, lances the places of stored trauma, restores glimpses of soul. The world offers too few such love and care. Violence persists.

Salvation also requires mourning. We must cross the raging rivers of grief to rest before the still waters of blessing. In grief, knowledge of loss finds its clarity. When Rita was able, after many years, to know the loss of her father, Roy, she began to mourn.

Grief knows that life has been altered with finality. Grief knows presence by its absence. It measures the weight of tragedy. It holds the memory of what might have been. The light of sorrow illuminates where life has been diminished, its missing faces, its torn photographs. Mourning deepens reverence for what is precious, what is already destroyed, what must be embraced with fierce determination, abiding faithfulness.

Those who cannot grieve fail to recognize when life is at risk. Mourning strengthens our ability to choose life and protect it, even as the pain of grief threatens to destroy us. Those who mourn experience the mystery of a presence that is not wholly lost, that accompanies the living with a tenderness and power that alters their lives. The world changes. The surface mask thins, life becomes luminous with fire. The heart expands its breadth. Love is as strong as death.

Grief is never overcome or removed, but remains part of living. To yearn for the return of the ones who have died, long after they have gone, is a sign to the living that love does not die with death, but lives on in those left behind. We know love in the relationships that sustain us, in the longest, most important friendships of our lives, the steady witnesses.

In grief the followers of Jesus found the advent of fire, the loosening of their tongues, the arrival of courage. Discovering that love endures, we come to the moment when we know that our hearts have room for more, that loss and regret have not snapped shut the clasp on our hearts. We unlock latches for repair and hope. If we are lucky, we discover this spaciousness of the heart in new loves that enter our lives and in acts of advocacy to change an unjust world.

Nothing can separate us from the love of God. We make this affirmation in concert with countless witnesses who affirm the same. For us, there is nothing new in this affirmation, except the newness of coming to know its truth in our own lives—not as a message passed on to us, but as a living discovery. With Job, we witness to a living truth:

> For I know that my Redeemer lives, . . .
> then in my flesh I shall see God. (Job 19:25–26)

Love encompasses life. Like an arc of fire across the night sky, Presence blesses those who await it. In sensing Presence, we embrace a passion for life. Love is a seal upon the heart, a hunger to create, to honor life, to protect it, and to see it flourish.

This passion for life burns fiercely and cannot be quenched by many waters. It is as strong as violence and death. As we see more deeply into the luminous depths, we draw closer to that astonishing fire at the heart of things.

This is God with us:

> quiet moments of mutual discovery by friends sharing coffee on a
>   sunlit afternoon,
> tears appearing on a frozen face,
> a community meeting that resists violence,
> an embrace that holds the other through the terrors of the night,
> a sheltering moon watching over an unblessed child,
> an old woman keeping faded photographs on a mirror,
> a dark ocean shimmering with diamonds.

Let us say that life shows us the face of God only in fleeting glimpses, by the light of night fires, in dancing shadows, in departing ghosts, and in recollections of steady love. Let us say this is enough, enough for us to run with perseverance the race that is set before us, enough for us to stand against violence, enough for us to hold each other in benediction and blessing.

If you are interested in further reading, we recommend the following books: *Violence Against Women and Children: A Christian Theological Sourcebook* edited by Carol J. Adams and Marie M. Fortune; *Making Waves* by Asian Women United; *Facing the Abusing God: A Theology of Protest* by David R. Blumenthal; *Christianity, Patriarchy and Abuse: A Feminist Critique* edited by Joanne Carlson Brown and Carolyn R. Bohn; *Constantine's Sword: The Church and the Jews* by James Carroll; *Who Killed Jesus? Exposing the Roots of Anti-Semitism in the Gospel Story of the Death of Jesus* by John Dominic Crossan; *Is Nothing Sacred? When Sex Invades the Pastoral Relationship, Love Does No Harm,* and *Sexual Violence: The Unmentionable Sin: An Ethical and Pastoral Perspective* by Marie Fortune; *Pornography and Silence: Culture's Revenge Against Nature* and *A Chorus of Stones: The Private Life of War* by Susan Griffin; *Crucifixion: In the Ancient World and the Folly of the Message of the Cross* by Martin Hengel; *Trauma and Recovery: The Aftermath of Violence—From Domestic Abuse to Political Terror* by Judith Lewis Herman; *Jesus and the Spiral of Violence: Popular Jewish Resistance in Roman Palestine* by Richard A. Horsley; *Mujerista Theology: A Theology for the 21st Century* by Ada Maria Isasi-Diaz; *Christianity and Incest* by Annie Imbens and Jonker Ineke; *Is God a White Racist: A Preamble to Black Theology* by William R. Jones; *Redeeming Memories: A Theology of Healing and Transformation* by Flora Keshgegian; *Sister Outsider* by Audre Lorde; *Women Resisting Violence: Spirituality for Life* edited by Mary John Manzanan, et al.; *Thou Shalt Not Be Aware: Society's Betrayal of the Child* and *For Your Own Good: Hidden Cruelty in Child-Rearing and the Roots of Violence* by Alice Miller; *The Journey Is Home* by Nelle Morton; *The Wounded Heart of God: The Asian Concept of Han and the Christian Doctrine of Sin* by Andrew Sung Park; *The Abuse of Power: A Theological Problem* by James Poling; *Why They Kill* by Richard Rhodes; *Suffering* and *Beyond Mere Obedience* by Dorothee Soelle; *Religion Is a Queer Thing* by Elizabeth Stuart; *Strangers from a Different Shore: A History of Asian Americans* by Ronald Takaki; *A Troubling in My Soul: Womanist Perspectives on Evil and Suffering* edited by Emilie M. Townes; *The Asian American Movement* by William Wei; *Battered Love: Marriage, Sex, and Violence in the Hebrew Prophets* by Renita Weems; *Wounds of the Spirit: Black Women, Violence, and Resistance Ethics* by Traci West; *Sisters in the Wilderness: The Challenge of Womanist God-Talk* by Delores S. Williams.

For films on Asian Americans, we recommend *Slaying the Dragon,* a film about stereotypes of Asian American women, *Who Killed Vincent Chinn* and *My America, or Honk If You Love Buddha,* documentary films by Renee Tajima about Asian American issues, and *Picture Bride,* a feature film by Kayo Hata.

ACKNOWLEDGMENTS

Our friendship made this book possible. Many others helped make it happen. Michael West first suggested to Rita in 1994 that she write a feminist critique of the atonement, planting the idea that metamorphosed into this joint project. The University of Puget Sound invited us in 1989 to give a joint lecture, which was our first collaborative effort on the atonement. In March 1999, Rita gave another lecture there on our research for this project. We returned to Puget Sound during Christmas 2000 and Epiphany 2001, to the shores of Wollochet Bay, to edit the manuscript for publication. There we found a cozy log cabin renovated and prepared by Bruce and Gretchen Parker, Rebecca's parents, whose unflagging generosity and hospitality provided us with dinners every night, periodic bridge lessons, occasional movies, and boundless encouragement.

Our lives are intertwined with many others. We thank those whose stories are included with ours in the book. We have used their names when we felt it was appropriate to do so, and whenever possible, obtained their permission. Those who are deceased or whose names appear in public documents are also named. For others, we have used initials or changed their names and sometimes altered their stories to protect their identities. Though we have not named them, we are grateful for their lives. For access to court records, we thank the Clerk of the Pacific County Courthouse, South Bend, Washington. For reviewing the stories and reflecting with us on their meaning, we thank Virginia Andrews, Huntley Beyer, Jo Ann and Ray Brock, Joy Clark, James Doti, Sandi Hedlund, Vilma Hoevertz, Leslie Knight, Rick Koyle, Carmen Morales, Bruce and Gretchen Parker, George Shangrow, Patricia Simpson, and Pritchy Smith. We thank the members of Wallingford United Methodist Church, Seattle, 1979–86, especially Will and Mary Brown, Sharon Moe, Chuck Richards, Colleen Simpson, and Carmen and Cecil Taylor. We also thank Glen Poling, Darren, Norma, Jim, Neil, Bernice, and the staff and youth of Brotherhood/Sisterhood USA, Los Angeles, 1974, 1978–88.

Supportive friends sustained us on the journey. Rebecca expresses particular gratitude to Rick Koyle for countless acts of encouragement, counsel on the writing process, and for the peace, refreshment, and focus provided by six weeks spent at Papakowhai, New Zealand. Over the course of many drafts, Claudia Highbaugh, Belva Brown Jordan, and Tonee Jordan provided Rita cat-sitting services and offered both of us hospitality and enriching conversations. Joanne Brown and Rosemary Bray McNatt gave encouragement and good advice.

The Board of Trustees of the Starr King School granted Rebecca a sabbatical in spring 1999 and the faculty and staff covered the work so she could go. President Linda Wilson and Dean Mary Maples Dunn at Radcliffe found ways for Rita to clear weeks each summer for writing, and the staff of the Bunting Fellowship Program protected her time. Thanks to Rosemary Chinnici, Eliyahou Farajajé, Clare Fischer, Alicia McNary Forsey, Patti Lawrence, Yielbonzie Charles Johnson, and Becky Leyser at Starr King and Julie Burba, Lyn O'Conor, Janice Randall, Beth Silverman, Paula Soares, Peggy Tuitt, and Jeanne Winner at the Bunting.

A variety of people challenged us and gave helpful feedback: Paulette Bates Alden and the members of the Split Rock writing seminar, July 1997, in Duluth, Minnesota; the members of University Congregational United Church of Christ, Seattle, who attended the July 1998 camp at Seabeck; Kwok Pui Lan, Joan Martin, and Gale Yee of Episcopal Divinity School; Rosemary Chinnici, Joanna Dewey, Marie Fortune, Richard Horsley, and Ann and Hugh Wire, who offered scholarly insights and suggestions; and Lindy Hess, who gave us savvy contract advice; Bunting Fellows Tamar Diesendruck, Pumla Gobodo Madikizela, Rachel Manley, Cecile McHardy, and Lori Roses; the audiences for Rita in spring 2000 at Wake Forest and Furman universities, and especially Keller Freeman and Lynn Rhodes; the New England Maritime Region of the American Academy of Religion; those who attended our lecture in October 2000 at the Harvard Divinity School; and the women and men who attended Rita's July 1999 lectures in New Zealand and Australia, especially her hosts Susan Adams, Jemma Allen, Gwen and Marcus Benjamin, Josie Dolan, Coralee Ling, Judith McKinlay, Kathleen McPhilips, Jill McRae, Rosemary Neave, John Salmon, Diane Strevens, Susan Sullivan and the Sophia Center staff, and Elaine Wainwright.

Of inestimable help have been the readers and editors whose suggestions have improved this project immeasurably. Critical engagement with the ideas came from the participants in Rebecca's seminar on violence and redemption at Starr King, spring 2000: Cristhal Bennett, Rebecca Brooks, Sandra Hart, Julie Kain, Sandra Millar, Alyssa J. Morrow, Claudia Nolte, Katherine Reis, Eva Schulte, Barbara Threatt, Julia Watts, Nancy Kay Yount, and Kinga-Reka Zsigmond. Christina Robb helped us restructure and focus the text, and Dan Moseley pushed us to make our theology consistent with our emotional insights and showed us the weak places in many of our stories. We found a great collaborator in our ever-encouraging, astute editor at Beacon, Amy Caldwell. Jocelyn Soutter prepared the manuscript for publication, for which we are deeply grateful. Finally, we thank three mentors who taught us to venture boldly: John Cobb, Jr., Bernard Loomer, and Nelle Morton. To the dismay of our excellent copyeditor, Arnessa M. Garrett, we have hidden flaws throughout this book for you to detect. We hope to hear from you.

Epiphany
February 2001